NEW COLLECTED POEMS

David Gascoyne by Gertrude Hermes, 1956 © National Portrait Gallery

DAVID GASCOYNE

New Collected Poems
1929–1995

Edited with a Preface by
Roger Scott

ENITHARMON PRESS

First published in 2014
by Enitharmon Press
10 Bury Place
London WC1A 2JL

www.enitharmon.co.uk

Distributed in the UK by
Central Books
99 Wallis Road
London E9 5LN

Text © Estate of David Gascoyne 2014
Preface, selection and editorial matter © Roger Scott 2014

ISBN: 978-1-907587-37-5

Enitharmon Press acknowledges the financial
assistance of Arts Council England and for this publication it is
particularly grateful for the support of Dr Roger Scott
and the beneficiaries of the estates of David and Judy Gascoyne.

British Library Cataloguing-in-Publication Data.
A catalogue record for this book is available
from the British Library.

Typeset in Bembo by Servis Filmsetting Ltd, Stockport, Cheshire
and printed in the UK by
Gomer Press Ltd

CONTENTS

UNCOLL. = uncollected poems; titles in italics are unpublished

Bibliography	xiv
Editor's Preface by Roger Scott	xix
Introductory Notes by David Gascoyne	xxvii
Acknowledgements	xxxviii

POEMS WRITTEN AT SCHOOL (1929)
Storm UNCOLL.	3
October Night UNCOLL.	3

From *ROMAN BALCONY* (1932)
Roman Balcony	7
Fading Avenues	7
Vista	8
Roman Ghosts	9
Summer's Echo	10
Rain Clouds	10
Prison	11
Transformation Scene	11
The Bridge	12
Psychological Fragment	13
Exhaustion	14
Seaside Tragedy	14
The New Isaiah	19

OTHER EARLY POEMS (1932–1935)
Sonnet to Alida Monro	
Hinterland	
By the Sea: Traditional Form & Modernist Forms UNCOLL.	25
Seaside Souvenir	27
On the Terrace	27
Slate	28
Susan: a carving by Eric Gill UNCOLL.	28
from 'Ten Proses'	29
2. 'In New York and other cities'	29
3. 'Shafts of pale light are directed'	29
8. 'They were hardly to be expected here'	29
10. 'The world of De Chirico'	30

From 'Automatic Album Leaves'	30
1. 'The Room is not very large'	30
In Perpetuum Mobile	31
Hommage à Mallarmé UNCOLL.	31
Oleograph UNCOLL.	32
Night-Piece UNCOLL.	33
End of Peace UNCOLL.	34
Perpetual Winter Never Known UNCOLL.	34
'Not having knife-edge to my ermine cape'	35
Landscape	35
Speculation	36
Sonnet: 'Progressing forward . . .' UNCOLL.	37
'They Spoke of a New City' UNCOLL.	37
'The Roots of Evil' UNCOLL.	38
Germinal	39
Gnu Opaque	39
Marrow	40
Baptism	40
Future Reference	41

MAN'S LIFE IS THIS MEAT (1936)

The Chariot	45
'The cold renunciatory beauty'	45
'Light of the sun over the arctic regions'	46
Morning Dissertation	46
The Unattained	47
Reintegration	48
No Solution	49
Direct Response	49
The Last Head	50
Purified Disgust	50
Charity Week	51
Reflected Vehemence	52
The End is Near the Beginning	53
Lost Wisdom	53
Unspoken	54
Yves Tanguy	56
'The Truth is Blind'	57
The Cage	58
Educative Process	59
Antennae	61
Lozanne	64

Salvador Dalí	65
The Diabolical Principle	66
The Rites of Hysteria	67
And the Seventh Dream is the Dream of Isis	68

SURREALIST AND OTHER POEMS (1936–1938)

A Sudden Squall	73
Competition UNCOLL.	74
'The entrance to that valley stands alone' UNCOLL.	74
Phenomena	76
The Very Image	
Asylum	
The Perpetual Explosion	
The Light of the Lion's Mane	77
The Great Day	79
The Very Image	82
The Cubical Domes	83
The Symptomatic World	84
The Supposed Being	88
Eau Sifflé (for Georges Hugnet) UNCOLL.	90
Goût du jour UNCOLL.	91
Cafard UNCOLL.	91
Récupération UNCOLL.	92
Fool's Paradise UNCOLL.	92
Symptomatic World UNCOLL.	93
Elegiac Stanzas I.M. Alban Berg UNCOLL.	93
'Chorus' to 'Procession to the Private Sector' UNCOLL.	98
The Hills and in the light, daily	
Compline for the Occident: a cantata for choir and solo voice	
The Moon Over London UNCOLL.	101
An Unfinished, Post-Auden Pre-War Proem (for J.S.)	101
Three Verbal Objects	103
'transparency of the vegetable world . . .' UNCOLL.	106
Two Untitled Fragments	
Phantasmagoria	107

From **HOLDERLIN'S MADNESS** (1938)

Figure in a Landscape	115
Orpheus in the Underworld	117
Tenebrae	118
Epilogue	118

POEMS 1937–42 (1943)
MISERERE   123
    Tenebrae   123
    Pieta   123
    De Profundis   124
    Kyrie   125
    Lachrymae   125
    Ex Nihilo   126
    Sanctus   126
    Ecce Homo   127

METAPHYSICAL POEMS:
Concert of Angels   130
Elsewhere   132
World Without End   133
Inferno   134
Lowland   134
Mountains   135
Winter Garden   135
The Wall   136
The Fortress   136
Dichtersleben   137
I.M. Benjamin Fondane   138
Mozart: Sursum Corda   138
Cavatina   139
Artist   140
Insurrection   140
Legendary Fragment   141
Eve   141
Venus Androgyne   141
The Dark's Fidelity
Post-Mortem UNCOLL.   142
Amor Fati   142
Signs   143
The Hero   143
The Fault   144
The Descent   144
The Open Tomb   145
The Plummet Heart   146
The Three Stars   146
Epode   148

PERSONAL POEMS:
Sonnet: From Morn to Mourning	149
The Fabulous Glass	149
Camera Obscura	150
Apologia	151
Epilogue to an Episode	
The Writer's Hand	152
Dead End	
The Sacred Hearth	153
To a Contemporary	154
An Elegy	155
From a Diary	157
Odeur de Pensée	158
Fête	159
Chambre d'Hôtel	159
Jardin du Palais Royal	160
Noctambules	161
Souvenirs de Paris (I): *A La Fenêtre*	
Epilogue 1940–1	
Sonnet: The Uncertain Battle	165
Lines	166
The Anchorite UNCOLL.	166

TIME AND PLACE:
Snow in Europe	169
Zero	169
An Autumn Park	170
The Conspirators. Prelude to an Unfinished Narrative	171
Come Dungeon Dark (III)	
Farewell Chorus	176
Spring Mcmxl	179
A Wartime Dawn	180
Walking at Whitsun	181
Oxford: A Spring Day	184
The Gravel-Pit Field	184
Requiem	186
Strophes Elégiaques à la Mémoire d'Alban Berg	189

***A VAGRANT AND OTHER POEMS* (1950)**
A Vagrant	195
Innocence and Experience	196

Photograph	198
Reported Missing	199
A Tough Generation	199
The Other Larry	200
Eros Absconditus	201
The Goose-Girl	201
Beware Beelzebub	202
Rondel for the Fourth Decade	202
September Sun 1947, updated 1983	203
The Post-War Night	203
Demos in Oxford Street	204
Evening Again	205
Three Venetian Nocturnes	206
1. Barcarolle	206
2. Lido Gala Fireworks	206
3. On the Grand Canal	206
Birth of a Prince	208
Rex Mundi	208
Fragments towards a Religio Poetae	209
The Second Coming	213
A Little Zodiak for Kathleen Raine	214
After Twenty Springs	217

LIGHT VERSE

An Unsagacious Animal	221
Le Déjeuner sur L'Herbe: a Pastoral	223
The Decay of Decency	224
With a Cornet of Winkles	225
Three Cabaret Songs	227

***ENCOUNTER WITH SILENCE: POEMS, 1950* (1998)**

Give Up Dead Words	231
Stele	231
Terminal	231
Fragment from an unfinished / unpublished poem	232
Untitled: 'Mist and damp . . .'	233
Saturnalia	233
The Bomb-Site Anchorite (fragment)	235

MAKE-WEIGHT VERSE

A Post-Card from Venice to T.S.E.	236
Who Are the Orthosexual?	236
L'homme assez moyen (pas très sensual)	236

OTHER POEMS 1950–1956
'Dear Thomas Eliot'
'The Porch before these poems is the entrance into Night'
'The Hand that in the Darkness'
'The Son of Man is in Revolt'
'When I am able to think at night'
Qu'est-ce que la Décadence? UNCOLL.	239
Yes, You UNCOLL.	239
Yes, thank you. Now I can start the day UNCOLL.	240
Remembering the Dead	241
Haiku: Urban Autumn After the War UNCOLL.	242
'My own sophistry' UNCOLL.	242
Ambiguous Haiku UNCOLL.	242
Cartesian Haiku UNCOLL.	242

'Rain globules on glass'
'And tell me, how is Christ preached now . . .'
Metropolis by Night UNCOLL.	243
Night-Watchers' Ruminations UNCOLL.	244
Night Thoughts UNCOLL.	246
Sentimental Colloquy	252
Elegiac Improvisation on the Death of Paul Eluard	253

NIGHT THOUGHTS (1956)
The Nightwatchers	259
Megalometropolitan Carnival	266
Encounter with Silence	278

LATER POEMS 1956–1995
The Grass in the Waste Places	287
Half-an-Hour	287
On ReReading Jacob Boehme's 'Aurora'	288
Three Verbal Sonatinas	289
Speechlessness	296
Whales and Dolphins	296
Prelude to a New Fin-de-Siècle	298
Variations on a Phrase	300
Rare Occasional Poem	301
Dodecatribute to Miron Grindea at 75	302
Arbres, Bêtes, Courants d'Eau: Improvisation (for Salah Stétié), UNCOLL.	302
Haiku for [Salah] Stétié, Hague Haiku UNCOLL.	304
Thalassa: the Unspeakable Sea	305

Entrance to a Lane	306
A Further Frontier	306
A Sarum Sestina	307
November in Devon	309
Three Remanences	310
A Summer Evening at Caesar's Tower (Drafts)	
Ivy UNCOLL.	311

APPENDIX A:
UNPUBLISHED POEMS, drafts and fair copies

Sonnet to Alida Monro	315
Hinterland	315
The Very Image	317
Asylum	317
The Perpetual Explosion	318
'The Hills, and in the light, daily'	323
Compline for the Occident: a cantata for choir and solo voice	324
Two untitled fragments	325
Come Dungeon Dark (Part III)	326
Dark's Fidelity	326
Epilogue to an Episode	327
Dead End	329
Souvenirs de Paris: A la Fenêtre	330
Epilogue 1940–41	331
'Dear Thomas Eliot'	331
'The Porch before these poems is the entrance into night'	332
'The Hand that in the Darkness'	332
'The Son of Man is in Revolt'	333
'When I am able to think at night'	333
Haiku: 'Rain globules on glass'	334
'And tell me, how is Christ preached now?'	334
A Summer Evening at Caesar's Tower	335

APPENDIX B:
DRAFTS, POEMS IN FACSIMILE, TYPESCRIPTS

Elegiac Stanzas I.M. Alban Berg, typescript	339
Ex Nihilo, handwritten	341
Mozart: Sursum Corda, typescript	343
The Plummet Heart, handwritten	344
Apologia, typescript	345
Epilogue to an Episode, typescript 1 & 2	346

Dead End, typescript	349
An Elegy, last page	350
From a Diary, pages 1 & 2	351
Chambre d'hôtel	353
Noctambules, page 1	354
Epilogue 1940–41	355
Sonnet: The Battle	356
An Autumn Park, typescript	357
The Gravel-Pit Field	358
Poems published 1941, Notes handwritten	360
Requiem, A1 & typescript page 1	362
A Vagrant, page 1	364
Rondel for the Fourth Decade, typescript	365
Barcarolle	366
Stele	368
Terminal	369
Elegiac Improvisation in honour of Paul Eluard, page 1	370
Entrance to a Lane	371

APPENDIX C:
NOTES TO THE POEMS   375

SELECT BIBLIOGRAPHY

POETRY
Roman Balcony and Other Poems (London: Lincoln Williams, 1932)
Man's Life Is This Meat (London: Parton Press, 1936)
Hölderlin's Madness (London: Dent, 1938)
Poems 1937-42 (London: Editions Poetry London, 1943; reprinted 1944, 1948)
A Vagrant and Other Poems (London: John Lehmann, 1950)
Night Thoughts (London: André Deutsch, and New York: Grove Press, 1956; Paris: Alyscamps Press, 1995)
Collected Poems, edited by Robin Skelton (London: Oxford University Press & André Deutsch, 1965; reprinted 1966, 1970, 1978, 1982, 1984)
Penguin Modern Poets 17, with Kathleen Raine and W.S. Graham (London: Penguin Books, 1970)
The Sun at Midnight : Poems and Aphorisms (London: Enitharmon Press, 1970)
Three Poems (London: Enitharmon Press, 1976)
Early Poems (Warwick: Greville Press, 1980)
La Mano del Poeta, bi-lingual selection of poems, edited by Francesca Romani Paci (Genoa: Edizioni San Marco del Giustiniani, 1982). Awarded the Premio Biella-Poesia Europa 1982
Five Early Uncollected Poems (Leamington Spa: Other Branch Readings, 1984)
Collected Poems 1988 (Oxford University Press, 1988; reprinted 1988)
Extracts from 'A Kind of Declaration' & Prelude to a New Fin-de-Siècle (Warwick: Greville Press, 1988)
Tankens Doft, selection of poems, edited by Lars-Inge Nilsson (Lund: Ellerströms, 1988)
Miserere: Poems 1937-42 (Paris: Granit, 1989)
Poems of Milosz (London: Enitharmon Press, 1993)
Three Remanences (London: privately printed, 1994)
Selected Poems (London: Enitharmon Press, 1994)
David Gascoyne selection, edited by Roger Scott with Nicholas Johnson, in *Maggie O'Sullivan, David Gascoyne, Barry MacSweeney*, Etruscan Reader III (Newcastle-under-Lyme: Etruscan Books, 1997)
Encounter With Silence, Poems 1950, introduction by Roger Scott (London: Enitharmon Press, 1998)

The Entrance to that valley stands alone, pamphlet poem c. 1936 (London: Enitharmon Press, 2001)
Poems by David Gascoyne, selected and introduced by Judy Gascoyne (Warwick: Greville Press Pamphlets, 2001)
Poems by George Herbert, selected and introduced by David Gascoyne, edited by Roger Scott (Warwick: Greville Press Pamphlets, 2004)

PROSE
Opening Day (novel; London: Cobden-Sanderson, 1933)
A Short Survey of Surrealism (London: Cobden-Sanderson, 1935; London: Frank Cass & Co., 1970; San Francisco: City Lights Books, 1982)
Thomas Carlyle (London: Longman, Green & Co., 1952; reprinted 1963, 1969)
Paris Journal 1937-1939, with a preface by Lawrence Durrell (London: Enitharmon Press, 1978)
Journal, 1936-37 (London: Enitharmon Press, 1980)
Journal de Paris et d'ailleurs, 1936-1942, translated by Christine Jordis (Paris: Flammarion, 1984)
Rencontres avec Benjamin Fondane (Cognac: Arcane 17, 1984)
Collected Journals 1937-42, introduced by Kathleen Raine (London: Skoob Books Publishing, 1991)
Exploration, preface and trans. into French of 'Death of an Explorer' and 'Self-Discharged' by Michèle Duclos (Bordeaux: Editions Dufourg-Tandrup, 1992)
Lawrence Durrell (London: privately printed, 1993)
The Fire of Vision: David Gascoyne and George Barker, edited and introduced by Roger Scott (London: privately printed, 1996)
Selected Prose 1934-1996, edited by Roger Scott, with an introduction by Kathleen Raine (London: Enitharmon Press, 1998)
A Short Survey of Surrealism, with a preface by Dawn Ades and introduction by Michel Remy (London: Enitharmon Press, 2000)
April: A Novella, edited and introduced by Roger Scott (London: Enitharmon Press, 2000)
Letter to an Adopted Godfather [Henry Miller], edited and introduced by Roger Scott (Etruscan Books, 2012)

TRANSLATIONS

Salvador Dalí, *Conquest of the Irrational* (New York: Julien Levy, 1935)

Benjamin Péret, *A Bunch of Carrots: Twenty Poems* (London: Roger Roughton, 1936; trans. with Humphrey Jennings; second edition published as *Remove Your Hat*, 1936)

André Breton, *What Is Surrealism?* (London: Faber, 1936)

Paul Eluard, *Thorns of Thunder*, Selected Poems edited by George Reavey (London: Europa Press & Stanley Nott, 1936; trans. with Samuel Beckett, Denis Devlin, Eugène Jolas, Man Ray, George Reavey and Ruthven Todd)

Collected Verse Translations, edited by Alan Clodd and Robin Skelton (London: Oxford University Press, 1970)

André Breton and Philippe Soupault, *The Magnetic Fields* (London: Atlas Press, 1985)

Benjamin Péret, *Remove Your Hat & Other Works* (London: Atlas Press, 1986, trans. with Humphrey Jennings and Martin Sorrell)

Pierre Jean Jouve, *The Unconscious, Spirituality, Catastrophe* (Child Okeford: Words Press, 1988)

Three Translations (Child Okeford: Words Press, 1988)

Pierre Jean Jouve, *The Present Greatness of Mozart* (Birmingham: Delos Press, 1996)

Selected Verse Translations, edited by Alan Clodd and Robin Skelton, with an introduction by Roger Scott (London: Enitharmon Press, 1996)

Despair Has Wings: Selected Poems of Pierre Jean Jouve, edited and introduced by Roger Scott (London: Enitharmon Press, 2007)

NOTE

Thanks to the dedication over many years of the indefatigable Michèle Duclos, and the commitment of the editor Anne Mounic, much of David Gascoyne's work is available online (both in English and French) in several of the sixteen issues of *temporel: revue littéraire et artistique*: http://temporel.fr

See, for example, the following, prefaced by my English versions:

David Gascoyne: poésie et environnement;

David Gascoyne à Henry Miller;

David Gascoyne et Benjamin Fondane;

Gascoyne traducteur / traduire Gascoyne.

In chthonic labyrinth where we now stray
Do Thou in us make peace, O Lightbringer.
Submerged in darkness glows the serene day.
David Gascoyne: from 'Variations on a Phrase' (1982)

The spirit that flickers and hurts in humanity
Shines brighter from better lamps; but from all shines.
Look to it: prepare for the long winter: spring is far off.
Robinson Jeffers, from *Selected Poems*

The true point of the spirit sways,
Not like a ghostly swan,
But as a vine, a tendril,
Groping toward a patch of light.
Theodore Roethke, from *The Notebooks*

In our time, more than ever before, poets are the transcribers of a kind of truth to which only they can give articulate expression, and without which society becomes eventually one vast undifferentiated Buchenwald. Even in the extermination camps, poetry struggled out of men's dumb suffering into articulation, because poetry is the native tongue of hope, – the language of possibility.
David Gascoyne, Commonplace Book, 1948,
Beinecke Collection,
Yale University (unpublished)

It is a terribly painful thing to feel oneself able to see and understand the truth about contemporary man's situation, the total human crisis in which we must all realize ourselves to be involved, and yet to feel oneself powerless to act in a way which will effectively contribute to the spreading of such understanding as can alone enable man to resist the subhuman forces threatening to destroy him from within and to produce in him that complacent indifference which can make him accept destruction and non-being as his destiny. The evil of the modern world is entirely the result of lack of faith. The kind of faith that is lacking is synonymous with love: this is not the kind of faith that expresses itself in dogma or ideology which are always substitutes for it.
From a notebook in the Gascoyne Collection,
McFarlin Library, University of Tulsa
(unpublished)

Certain writers and poets manage to remain 'balanced' by separating their high spiritual thought or the exploration of the depths from their lives – they do not Surrealistically synthesise the dark and the light, the man and the poet, but remain sane by dichotomy. Certain writers and poets like Blake – and Gascoyne refuse this escape.
Brian Merrikin-Hill, 'The Transparent Mirror'

David Gascoyne in the 1930s

EDITOR'S PREFACE

The poet and critic Peter Levi wrote that 'It is still impossible for me to recall certain lines by Auden without a physical excitement,' and he went on to quote an example: 'O Love, the interest itself in thoughtless heaven [. . .]'[1] The spark which ignited the thrust of my research emanates from the frisson of my first encounter with David Gascoyne's poetry in the form of lines from his poem 'Tenebrae'[2]:

> The granite organ in the crypt
> Resounds with rising thunder through the blood,
> With daylight song, unearthly song that floods
> The brain with bursting suns:
> Yet it is night

lines which still resonate rhythmically down all the years since my days in the Lower Sixth in the 1950s. Trying to get to grips with an essay on diction in modern English poetry, my reading had brought me with a marked degree of excitement to a discovery of poems by the Auden of *Look, Stranger!* and *Another Time*, George Barker, Stephen Spender and the line, 'Crowns and head bounce like hoops down stone steps', Dylan Thomas and Gascoyne. It was to Gascoyne that I returned most frequently at university and afterwards, collecting first editions of his work and literary magazines with his contributions. Many years later in the 1990s we became friends, exchanging letters and telephone calls, and I visited the Isle of Wight on several occasions. He asked me to edit for publication several poems and a novella, long-forgotten and unpublished works which I had found in notebooks in the New York Public Library and the British Library (other books, such as *Selected Prose 1934–1996*, would follow as part of Enitharmon's ongoing Gascoyne project). I had embarked by then on my PhD thesis, *David Gascoyne: From Darkness into Light. A study of his poetry 1932–1950*, researching his published, unpublished and uncollected work.

I have commented elsewhere on Gascoyne, Barker and Thomas in the context of 1930s' poetry.[3] Here is a cultural terrain which the

---

[1] *The Noise Made by Poems* (London: Anvil Press 1977, 1984), p. 53
[2] *Hölderlin's Madness* (London: J.M. Dent, 1938).
[3] Introductory essay, *The Fire of Vision: David Gascoyne and George Barker*, edited and introduced by Roger Scott (Tragara Press for Enitharmon Press, 1996), pp. 5–21.

prevailing critical concensus by and large still tends to characterize as the province of 'the Auden generation'. There were arguably three generations of poets writing during the decade. Gascoyne, Barker and Thomas belonged in their precocious and prodigious productivity to the youngest. Gascoyne wrote of 'feeling a great gap' between his own work and that of Auden and his circle in the 1930s, while acknowledging that 'the *New Country* poets of the generation before mine were exciting because of their awareness of society's urgent need of drastic change, their expression of a longing for "new styles of architecture, a change of heart"'.[4]

For me, there was from the outset the spur of researching a body of work about which there is no book-length study in English,[5] and a strongly felt need to try to redress the critical balance and rehabilitate a writer who has been unjustly marginalized. Initially, my central concern was to examine Gascoyne's poetry and the way it intersected with Surrealism, the avant-garde connection allied to the 1930s' context. However, a re-framing rapidly became necessary as my perceptions changed. Gascoyne's involvement with Surrealism was a necessary but brief journey of liberation. That phase, as he told me, tended to hang like an albatross around his neck in the public consciousness until the remarkable scope of his lifetime's work became apparent in the 1990s. My focus became Gascoyne's development from precocious avant-garde theoretician and practitioner of Surrealism into a religious poet of major significance.

Other areas and issues rapidly assumed centrality not least my growing awareness of the significance of specific texts: *Roman Balcony and other poems*; *Hölderlin's Madness*; the *Collected Journals 1936–42* as a major document both for research and, more broadly, in terms of the map of twentieth-century literature and cultural history; *Poems 1937–42* and the need to investigate the context and genesis of its production. There was, too, the shift in his poetry after the crucial encounter in 1937 with the work of Pierre Jean Jouve and the Romanian Benjamin Fondane, both of whom became friends and

---

[4] 'Afterword' to *Collected Journals 1936–42* (London: Skoob Books, 1991), p. 391.
[5] There is the monograph by Professor Michel Remy, *David Gascoyne, ou l'urgence de l'inexprimé* (Presses Universitaires de Nancy, 1984), but there is no English translation. Remy is also the acknowledged expert on British Surrealism. In 2012, Oxford University Press published Robert Fraser's biography *Night Thoughts. The Surreal Life of David Gascoyne*.

mentors,[6] and later, the engagement with the mystics, especially Jacob Boehme, and the existential philosophers Kierkegaard, Chestov and later Heidegger. Gascoyne's was a truly European sensibility: like T.S. Eliot's, his verse reflects the presence of 'the mind of Europe'.

Darkness is represented in: Gascoyne's mental state described with excoriating honesty in the *Collected Journals*; the notion of 'la bouche d'ombre', the Orphic voice;[7] the inescapable awareness of the Void; his characterization of the *Zeitgeist* in the late 1930s as 'The Time of the Open Tomb'. *Light*, or the search for it, is present in the brightness and warmth of the sun (even at midnight); in the visionary quality so prominent in a number of poems; above all in his articulation of the need for man to acknowledge his lack of faith and to embrace the spiritual.

'*From Darkness into Light*' signified for Gascoyne an on-going, an incomplete journey, but one that mankind must make. Like Hölderlin, he saw his, and successive generations, 'walk[ing] in Night, dwell[ing] as in Hades, without the Divine'.[8] In 1992 Gascoyne asserted, citing Hölderlin again, that 'It is the job of the poet to go on holding on to something like faith, through the darkness of total lack of faith, what Buber calls the eclipse of God'.[9] Gascoyne's was a constant quest, clearly expressed by the Solitary in *Night Thoughts*: 'I am a man of a benighted century, famished for light and praying out of darkness in the dark', and informing all his mature poetry.

Gascoyne was attuned to the spiritual ambience of his age. His poetry, essentially religious, continues to be discovered by successive generations, and has a particular relevance to the twenty-first century. He articulates the human condition profoundly but yet with such

---

[6] See *Despair Has Wings*. Selected Poems of Pierre Jean Jouve, translated by David Gascoyne, edited with an introduction by Roger Scott (London: Enitharmon Press, 2007), and my dossier, 'David Gascoyne and Benjamin Fondane' / David Gascoyne et Benjamin Fondane (translated by Michèle Duclos) in the ejournal *temporel, revue littéraire & artistique*, Num. 9, 26 April 2010, online at http://temporel.fr

[7] 'There is a poem by Victor Hugo called "*Ce que dit la bouche d'ombre*", the mouth of shadow; the poet is a mask, through whom words from beyond come. Baudelaire is an example and Rimbaud and Mallarmé.' Lucien Jenkins,'Gascoyne in interview': *Stand*, Vol. 33, no. 2 (spring 1992), p. 21.

[8] Gascoyne's epigraph for *Night Thoughts*.

[9] *Stand*, op. cit., p. 25.

visionary clarity,[10] seeking an accommodation with the agonizing problems of living in the modern world.

★ ★ ★ ★ ★

David Gascoyne's first *Collected Poems*, edited by Robin Skelton, was published by Oxford University Press & André Deutsch in 1965. It was succeeded by the more substantial *Collected Poems 1988* (Oxford University Press), and a *Selected Poems* was issued by Enitharmon Press in 1994, all appearing in his lifetime. Thirteen years after his death, the *New Collected Poems* is a comprehensive edition, which incorporates in one volume a selection of his published and unpublished verse together with previously uncollected poems, reinstating others omitted from the three previous collections. Unlike Archie Burnett's recent, exhaustive if not 'forensic' *Philip Larkin: The Complete Poems*, this Enitharmon edition does not reprint every poem Gascoyne ever wrote, but represents an attempt to set his achievement as a poet in a clearer and more accurate perspective, and add considerably to an overall understanding of his identity as a poet.

In compiling the *New Collected Poems*, I have referenced the notebooks and manuscripts in the British Library, the Berg Collection in New York Public Library, the McFarlin Library at the University of Tulsa and the Beinecke Library at Yale University.[11] I have chosen to retain the volume-arrangements of poems published between 1932 and 1956 so that the reader finds them in their first context, and I have wherever possible presented them in the order of their composition or first publication. The dates appended to each poem in the main text are extracted from a number of printed sources together with details from the numerous notebooks kept by Gascoyne throughout his life. I have found it useful to employ Skelton's system of dating in his *Poetry of the Thirties* at the end of each poem as follows: 'w' showing the date of composition; 'p' before a date, indicating a poem printed in a periodical or anthology of that year; 'c' before a date, marking a poem first published in a collection of the poet's work at that time. A few errors in the chronological order in previous editions have been corrected.

A number of unpublished poems are here in print for the first time.

---

[10] I have quoted here from my article, 'Gascoyne, David Emery (1916–2001)' in the new *Oxford Dictionary of National Biography* (Oxford University Press).
[11] *David Gascoyne. A Bibliography of His Works (1929–1985)*, compiled by Colin Bedford, though incomplete has been invaluable (Ryde, Isle of Wight: Heritage Books, 1985).

To avoid raising their profile in the absence of Gascoyne's imprimatur, I have resisted the temptation to place them in the main text alongside uncollected and previously published titles. They are referenced *in italics* in the list of contents but located in **Appendix A** between pages 313 and 335. While a few of them have come to light since his death in 2001, I was able to show Gascoyne several of the early notebook poems I had found in the 1990s. Although he possessed a remarkable memory for details of people and places throughout his long life, he had no recollection of any of these MS drafts. Uncollected poems are clearly indicated by the letters UNCOLL.

I have borne in mind as far as possible Christopher Ricks's observation that it is not the job of an editor to issue 'critical pronouncements or appreciations, but the provision of such information, textual and contextual, as makes possible the common pursuit of true judgment.'[12] The notes are selective only, offering information not easily accessible now, and drawing attention to the genesis of specific poems, or to modifications made between the notebook drafts and/or first printing(s), and their first book publication; they may reveal aspects of Gascoyne's personal life and artistic development.[13] I have drawn on his journals, his contributions to anthologies, talks and BBC radio programmes, and on comments made to me and to his principal interviewers Michel Remy, Michèle Duclos, Lucien Jenkins and Mel Gooding.[14] These notes may be read in conjunction with Gascoyne's own 'Introductory Notes' (pp. xxvii–xxxvii). Unlike Auden or Yeats,

---

[12] 'Desired Reading': his review of *The Complete Poems of Philip Larkin* in *The New York Review of Books* (7 June 2012).

[13] All references to specific notebooks in the David Gascoyne collection in the British Library Manuscript Department are indicated by the following, **Add. + number**, e.g. Add. 56043.

[14] *Collected Journals 1936–42*, op cit. Cited as **CJS**.

Michel Remy, op. cit. 'Notes et Commentaires de David Gascoyne sur les *Collected Poems*' [1965], pp. 119–137. Cited as (**MRUI**). My translations.

Michel Remy, 'Extracts from an interview with Michel Remy', translated by Kathleen Raine in *Temenos* 7 (1986), pp. 273–84. Cited as (**MRT**).

Michèle Duclos, editor, *Cahiers sur la Poésie, numéro spécial: David Gascoyne*. Groupe d'Etudes et de Recherches Britanniques (GERB), Université de Bordeaux III, 1984. 'Entretien avec David Gascoyne', Londres, juin 1984, pp. 9–61. Cited as (**MDC**). My translations.

Lucien Jenkins, 'David Gascoyne in Interview' in *Stand*, op. cit, and in *Selected Prose 1934–1996* (London: Enitharmon Press, 1998). Cited as (**LJI**).

Mel Gooding, 'David Gascoyne, 1916–2001', Artists' Lives collection, recorded 1991, available online at http://sounds.bl.uk Cited as (**MGI**).

Gascoyne chose not to revise previous work in the editions of his collected and selected poems.

While a small proportion of individual poems (fifteen out of forty-one) in *Roman Balcony and other poems* had appeared since 1932 in various books and anthologies,[15] Gascoyne had firmly resisted the re-publication of any others or of the collection as a whole. The nine poems he included in the *Collected Poems 1988* were reduced to five in the *Selected Poems* of 1994. This was in the face of strong opposition from those of us involved in the selection who were convinced of the quality of the poems in that first collection by an adolescent and of their significance for the more mature work that was to follow. We very much wished to bring others to light and see them in print.

A year later in September 1995 I spent an afternoon with Gascoyne at his home when, out of courtesy but with a lack of enthusiasm he did not attempt to conceal, he started to leaf through the collection, flicking aimlessly it seemed through the eighty-seven pages. I watched as his attention became less and less cursory and his interest grew rapidly; he began to look intently at particular poems. After we had discussed several of them briefly, he suddenly turned to me and said, 'I'm surprised to say that some of these are rather better than I've always thought.' In the light of his response, I have felt justified in making the editorial decision to bring back into print for the first time a small number of poems from that 1932 publication.

At one point in our discussion Gascoyne had commented that the collection 'does show a considerable knowledge of and familiarity with music.' His lifelong love of and engagement with music was nurtured at Salisbury Cathedral choir school which he attended as boarder and chorister. He was playing Satie and Schönberg on the piano at fourteen. In Gascoyne's 'Commonplace Book, 1948', a short passage headed 'Music' begins: 'I recognize more and more clearly that music is the expression of the highest development of the (mental) spiritual life of man. In a future incarnation, if I shall be granted one, I hope I shall be able to be a composer [. . .]'[16]

He always believed that one of the strongest links in his friendship

---

[15] 'Mood' in Jon Stallworthy (ed.), *First Lines* (Manchester: Carcanet, 1987), pp. 107–8; 'Vista', 'Rain Clouds', 'The Bridge' in Allan Rodway (ed.), *Poetry of the 1930s* (London: Longmans, 1967), pp. 174–6; 'Rain Clouds' also appeared in A.T. Tolley, *The Poetry of the Thirties* (London: Gollancz, 1975), pp. 231–2; 'Prison' in Robin Skelton (ed.), David Gascoyne, *Collected Poems* (Oxford University Press, 1965), pp. ix-x of the 'Introduction'.

[16] In the Gascoyne Collection in the Beinecke Library, Yale University.

with his mentor Pierre Jean Jouve was their mutual admiration of Mozart and Bartok but, more particularly, their shared passion for Berg. Gascoyne's long poem in French, 'Strophes Elégiaques à la mémoire d'Alban Berg', was written in 1939, and his poems 'Cavatina', 'Concert of Angels', and 'Mozart: Sursum Corda' (dedicated to the South African composer Priaulx Rainier), between 1937 and 1938. He presented 'Requiem' to Rainier in 1940 to set to music. In an article written for *The Listener* in 1972, she recalled a walk in the Tuileries when 'he expressed a wish to find words for a long poem suitable for vocalising, which he would lay out in some musical format that would help to intensify its meaning.' Later she saw the first draft in Gascoyne's attic 'looking across the Seine to the flying-buttresses of Notre-Dame.' He had described how 'Requiem' was 'conceived as a libretto with words chosen specially for singing.'[17] It wasn't until 1945 that she felt able to write the music first performed at the Aldeburgh Festival in 1956.

Rainier, born in Natal in 1903, had won the Cape University Scholarship to the Royal Academy of Music for her violin playing in 1920. It seemed then apposite as I was drawing up what was to be the definitive version of the Contents list that I should by chance discover that among the Priaulx Rainier Papers in the Royal Academy of Music Library in London there are two files holding poems by Gascoyne.[18] The first contains fourteen 'New Poems' in typescript (most of which are signed), including the unpublished 'Dead End' and 'Epilogue to an Episode'. I have added them to this new edition, together with an alternate version of 'Mozart: Sursum Corda', one of five poems in the second file.

★   ★   ★   ★   ★

It is plain to all who are familiar with Gascoyne's verse that his output as a poet was slender in comparison with that of Auden, say, or Lowell. Like Larkin, he was astonishingly prolific from his mid-teens to his late twenties, but less so in the following decade and after when the creativity which he had richly enjoyed began to desert him due in no small measure to the crippling effects on his mental and physical health of his methedrine addiction, which led to a series of breakdowns. Although *Night Thoughts* was completed in the mid-1950s

---

[17] 'Priaulx Rainier writes about her setting of David Gascoyne's "Requiem"', 10 August 1972, p. 185.
[18] Files IPR/6/1/1 and IPR/6/1/2 [c. 1940].

after writer's block, he was unable to write more than a small number of poems in the last forty years of his life, developing instead a remarkable facility as a very accomplished translator, essayist, memoirist, obituarist and reviewer.

I feel immensely privileged to have known David and his wife, Judy, and to have been asked by him to edit some of his work, both poetry and prose. Privileged, too, to have been part of the ongoing Gascoyne publishing project, set in motion devotedly by the late Alan Clodd in 1978, and continued with an enduring commitment into the present century by Stephen Stuart-Smith who took on the running of Enitharmon Press in 1987.

INTRODUCTORY NOTES (1988)

THE first poem of mine to be accepted for publication was entitled 'Transformation Scene', and appeared in the literary weekly *Everyman*. In 1932, while still a day-boy at a West End secondary school, I persuaded an obscure publishing firm in a Court off the Charing Cross Road to publish, under the title *Roman Balcony*, a collection of poems including 'Transformation Scene'. My mother (who never considered herself to be much of a judge of poetry) told me: 'You'll only regret it later.' Before long this proved to be true. For many years after the mid-'30s, I did not wish this early 'slim volume' ever to be alluded to. During recent decades, however, *Roman Balcony* has from time to time appeared as a rarity in bookdealers' catalogues at ever more extravagantly high prices; which has encouraged me to reprint in the present collection nine of the forty or so items it comprises, though my choice includes neither 'Transformation Scene', 'Prison' (reprinted in Robin Skelton's Introduction to my *Collected Poems*, OUP 1965), nor 'Mood', republished recently in Jon Stallworthy's anthology *First Lines* (Carcanet 1987).

In April 1933, a weekly column called 'Poets' Corner', run by Victor B. Neuburg (an endearing eccentric once involved with the black-magician poet Aleister Crowley), began to appear in *The Sunday Referee*. Among the younger poets whose work subsequently appeared in this column were Dylan Thomas, Pamela Hansford Johnson, Ruthven Todd, Julian Symons, Laurie Lee, and myself. 'Slate', the first poem in *Collected Poems* of 1965, was first printed in *The Sunday Referee*. I now reprint for the first time 'Seaside Souvenir' and 'On the Terrace' (Richmond Terrace, near where I then lived), both of which also first appeared on a 1933 Sunday.

One of my mother's best friends had lodgings for many years when I was a boy in the house of Alida Monro, who with her husband Harold ran the Poetry Bookshop in Bloomsbury. I was first introduced to this shop at an early age, and once heard T. S. Eliot give a reading there, not of his own poetry but of Christina Rossetti's. In 1933 Mrs Monro, then not long a widow, edited *Recent Poetry: 1923–1933*, in which she magnanimously included three poems of mine, one of them 'Slate'. Barely seventeen, I must have been the youngest contributor to this anthology, arranged in alphabetical order and intended to represent a sequel to the *Georgian Poetry* series of Edward Marsh, and was undoubtedly gratified to find myself in the company of Yeats and Eliot, as well as of the poets of Auden's generation, and of George Barker, whose *30 Preliminary Poems* had just been published by David Archer's Parton Press, which three years later was to publish a small collection of my own.

1933 was something of an *annus mirabilis* for me. It was the year when Geoffrey Grigson, at that time working for *The Morning Post*, began publishing from his Keats Grove home his small, adventurous, and soon influential periodical *New Verse*. In one of its earliest issues Grigson published 'And the Seventh Dream is the Dream of Isis', the result of my first attempt to produce a sequence of lines of poetry according to the orthodox surrealist formula: 'Pure psychic automatism by which is intended to express . . . in writing . . . the real process of thought . . . in the absence of all control exercised by the reason and outside all moral or aesthetic preoccupations', in the words of André Breton, instigator of the surrealist movement. I was not to become a fully-fledged and committed member of this movement until two years later; but already before leaving school earlier that year I had been in the habit of visiting Zwemmer's bookshop in the Charing Cross Road, on my way home via Waterloo, to purchase not only back numbers of Eugene Jolas's avant-garde *transition* but also previous issues of *La Révolution surréaliste* (1924–9) and then of the more recent *Le Surréalisme au service de la Révolution*. In November 1933, A. R. Orage published in his *New English Weekly*, to which I was to become for a few years an occasional contributor, the series of short surrealist texts that in the present volume I have retitled 'Automatic Album Leaves'.

The semi-autobiographical stream-of-consciousness account of a day in the life of an adolescent literary aspirant to be found in *Opening Day*, my only novel, completed the year I left school, gives no indication of an awareness of Surrealism, though it contains a passage of enthusiastic reference to Rimbaud. After finishing it I had given it to Alida Monro to read, and she eventually decided to submit it to Cobden-Sanderson, who had just become the publishers of Harold Monro's posthumous *Collected Poems*, prefaced by Eliot. The novel was duly accepted; and the advance royalties I received on its publication from Cobden-Sanderson contributed to financing my first visit to Paris, where I was able to spend the last three months of 1933.

At this point I am tempted to digress into a detailed account of what was for me a momentous first encounter with France, a country in which I was subsequently to spend, on and off, at least fifteen years of my life. For the purpose of introducing the poems in the present collection, however, I must restrict myself to recording that although I did not then make initial personal contact with any of the representative writers of the surrealist group, I did visit Max Ernst's rue des

Plantes studio for the first time, and brought away with me from it one of his gouaches, a *Oiseau en forêt*; and from a visit to the shop at the foot of Montmartre of the official surrealist bookseller and publisher, José Corti, I brought away copies of recent collections by such poets as Breton, Eluard, and Tzara.

Some of the poems arranged together for the first time in the present volume under the general heading 'Surrealist' were first collected (confusingly accompanied by a certain number of non-surrealist items) in the little book published under the title *Man's Life Is This Meat* in the summer of 1936 at the time of the London International Surrealist Exhibition. All these poems are united by the basic aim of achieving the greatest possible spontaneity, but this aim can produce results of considerable variety. In 1935, Geoffrey Grigson published in *New Verse* 15 a group of short pieces of a type quite dissimilar from the apparently incoherent pellmell outpouring of images and phrases characteristic of 'And the Seventh Dream . . .'. Each of them appears to have some underlying theme or subject, though never a preconceived one. The title was usually added after the poem's completion, as is said to have been the case with the poetic pictures of Paul Klee. 'Gnu Opaque', for instance, was the watermark faintly distinguishable in the paper on which it was written. The title of the 1936 Parton Press collection was the result of a meeting with Geoffrey Grigson during which he produced a sample-book of printers' type-faces, which when opened at random showed the words 'man's life is' in one sort of type at the end of the bottom line on the left-hand page, and 'this meat' in a different type of lettering at the beginning of the top line of the page opposite: as an example of what the surrealists described as 'objective hazard', this seemed at the time an ideal title. 'The Truth is Blind' is a title applied without reflection to the result of an attempt to create a poem by adopting the technique of collage: three cuttings were selected at random from *Argosy Magazine, The Listener*, and an evening newspaper, which happened to be the sources nearest to hand at the time, and then stuck on two sheets of paper with spaces left between them to be filled in such a way as to link them into a more or less coherent whole, while avoiding stopping to consider anything like a normally logical connection between the three disparate component elements. A scarcely avoidable presupposition in this case was that the result would read like the account of a specific dream.

A French professor of English once asked me: Why did you call one of your poems by the name of a village near where I live outside Lyons? He was referring to 'Lozanne', the result of a specific conscious premeditation, to elucidate which requires some explanatory gloss. In 1933 there occurred in France a *cause célèbre* that, while scandalizing the general public, so aroused the indignation and sympathy of the surrealist group that its members collaborated in producing a collection of poems and drawings inspired by it. This was the case of Violette Nozière, put on trial for parricide and sentenced to life imprisonment. When in 1977 Louis Malle made a film based on the Nozière affair, portraying it as a classic instance of the triumphant hypocrisy of bourgeois morality, he made a point of referring in it to the poem contributed by Paul Eluard to the Surrealists' collective *plaquette* of protest and homage to the accused. In the summer of 1935, England was for weeks shocked and electrified by the Rattenbury/Stoner case (to be dramatized by Terence Rattigan in his last play, *Cause Célèbre*). Readers of any British newspaper at the time would have been aware that Mrs Rattenbury had already made a name for herself as a composer of light music under the pseudonym 'Lozanne'; they would also have seen photos of her invariably wearing a slim bandeau across her forehead. After a trial resulting in her acquittal and the sentencing to death of her young chauffeur lover, Alma Rattenbury committed suicide by drowning. Though genuinely touched by her fate, I doubt whether I should have written 'Lozanne' had I not recently seen a copy of the Surrealists' *Violette Nozière*.

As it is no longer possible to present the poems in the Surrealist section of this book in strictly chronological order, I have found it preferable to place together the four poems inspired by or dedicated to painters. 'Charity Week' is inspired by the sequence of Ernst's collages entitled *Une Semaine de Bonté*, the 'hero' of which is the Lion of the Place de Belfort. 'Yves Tanguy' attempts to evoke the atmosphere of his earlier unearthly landscapes. 'Salvador Dalí' was originally entitled 'In Defence of Humanism'; it does not attempt to present in verbal terms the imagery to be found in Dalí's best-known works, but to provide some sort of parallel equivalent of the personal 'mythology' his paintings embody. To each of the six stanzas of 'The Very Image' the title of one of Magritte's pictures could be affixed, though I had no idea when starting the poem what images were going to occur to me in the course of writing it: I had decided in advance only that each stanza should have five lines.

A similarly convenient grouping together is that of all the items in prose. I hesitate to designate them 'prose poems', since this category has been denounced cogently and with wit by George Barker as representing a 'Jubjub Bird'. The sequence now retitled 'Automatic Album Leaves' is no more than early exercises in uncontrolled word-play. 'Reflected Vehemence' probably represents the most successful of my attempts to register what Breton called '*le fonctionnement réel* de la pensée'; it was written in haste, without hesitation or the least intention to mystify, though its content defies analysis. The longest piece, 'The Great Day', was obviously written in emulation of the texts in *L'immaculée conception*, produced in collaboration by Breton and Eluard with the intention of simulating various types of mental disorder. Paranoia would appear to be the most easily imitable of such derangements. The pieces retitled 'Three Verbal Objects' were first published in the catalogue to an Exhibition of Surrealist Objects at the London Gallery in the winter of 1937, by which time I had moved to a Paris attic and virtually ceased writing in the surrealist vein. They are posthumously dedicated to Humphrey Jennings, in acknowledgement of the influence that his 'Reports' and other admirable short texts, first published by Roger Roughton in *Contemporary Poetry and Prose*, undoubtedly had on me.

'The Supposed Being' first appeared in the original *Faber Book of Modern Verse*, edited by Michael Roberts and published in 1935. 'The Symptomatic World' was originally planned as a sequence of a dozen parts, each to be written at a session. Some appeared in the short-lived review *Janus*, some in Roger Roughton's magazine; the remainder appear to have been lost. 'Phantasmagoria' was written early in 1939, when I had returned from Paris and was no longer writing poetry classifiable as surrealist. A young friend of friends insisted that I should write a poem especially for her. Unable to produce a suitable poem to order, I proceeded to employ the formula of quasi-automatism I had been accustomed to use during four previous years. The deliberate repetition of such a motif as a little black town on the edge of the sea is a device I would not formerly have allowed myself (except perhaps in the poem about sleep, 'Unspoken'). John Lehmann included it in the 1942 issue of *Poets of Tomorrow*, together with other poems of a quite different description.

In the autumn of 1937, my discovery of a copy of the 1930 edition of Pierre Jean Jouve's *Poèmes de la Folie de Hölderlin* in a book-dealer's box on the Paris quays marked a turning-point in my approach to poetry. I had not so much become disillusioned with Surrealism as begun to wish to explore other territories than the sub- or unconscious, the oneiric and the aleatory. Jouve's Hölderlin translations led not only to my essay, poems, and translations published by Dent the following year as *Hölderlin's Madness*, but to an excited first reading of Jouve's own poetry and prose, and before long to an acquaintance with the poet and his psychiatrist wife that was to last nearly thirty years. The use of lines quoted from Jouve as epigraphs to certain sections of *Poems 1937–1942* is insufficient indication of the enormous influence that his poetry, outlook, and conversation were to have on me for many years to come. Anyone familiar with Jouve's *Sueur de Sang, Matière Céleste* or *Kyrie* will recognize this influence in such poems of mine as 'World Without End', 'The Fortress', and 'Insurrection'.

This is not the place to pay further homage to a poet I still regard as the greatest it has been my good fortune to know. I should however add that 'The Fabulous Glass' now appears, as it should have done from the first, with a dedication to his wife, Dr Blanche Reverchon, as it represents a half-rhyming versification of a sequence of images that actually occurred to me during a psychoanalytic session with her in late 1938 and noted down immediately after: the Virgin and child in an alcove were in fact a medieval statuette of the Virgin with her child's face obliterated by an iconoclast or time, treasured by Jouve and kept in a recess in the study adjacent to his wife's consulting-room, to become the inspiration of his collection *La Vierge de Paris* (1939–44).

The place of 'The Conspirators' in the present collection should strictly speaking be between 'Snow in Europe' and 'Farewell Chorus'. I first read W. H. Auden's paperbacked *Poems* and his *The Orators* soon after their appearance, the *New Signatures* and *New Country* anthologies likewise; and it is not improbable that, had I not been carried away by enthusiasm for contemporary French poetry, and for *le surréalisme* in particular, I should have endeavoured to find a way of my own to express the politico-social awareness cultivated by many of my contemporaries and their immediate predecessors. I was as keenly conscious as they were of the meaning of current events in Europe, as well as of the hunger marches, and the menace of Mosley at home. In the summer immediately preceding the outbreak of war with Germany, in my family's home at Teddington, I was seized by an anomalous impulse to embark on a long narrative poem to be entitled 'Come Dungeon Dark'. Its setting was an imaginary European country on the brink of a fascist coup and the installation of a reign of terror and tyranny. The hero was to be a left-wing social scientist with the impossibly romantic name of Flambow. If my memory still serves me faithfully, this character, after the take-over of his country by dictatorship, was to retreat with a band of his comrades into hiding in a disused mine, finally to emerge, after numerous Resistance-type sorties and forays followed by a disastrous flood, to inaugurate the triumph of socialism after the dictator's downfall. That I could ever have carried out such a scenario in verse was of course a delusion; but I reprint the pages I did succeed in writing because they not only convey something of the atmosphere peculiar to the period, but also represent a reminder of my brief involvement with Mass Observation during those evenings in Blackheath in late 1936 when Charles Madge and Humphrey Jennings were about to launch it as a movement (in which later I took little part). The introductory episode of this unfinished epic was published by John Lehmann in the new series of his *New Writing* in the winter of 1939, and remained unreprinted and forgotten until recently.

A couple of poems that remained similarly forgotten until recently are 'Elsewhere' and 'Concert of Angels'. They appeared originally in Miron Grindea's *Adam International Review* just after the end of the War, though they may have been written earlier, perhaps at about the same time as the 'Requiem' later set to music by Priaulx Rainier. The second is recognizable as having been inspired by one of the panels of Grünewald's Isenheim altarpiece. The 'horrifying face, discoloured, flayed', in 'Ecce Homo' was likewise the result of having been impressed by the central figure in the black-and-white reproductions of this masterpiece that I first saw before the War. It was not until at least ten years later that I was taken to Colmar to see the original. 'Elsewhere' is an unmitigated overstatement of an underlying theme that has remained constant in almost everything I have written since then: the intolerable nature of human reality when devoid of all spiritual, metaphysical dimension.

I first returned to Paris after the War in 1947, and remained there for a year. At least half-a-dozen of the items collected in 1950 as *A Vagrant & other poems* were written during this visit or as a result of it. 'A Vagrant' represents the apologia of a premature beatnik or dropout, and is partly based on the idle, hotel-room existence I led at that time, increasingly disappointed with post-war governments' failure to implement the dreams and promises of a radically improved new future that had helped the Allies bring the Third Reich to an end. In my case this disappointment was compounded by the realization that I could no longer depend on the untramelled spontaneity of inspiration I had assiduously cultivated before the War. During the War, Tambimuttu's Poetry London Editions had published my *Poems 1937–42*, illustrated by Graham Sutherland; after which I had little time to write poetry as, unfit for military service, I turned professional actor for a couple of years, adopting Emery as my stage-name after that of my mother's family. The return of genuinely gifted demobilized young actors after the War meant that I was soon once more out of regular employment. I mention this in passing only because my intention during this period was to prepare myself through first-hand experience to contribute something to the revival of poetic drama that was still in the air at that time. The only result of this ambition was the production in 1950 of a satirical one-act piece concerned with the state of English theatre just before the abolition of censorship and the renaissance brought about by John Osborne and his contemporaries and successors. All that remains of *The Hole in the Fourth Wall*, as this production was called, is one of the Cabaret songs to be found here under the heading Light Verse.

The city setting of 'A Vagrant' is identifiable as Paris from its reference to straying 'slowly along the quais towards the ends of afternoons'. Young visitors to present-day France may no longer come across the 'cosy-corner', a franglais expression applied to a combined bed-head and book-shelves once a familiar feature of Parisian hotel rooms and bed-sits, and so fail to understand the allusion to a 'cosy-corner crow's-nest' also occurring towards the end of the poem. One or two other poems of this period require slight elucidation. The intention behind 'Innocence and Experience' was to produce something in the tradition of Eliot's early 'Portrait of a Lady', modelled on my experience of a couple of meetings with a certain Mme X, the wife of the owner-director of one of the best-known Parisian department stores. The line 'I still knew of her nothing less than this' leads to a complicated image intended to suggest a combination of two well-known portraits, one of Ellen Terry in the role of Portia, the other of the cellist Suggia by Augustus John, each of them intimating an aspect of Mme X's character and appearance. The imagined incident from her childhood is purely speculative. The setting is the *hôtel particulier* in the Faubourg Saint-Germain district in which she had lived for many years. The occasion narrated is close to what actually occurred when another lady belonging to her circle took me with her to call on Mme X again, for the first time in ten years. The works of art referred to were almost exactly as described.

The following piece, 'Photograph', was inspired by a portrait of Philippe Soupault in his prime by the American photographer Berenice Abbott. When I wrote this poem, which deliberately avoids anything visually concrete except the subject's eyes, I had still never met Soupault, who at the time of my frequenting the surrealist group in 1935/6 had fallen out of its official favour, having begun to write travel journalism and novels that might have been intended to be commercially successful. When I was finally able to visit him, he was in his mid-eighties. He will be ninety-one this year, the last survivor of the original surrealist movement, except Dalí. A final explanation here: 'The Other Larry' refers to Lawrence Durrell. How I can have expected the reader to realize this in the absence of footnote or formal dedication, I don't know. The poem is in a sense an answer to one by Durrell, dated 1939 and addressed to me (his 'Paris Journal': *Collected Poems*, Faber & Faber 1957), and it attempts to sum up certain differences between our points of view that had first become apparent during our discussions in pre-War Paris. It is republished in the hope that its argument is of sufficient interest to be appreciated without consideration of the specific persons involved in it.

In the autumn of 1951, I accompanied Kathleen Raine and W. S. Graham to America, where we gave a series of readings in New York and certain NE States under the guise of 'Three Younger British Poets'. I returned to England a year later, having first gone on from the States to Vancouver Island BC to visit my parents who at that time were living in retirement there. It was immediately after arriving back in this country that I learnt of the death of Paul Eluard. I had met him again only once since the War, during which his fame and popularity had increased enormously. So had his commitment to the PCF and Stalinism, largely, it seemed to me, as a result of his third marriage. The 'Elegiac Improvisation' I wrote after his death was an expression of the admiration of him I had first felt when not yet twenty. Passages of the poem use brief lines imitative of his *Poésie ininterrompue*; others introduce imagery derived from the kind of French painting he loved and interpreted so well. It refers to him as the great poet of the Resistance that he was commonly supposed to be. It was not until quite recently, on reading Milan Kundera's *Book of Laughter and Forgetting*, which contains a bitterly ironic account of Eluard's inexcusable failure to speak out in defence of his one-time friend the surrealist Zavis Kalandra, who was hanged in Prague in 1950 during the French poet's visit to the city at the invitation of the Czech authorities, that I fully realized what kind of man he had become at the end of his life. If I had been aware of this incident at the time, and fully understood the way authoritarian politics can transform even so fraternal a poet as Eluard, it would not have been possible (or, at least, I hope not) for me to write the kind of poem that the 'Elegiac Improvisation' turned out to be. The poem was intended for recital and I first read it at the Institute of Contemporary Art, then still located in Mayfair; it was later published in the review *Botteghe Oscure*.

Soon after my return from America, Douglas Cleverdon of the BBC commissioned me to write a work for voices and music for the Third Programme. This turned out to be *Night Thoughts*, written in a relatively short space of time, and with the exception of the Eluard elegy the only poem of any kind I had been able to write since 1950. It was finally broadcast in December 1955, with music specially composed by Humphrey Searle. By that time I had gone to live in France, and was to spend the summer in Aix-en-Provence, the winter in Paris, for ten consecutive years, except for occasional brief return visits to England. During this period I was incapable of writing a line due to the block, or *crampe* as the French call it, that had resulted from a long abuse of amphetamines dating from as far back as the beginning of the War. In one of the 50-odd 'aphorisms' collected in *The Sun at Midnight* (edition limited to 350 copies, Enitharmon Press 1970), I discuss this addiction at some length, explaining that amphetamines 'have powerful and most undesirable side-effects which probably were responsible for reducing my output to the strict minimum of work on which a poet's reputation can plausibly rest'.

The title of the fragment entitled 'Half-an-Hour', dedicated to my generous hostess during those years of unproductivity, derives from one of the most mysterious phrases to be found in the Book of Revelation: 'And there was silence in heaven for the space of half-an-hour.' It is all that remains of an attempt to break my silence of years by exploring its nature and conditions. 'Remembering the Dead' was my only contribution to David Wright's review *X*, in which it appeared in 1959. The poem first published in 1970 in *Penguin Modern Poets 17*, under the optimistic title 'Part of a Poem in Progress', now changed to 'Unfinished Poem from Elsewhere', had suddenly emerged as though by dictation from the unconscious, unexpected and inexplicable, in 1964, just before the onset of a severe nervous breakdown, as a result of which I had to return permanently to England.

The 'Three Verbal Sonatinas' (which conclude the Light Verse section) were written in 1969 when I was convalescing in a psychiatric hospital from a further breakdown as chronic as that of five years previously. Several of the small number of poems produced since my final recovery from a third breakdown and my marriage in 1975 were written as a result of requests from editors. 'Whales and Dolphins' was produced for the Greenpeace organization's enormous anthology *Whales A Celebration* (Hutchinson 1983). The tribute to Miron Grindea was composed on the occasion of his seventy-fifth birthday, and printed on the cover of a special 45th anniversary number of his *Adam International Review* (also 1983). Its title is intended to indicate that it is what could be called a 'verbal square', consisting of twelve dodecasyllabic lines, or alexandrines, a form I had used the previous year to contain a comment on the Falklands conflict. The latter appeared at the end of a contribution to a compilation called *Authors Take Sides on the Falklands*. 'A Sarum Sestina' was written specially for Satish Kumar's anthology *Learning by Heart*, published in 1984 to raise funds for The Small School founded by him in Hartland, near Bideford in Devon. Similarly, 'Thalassa: The Unspeakable Sea' was written simultaneously in English and French for the international anthology *Thalatta (Hommage à la Mer)*, published by Editions Internationales Eureditor of Luxemburg on the occasion of the 8th Congress of the World Organization of Poets held in Corfu in 1985, though it did not reach the editor in time to be included in it; the French version ('*Au delà de toute expression*') eventually appeared later that year in no. 35 of the review *Phréatique*, and the English in *Temenos* 7. It is dedicated to Mimmo Morina, Secretary General of the World Organization of Poets. Finally, 'Entrance to a Lane' resulted from a request for a contribution to the anthology *With a Poet's Eye* (Tate Gallery, 1986).

The seventh verset of 'Thalassa: The Unspeakable Sea' combines allusions to Prospero's book of magic spells, to two of the Fragments of Heraclitus, and to Tennyson's early poem 'The Kraken'. 'A Further Frontier' was inspired by the view to be seen from the North of the isle of Corfu of the frontier dividing mainland Greece from Albania. Greek-hay is a variant of fenugreek, a herbal plant the green of which is distinguishable from that of coniferous foliage. The last lines of the poem derive from the conclusion of Schiller's lyric *Gruppe aus dem Tartarus*, set as a *lied* by Schubert. 'November in Devon' contains a reference to an autumn landscape clad in the colours of DPM, the military term for 'disruptive pattern material', in other words the camouflage-type stuff of uniforms now worn by troops and guerrillas throughout the entire civilized world.

In addition to those I have already acknowledged throughout these introductory notes, I would like to thank particularly my bibliographer Colin Benford, Alan Clodd of the Enitharmon Press, and Professor Norma Rinsler of King's College, London; and belatedly, Robin Skelton, whose edition of the first *Collected Poems* has paved the way for this fuller and more complete edition of my poems from 1932 to 1986.

DAVID GASCOYNE,
Isle of Wight, July 1987
Collected Poems 1988.

ACKNOWLEDGEMENTS

I would like to record my deep gratitude for the friendship, unfailing help, kindness and encouragement shown throughout the gestation of this book by the following: Allan Ingram, Anthony Astbury, Colin Benford, Yves Bonnefoy, Robert Fraser, Anne Goossens, Jeremy Reed, Anthony Rudolf; Michel Remy and Michèle Duclos who continue to keep Gascoyne's work alive in France; booksellers James Fergusson, Peter Ellis and Charles Seluzicki; the late Alan Clodd, Yves de Bayser, Michael Hamburger, Peter Jolliffe, Alan Smith, I.D(avid) Edrich and Kathleen Raine.

Stephen Stuart-Smith's gentle guidance and sympathetic understanding, as always, have been crucial.

I am indebted, too, to Sally Brown and Chris Fletcher, formerly of the British Library Manuscript Department; to Erin O'Neill at the BBC Written Archives Centre; to Melissa Burkhart and Ruth Carruth at the McFarlin Library, University of Tulsa; to Kevin Repp and Becca Lloyd of the Beinecke Rare Book and Manuscript Library at Yale University, and to Andrew Morris at the Royal Academy of Music Library. Their prompt, patient and friendly response to my numerous queries and requests has been of immense value.

And finally, for the constant support given and time taken, my inadequate thanks to my wife, Pat, and to our daughter Kate and son Mark.

R.S.

POEMS WRITTEN AT SCHOOL
(1929)

STORM

With a mighty rush the wind goes by,
Singing a weird sad prelude of the Soul,
Driving black clouds before the moon,
With its thunder in a mighty roll.
In fitful rush the rain comes streaming down
Filling with water the streets of the old town,
And round the steeple the wild gale howls,
Catching the laughter of fiendish ghouls,
Throwing higher the dreary song
The dreary wild song of the storm.

OCTOBER NIGHT

I stood outside that October night
I stood outside in the dim half light
'Dark deep clouds the moon half obscure
Clearing the sky a few stars fewer
The Wind that rustles in the leaves
Rises sighing to the eaves.'
I took a breath of the sharp clean air
The Autumn tang was rich and rare
'A clanging peal breaks forth from the spire
Offering the stars its musical fire
The lawns of the Close, dim white outspread
Are a mist on the sea' I said.
'This Autumn is but a stage
A step, on the house of my pilgrimage.'

From **ROMAN BALCONY AND OTHER POEMS**

(1932)

ROMAN BALCONY

Far-off, palpitating tide!
In the pale light I sit here,
Sad with sin, gazing on the city,
On the yellow waters of the distant Tiber,
On a stone sphinx at the gate of my villa.

A wild pipe-tune climbs through the cold air
From the rain-beaten roses under the balcony,
Like the vast, tumbling cloud that sweeps
Whirling over the faded sky,
Full of the shadow of death.

Far-off, palpitating tide!
There is a fluttering of wings
As a withered petal falls from the trellis,
Creating a swift, fantastic shadow
Across the purple wine within my golden cup.

FADING AVENUES

At my feet, trembling in the wind,
lies a rusty and serrated leaf,
alive with sun-caught moisture,
with a scarlet stem.
Above my head as I stand, cold, dreaming,
a tattered projection of black-spotted leaves
on a branch.

The avenues are fading
and my sight is fading fast as they
for I see but vaguely the figures that pass:
. . . There is a crimson coat . . .

The sound of the wind is like water; . . .
(water falling only in dreams,
for the fountain is choked, the fountain is stained,
at its food a few burrs rotting lie).
The sound of the wind is fading,
and fading the sad sound of feet

drifting over the lawns
where grey's on the sheen of green.
The sound of the wind is fading . . .

The wind creeps slowly up my spine
and creeps up the boles of the trees.
The trees stand brooding over their disintegration:

The ichor within grows lifeless and cold.
Above them one pine exulting stands
for the green of its foliage never fades.
But the avenues are fading
and the mould of the flower-beds is sour and dark
and the stems of the shrubs are black
with a sudden ignition of leaves at their tips.
The avenues are fading and sounds drift from afar.

Whose tomb shall we discover
in the dun shade of the woods
at the end of the fading avenues?

VISTA

A clatter of geese
fantastically waddling
over the jade silk lawn.

Behind them dark trees
genii clad in a green smoke
of leaves.

Under the trees,
warm and silent,
the mysterious, placid colours
of rhododendrons burn,
faintly,
electric blossoms,
like calm, pale,
subaqueous coral, . . . anemones.

Beyond,
stretching into sightless, unknown regions,
up the slope of a summitless hill,
a vista of low, contorted trees,
under a lavender sky.

What secret is hidden
at the end of the avenue?
A temple?
An iron gate?
A fragrant wilderness with briars?

ROMAN GHOSTS

THE trumpet's echo
stirs the vast
shining plain of the shore.
The noisy sun
clashes its swords
on the horsemen's armour
that ride here to dip
their misty, snorting steeds
in the sharp brink of the sea.

A metal-clattering cavalcade
advances
across the beach
where shallow pools
mirror the sky.

The ostrich feathers
of the waves
that flap against the shore
mimic the plumes
that wave from the helmets
of the Roman ghosts
who ride across the sand
to vanish in the mist.

SUMMER'S ECHO

Cold is the day,
colder than fires of water,
colder than ashes of a forgotten moon.
In the dark room under the tower
the shutters flap in the draught.
The hollyhocks hang broken.

Empty
void in space a sound (trickling
through colossal stretches
of arid air) intimating
some tremendous music
beyond our consciousness.

Some white figure with long hair
walks through the mist
sighing and stirring the branches
of sleep, walks through the room
raising the dust from the stones
of the cold-paved floor.

RAIN CLOUDS

The garden is cold.
Winds stir
over the green hollow of the lawn.
Faded roses
tumble delicately over the old brick wall.
Marigolds burn
on the margin of the green.
Here is colour,
but behind the darkling trees
clouds rear,
dark and ominous, rain-burdened,
like shreds of an old dream
which tumbles out of its chilly case
when the door of the mind
is opened by memory.

PRISON

It is dark and stifling within this cupboard.
I cannot open the door.
In the faint light I see a Chinese mask
That glares down upon me
From one high corner.

When I move, the walls move.
They follow my movements like the moon.

Like the unfolding of a rose,
Within no prefixed hour, a window opens.
In the clear air outside I see the plain
Rushing to join the distant sky.
Over the sun-scorched grass of the plain
Red-robed riders pass on tall horses.

The window closes.
I hear a gramophone.

If I put out my hand in the darkness
I know that my trembling fingers will meet
The leaves of the tree that grows in this cupboard.

If I open my eyes again
I know that my eyes will always see
The Chinese mask or the vague window.

If I move my body from this spot
I know that the walls will follow me,
Moving always like walls in a mirror.

TRANSFORMATION SCENE

The fire-lit room fills itself with shadows,
And with indistinct wall-paper,
And with a bowl of chrysanthemums,
Freshly gathered from the wet garden.
On the oak sideboard are oranges,
And a book with a bright cover.

A web descends upon the room,
Woven of aerial texture:
A veil of semibreves and minims,
A melody pensive – now plaintive,
A nuance of subtle colourings.

We will dance a slow pavane
down a dark alley of cypresses.
We will let our brocades trail through the dewy grass.
We will let laughter and low lute-notes float across the lake.
In this antique but newly discovered paradise
we shall meet apes and parrots.
The light shall be subdued.
We shall suspend our dream-balloons
by silken threads on the cold, sweet air.

As we glide lightly through the willow's foliage,
fixing our eyes on some white statue through the leaves,
we shall discover that the oranges on these branches
are only oranges on the sideboard.

We slide back into the warm room.
The bright web fades . . .
The fire crackles and I see its light
Glittering on the firm flesh of your hand.

THE BRIDGE

Under the cruel and steely water
Lie the soft, white bodies of the suicides.
Their hair is green river-weed.
Bright pebbles are their eyes.
Strange lilies grow out of their breasts,
And through the long-nailed fingers
Glide the silver-shining minnows.

Slowly the decaying moon
Slides up behind the shadowy palaces.
Soft flame-red is her puppet's face,
And soaked with the sins of the City.
As she climbs painfully through the darkness

Her light falls across the water of the river,
And makes thereon a hard, bright bridge of beaten copper.

The tall, powdered courtesans
Come out from the wicked City
With crimson ribbons floating from the shadows of their hair,
And above the river where the suicides lie
They strut to and fro across the copper bridge,
Holding hard iron roses in their hands
With wooden leaves.

PSYCHOLOGICAL FRAGMENT

INDEFINITE horror . . .
O unquiet water
you cannot be calm.
The volcano that stands
in the ultimate desert
is your fullest expression.
(Arabia, shadowy, veiled,
silent, yet singing).
That urge of faint terror
in unquiet water
is your confession.
For hark! as it falls
the yellow water mingles with the sky
and rocks are opened suddenly
in the dark solitudes
and blossoms strange
wander vaguely into sight
and unknown words
form in the air.
The air (pale, secret as flowers),
is as green as the sea
and as blue as the soul
which is filled with indefinite horror
O words which form in the air,
free me from this subtle terror!

EXHAUSTION

THE hall is darkening.
New possibilities stir in the dusk.
New hills rise behind the newspaper.
Withered poppies descend the stairs.

When will the noises in the street
Break down these walls?
At night the street-lamps send long tentacles
Which slide through the dusty window-panes,
Pulling off the withered petals
Of the poppies which perpetually descend the stairs.

SEASIDE TRAGEDY

'A Verdict of Suicide while of unsound mind was
returned at the Inquest on Mrs X, a widow, at Bournemouth
today. Mrs X was the Proprietress of a Boarding-house, and
it was stated at the Inquest that financial and other troubles
had been weighing on her mind for some time.'
– *Daily Paper*.

'LONG, long ago it was remembered
on the seashore
(by one of those who find it possible to remember),
it was remembered that
black is never white
and that the snow
will fall into the sea
and at once become part of the sea;
and that a door will open
and let fall upon the linoleum
a square of light,
white against the black of the shadow.
So how can one remember clearly?
It has become impossible to distinguish
between the sea and linoleum.
I will think of black and white
until I see them mingle in the sea
and intertwine and die.

Candles must rise out of the waves
heralding the birth of a new sunrise.
Across the waters pass the feet
of one, of five, of nine: –
How the light is white!
And how the green is in the sea!
And how it falls!'

'Let us exploit a vegetarian activity.
Let us resolve the chords of the barrel-organ
playing in the street outside my window
at half-past two in the morning
    into thirds and fourths
    and sharps and flats.'

'Among the waves
(gambolling upon the deserted shore),
so many barrel-organs . . . .
They glide like stately swans
over the surface:
And their candles are reflected in the mirrors at
    their feet.'

'I must each day say o'er the very same.
I must each day say o'er the very same.'

'I would pay one-and-nine
for an artichoke,
provided that it was fresh,
and gathered between half-past one
and half-past two in the morning
by an old man with a glass eye . . . .
I would indeed pay one-and-nine
for such an artichoke.'
'This is perfectly serious,
perfectly serious (I mean it);
Measures may have to be taken.
Something ought to be stopped.
This kind of thing ought not to be allowed.'

    .   .   .   .   .   .

Wandering among Paul's serpents
She expressed a faint desire
To start her life afresh.
She said she was tired of playing bridge;
And of removing her teeth last thing at night before
    going to bed;
And of buying chrysanthemums
For her husband's grave
Every ninth of October: . . .
. . . Poor thing!
She really deserves no pity,
But yet one grudgingly gives it her.
She sits in the bathroom
Staring at her distorted reflection
On the curved copper side of the geyser.
There is still a disturbing memory
Of last Sunday's breakfast,
When the eggs had not been boiled properly,
And she had had to speak severely
To the Cook.

She went out of the bathroom.
She ran downstairs.
She went out by the French windows.
She felt the cold sea-air on her face.

    .   .   .   .   .   .

'Immeasurably wan
the grace of women,
. . . distant, . . . distant; . . .
and rose-petals lying fading on the grass;
and the hush and the sway of the sea,
which seems like dew dying the fruit
with ermine and jasmine.'

    .   .   .   .   .   .

She went across the lawn
Towards the sea.

    .   .   .   .   .   .

'This is perfectly serious,
perfectly serious (I mean it);

Measures may have to be taken.
Something ought to be stopped.
This kind of thing ought not to be allowed.'

'I must each day say o'er the very same.
I must each day say o'er the very same.'

.   .   .   .   .

She saw the sea.
She heard the barrel-organs
Playing eternally
At the bottom of the sea.

She remembered,
(As she approached the sea),
The linoleum,
And the artichokes,
And the geyser.

Sad wraith,
Thy hair (white, . . . white),
Flowing out like a towel,
Rises and becomes part of the texture
Of the tower of your thoughts,
Flickering solemnly, like your hair,
Round your head.

.   .   .   .   .

'The beach is a chess-board.'

'Among the waves
(gambolling upon the deserted shore),
so many barrel-organs . . . .
They glide like stately swans
over the surface:
And their candles are reflected in the mirrors at
    their feet.'

'The beach is a chess-board.'

.   .   .   .   .   .

She remembered her husband.
She saw the chrysanthemums
Burning yellow in the rain,
(Like the barrel-organ's candles),
In the grass above his grave.

.   .   .   .   .

'The grave is dark.
There is no death.
The sea shall give up its dead.'

.   .   .   .   .

She sits on the beach,
Staring at her reflection
On the curved glass side of a wave.

.   .   .   .   .

'These feet are feet (yes, indeed feet),
they are covered with sand,
they are cold,
they are feet,
feet, feet,
feet.'

'I must each day say o'er the very same.
I must each day say o'er the very same.'

'Little drops of water, little grains,
trickle in a slow stream
down my back and through my nose,
and tingle in my eyes,
and turn my feet into cement.'

'Death has nothing whatever to do
with linoleum or artichokes or the geyser.'

'The barrel-organs
shall play my funeral march,
and the drums of the sea
shall roll at my departure.'

'Unending, unending,
Beyond the veil
there is no death,'
(The waves cover her),
'linoleum, artichokes, the geyser
   so damp, so distant,
      rose-petals and skeletons
         unending, unending,
            unending.'

'I must each day say o'er the very same.'

THE NEW ISAIAH

To Oswald Spengler

ALONG the highways strewn with ashen filth
the ragged pilgrims come to the new Metropolis,
that cruel City, built of stone and steel,
where unveiled passions, unashamed crimes,
the windy avenues traverse, where lust
wars bitterly with lust, where naked lights
illumine nightly what the day concealed.

They come in hordes, they come all day,
the oafs, the ignorant, the louts,
who tire at last of retch and sweat
on farms, on all-too-barren fields,
whose crude desires, unsatisfied
by buxom cheek of dairymaid,
by greasy thigh of country-wench,
come hither in an eager rout
in search of painted lips and faces,
of limbs by nightly libertines embraced.

They come to toil at City desk,
to serve in cafés or in shops,
to balance on the scaffolding
of building-sites, to dig the roads,
to wait in the weary, rain-drenched queues
that straggle outside the Labour Exchanges;
or, if the City finds them fools,
they sit and sleep like sodden sacks
on the rusty seats of embankments or suburbs.

When night descends, when the last toil is done,
the City streets, garbed in beguiling lights,
invite the labourer to every vice,
and laughter squalls, and crowds go arm-in-arm,
the whores come out to wait in alleyways
where sudden drunks from hidden corners lurch,
and Pleasure Palaces and smoky dens
alike proclaim their divers cheap attractions.

In stinking sewers open to the sky
the worn-out profligates lie down to die;
and rank contagion fills the germ-laid air
from poisoned corpses that the wind strips bare.

Midst clawing shadows and the web of crazy nights,
in stuffy rooms that paralyse the mind,
the weakened bodies of this later race of men
beget a stunted and deformed mankind.

Nor art nor music flourishes in this decline;
the world degenerates, has lost its mind.
We hang our harps upon the trees to weep
and with our brushes paint disintegration's signs.

All aim and faith has gone. Men do not grope
within this xanthic fog, nor do they hope,
but toil and grovel as the years proceed.
They toil for nothing; nor do they feel need.

The ranting whirligigs revolve and scream
in acrid breath of smoke or steam;
the lights are harsh and dazzle every eye
to signs of omnipresent Destiny.

But Destiny's brass trumpet wakes the wise.
They see decay, they see the falling globe,
they see the slow inevitable decline
of nations, and the twilight of the West.

A new Isaiah walks the City streets
with burning coals of fire on his head
who cries his warnings to the careless crowds
who heed him not but arm themselves for wars,
who whet their swords for one another's blood,
who go a-whoring with their own inventions
deaf to the cries of one who sees their fate:
'As Rome fell, ye shall fall,
as falling ye are now.'

A new Isaiah walks the City streets
with burning coals of fire on his head:
'The world-metropolis is built on dust,
with fruitless labour, by the sweat of lust.

To dust it shall return nor shall it rise again
till the world writhes in the tremendous pain
of a new birth in a far-distant dawn,
nor can you hope to see that new world born.

'You cannot turn to God for there is no God left:
Your god is the Machine, of soul bereft.
Through all the discords of a striving host
the Machine drones on, a steel ghost.

'Out of the foul refuse that the mob ignores
old vices rise that no one now deplores.
New Sodoms and Gomorrahs flourish in the dusk
which suck their foul fruit dry and fling away the
   husk.

'You cannot check the wheel of Fate.
The years are late,– the years are late.
The West declines, Metropolis is falling . . .'
through the loud shade the prophet-voice calling.

The sun has gone. The City's lights
shine out with fevered brilliance.
When at the last these brilliant lights shall fail
how dark and terrible the Winter night!
E'en now, above the giant roofs
rises a pale and waning moon –

Tis but a few can read the signs.

OTHER EARLY POEMS

(1932–1935)

BY THE SEA

TRADITIONAL FORM

The sea rolls to and from the land,
Leaving white patterns on the sand.
To watch the waves I wander here
Along the water's edge – I hear
The whole world crying out in sleep,
With voice of winds and waves that weep.

BY THE SEA

MODERNIST POEM

(1)
the whiskey windwhite
                         waves spit in my
   face they are so grey so stony cold the
                      waves
          are grey stone walls the
   sea is an old washerwoman's wh
O (ooo)spitsand flings grey stones   atm
e (eee)

(2)
Bluer and blue   meeting
bluer the sea rushes and
retreats folding   (o) and
ex pan ding l ike a
concertina.

(3)
Lettuces are grow
ing in the blue   c
       averns
       little f
       ish sw
       ish in
       and out of them

```
                           (4)
   LOOK!
            it is the shark
            with the little    no
            selike        al
                      umpo
            fsugar he jumps)
            out of the water) (sh-) . . . spl . . . ash . . . ashing
            us with spray likes
            ilver tea-leaves
                           (5)
      awave   touches
              aus Trali A
              and anothe
              r touches C
              hinajingl
              ing likech
              ains the   waves   join   am
                                        er
              (booo . . . o . . . oom)  ic
                                        a
   to Europe where the flags            fly
   but no wave touches Switzerland
   where the mountains like taller
   waves only whiter reach for the
                                        sky

                           (6)
   the sea is an old washerwoman
   forever folding and unfolding
   her blue with cold enormous
   arms
   forever rolling and unrolling
   her white froth with enormous
   eyes.


   p. 1933
```

SEASIDE SOUVENIR

The pattern the jelly-fish left behind,
a pocketful of sand,
a dead, pressed leaf,
the woven rhythms of three days:
these are their traces, faded, indistinct.

The cliff's wide boulders, the immense
rocking of ocean through the bay,
the lighthouse beam stabbing the rainy night:
these are the memories of three days and more,
not separate, but one – and quite distinct.

p. 1933

ON THE TERRACE

A heavy day: so old the sky
That covers up the treegrown leagues below;
So cold the figures up and down
The terrace where the gusty fountains blow.

Here comes a colonel, at his side
His wife, with drooping shoulders, dressed in black.
They neither of them speak a word.
The colonel walks with hands behind his back.

The woman wears a fading rose
Upon her breast. She and the colonel stare,
Dumb, at the footworn pavingstones
As they walk on. A sigh disturbs the air.

Stirred by no dull regrets for youth,
Or love now dead that once in Spring was new,
Too tired to speak of memories,
They pause and turn to contemplate the view.

Then they pass on. A fountain leans
To drench the stones on which they stood with spray;
And from an ironrailinged tree
A bird looks after them – then flaps away.

p. 1933

SLATE

Behind the higher hill
sky slides away to fringe of crumbling cloud;
out of the gorse-grown slope
the quarry bites its tessellated tiers.

The rain-eroded slate packs loose and flat
in broken sheets and frigid swathes of stone,
like withered petals of a great grey flower.

The quarry is deserted now; within
a scooped-out niche of rubble, dust and silt
a single slate-roofed hut to ruin falls.

A petrified chaos
the quarry is; the slate makes still-born waves,
or crumbling clouds like those
behind the hill, monotonously grey.

p. 1933

SUSAN: A CARVING BY ERIC GILL

The fingers of the air caress your face;
you are so smooth and yet your stone is firm,
inevitable, like volcanic rock
that bursting molten through to air
at once sets firm and is unalt'rable.
The rock has formed spontaneously your face;
and natural as the waves that run through corn
your curved and flowing hair; your petalled lips;
and empty eyes that show no soul although a soul is there.

p. 1933

From: TEN PROSES

2

In New York and other cities, cities of the Future, there are overhead railways along the sides of buildings. The windows of the trains glint in the sunlight or the frenetic glare of enormous electric signs as they pass, dizzily, leaning swiftly outwards as they swerve sharp corners.

Far, far above, writhing away from the cutlery-canteen-crescendo of the interminable traffic passing in the canyons below, a few jets of smoke or steam spurt upwards into the indigo sky, the once-enormous sky now dwarfed by the overwhelming presence of the Present.

3

Shafts of pale light are directed across vari-surfaced planes set at conflicting angles. We become aware of a mysterious and inhuman figure gradually moulding itself into actuality against this faceted background: Titan's forehead, bull's eyes, ultra Romano-Semitic nose, bald, lipless mouth, chin vanished or never existent. When fully materialised, this neo-Gothic gargoyle speaks:

"I carry in my breast the secret of renunciation."

And we have to acknowledge that this strange mask possesses at least one thousandth part of the world's total beauty.

8

They were hardly to be expected here, but it is not necessary to explain the long strings of telephone wire looped unexpectedly among the branches of the lane. – Red blotches. – "Now Edinburgh is a place I'd like to go to," said a voice; and then there was another voice beneath the dark windows, talking about dogs. But now the jabneedles in perilled sockets, candles of pain twisted back in the sockets of eyes.

The fair-ground melodiously awoke beneath the Entry of the Gladiators March. A little steam trickled from the funnel in the middle, against the trees. You couldn't see it from the top of the hill, where I sat thinking: Supposing I wanted to sign my name across the fields? Wasn't it like looking into a cup to see that harrow? A horse harrowing an earthcup's bottom. Undoubtedly a horse.

And now the old beams die, or are chalk marks on white chalk. After dark a sudden and terrific hootwhistle-hoot. People *rush* past the window which is not yet but soon will be lit.

THE WORLD OF DE CHIRICO

We cannot tell the hour, for these elongated shadows across the square are not those of sundials; beneath the arches of the colonnades they are mystery. Against the infinity of the horizon a train moves towards Nowhere, releasing phantom plumes of smoke.

Beyond the immobile equestrian statue which has stood at the edge of the square for so long that one has forgotten whom it commemorates, the sea lies waiting for the hour when it shall rise to overwhelm this dead and empty city. Roman soldiers wander and terrific horses gallop over the sands.

We enter the colonnade and find our way into a white-washed room. Here there are plaster casts of heads of a type of beauty now extinct, there are gloves, T-squares, cornices, laths, picture-frames, handles of violins, biscuits and strangely-marked wands.

Coming towards us from the doorway with slow, agonising movements is a menacing and abnormally tall figure, swathed, its head featureless as an egg, with bricks, scaffoldings, models of buildings and little arches tumbling from its dreadful breast. Its arm creaks as it raises its rubber hand to point at us, meaninglessly . . . .

p. 1933

AUTOMATIC ALBUM LEAVES

1

The room is not very large, plaster has begun to flake from the ceiling, the windows are draped with whorled lace, under the windows there are little orange trees growing in patent-leather shoes instead of pots. On the plain walls there are hundreds of crosses hanging, made of rotting, worm-eaten wood, and to each one is nailed a small flat figure cut from rose-coloured tin. On the table there are bundles of hair, paper-knives, photographs of angels kissing, bottles of chlorine, miniature facsimiles of the Discobolus in cork, and specimens of the handwriting of children. A tattered shadow floats upwards towards the ventilator and bursts there like a silent bomb; portfolios open on all the shelves and coloured plates showing embryonic development flutter down in slow-motion to the cement floor, faintly phosphorescent and smelling of sweat.

p. 1933

IN PERPETUUM MOBILE

Too tightly tangled are mixed notions;
Wide ocean's wrack-worn tracks trace whorling wheels,
The vampire sun sucks up the sea's salt scum
And twists it into cloud that rolls or reels
In woven webs across the crystal sky;
The sun's barbaric cockerel comb of fire
Royally rages, reaching myriad miles,
Revolving regent rays that outwardly expire;
The system which has sun for centre spins
Round other systems that are cogs for more
Which act on others to the orbit's end, –
Continual correlation, endless war.
Unending Motion changes as it goes,
Like glyptic flame or shifting waterfall;
One moment is, then metamorphosis
Alters what was before to not at all.
Disintegration is the uncertain seed
Of Motion, making all seen things seem
A nystagmus, leaving no proof to show
That what we saw or shall see is not dream.

p. 1933

HOMMAGE À MALLARMÉ

Returning from pure space, undazzled, to
this calm square room where, sitting quite alone,
I am within white walls; attaining through
lack of motion the quietness of stone;

(too absolute is cold, this hanging air
is null; outside the window no clouds pass;
immobile is this table and this chair;
here dreams a single rose within a glass);

returning to my room from emptiness,
my slowly-moving eyes rest on a page
where clear-cut words are printed, motionless,

and through these crystal words, sans youth, sans age,
to space I now return, expressionless,
from which my sight had made its pilgrimage.

p. 1933

OLEOGRAPH

                                      the sun
going about like a gymnosophist
being so big and strong and full of his own importance
                                      licks
the trees and the wind
                                shows
their underclothes
                     (straw in the sun
                          spindrift
                moths and wood-bugs
              crumbling wood in lofts
            motes shimmering in the
            violent ray let in by the
          hole in the roof of the barn)
                    . . . .
                      the sun
talking about SOLAR MYTHS
and the   LEGEND OF APOLLO
                      the sun
claims to be descended from
                  EGYPT

                              in the desert
the sun discloses with surprise
the thighbone of a
                      GODDESS
buried in the sand

p. 1934

NIGHT-PIECE

Sea Voice: With these my massive arms of water flung
Wide and afar about the darkened globe,
I grasp in grim despair at frigid shores
Of islands that repulse my wild embrace.
Then I would smash them. Hatred in my waves
Surges against the allied stubborn cliffs;
And I will on, will ever onwards crash,
Blind as the night reflected in my deep,
Against the stone limbs of these lands that love me
   not.

Bird Voice: My flapping pinions catch
Dissolving snow with which
The air quivers; is taut
The fragile bone beneath my feather;
My meagre bird-flesh hates
The sharp kiss of this winter weather

The cloud-hung heavy spate,
Across the sky, of night
Chills my frail heart with fear;
Buffeted, deafened by the hollow
Howl of the sea, how fare
Shall I, with no star left to follow?

Man Voice: Silence I cannot this sorry yearning
Which with each winter night returns,
Finding a voice in waves' and wild birds' calling;
Distress commences as first darkness falls.
Sea-spume and wind-blown mist above the
   seething
Ocean meadows, with each breath I breathe
Enter my open heart, as I stand staring,
To mimic night's empty panic there.

   p.1934

END OF PEACE

The silhouette of a German count has been pasted
to the door; three families to one room; guns
ready in hippockets.

The rosegarden is decaying in spite of the patent
fertilizer we bought last Spring. The tin lies
rusting on the heap beside the pottingshed.

POISON: – To release and to dispose; a clearance
of the unwanted and an escape.

A loop. A metal design. An air-pocket.

p. 1934

PERPETUAL WINTER NEVER KNOWN

When the light falls on winter evenings
And the river makes no sound in its passing
Behind the house, is silent but for its cold
Flowing, its reeds frozen stiffer than glass
How can one anticipate the dawn, a sudden
Blazing of sunlight thawing the harshest sky?
How can one remember summer evenings?
Must not the tired heart sink and must not fear
Bite, like an acid, wrinkles in its stone?

Behind drawn curtains, gazing at the fire,
Think how the earth spins dumb and bound
By iron chains of frost through death-still air;
And how in every street the sealed windows
Are orange cubes of firelight, how in houses
Cuckoo-clocks imitate the spring, candles are
Suns. Perpetual winter never known,
Families warm their hands and wait, nor
Ever doubt the season's transience.

p. 1934

'NOT HAVING KNIFE-EDGE TO MY ERMINE CAPE'

Not having knife-edge to my ermine cape,
Like smoke I float down passages of
Dust and rust and leave not cut or smouldering
Trace. Tick-tock. Didactic. Vague.
And now stop short
                         to scatter
A careless crumb or two of imagery.
For you a rose, madame; (so simple).
For you, sir, a factory, or a star perhaps.
But now
           what desperate effort and what
Damp nail-wounded palm, what peevish squealing rage,

When as the future raises barricades
I find myself too late to be inside.

p. 1934

LANDSCAPE

Across the correct perspective to the painted sky
Scores of reflected bridges merging
One into the other pass, and crowds with flags
Rush over them, and clouds like acrobats
Swing on an invisible trapeze.

The light like a sharpened pencil
Writes histories of darkness on the wall,
While walls fall inwards, septic wounds
Burst open like sewn mouths, and rain
Eternally descends through planetary space.

We ask: Whence comes this light?
Whence comes the rain, the planetary
Silences, these aqueous monograms
Of our unique and isolated selves?
Only a dusty statue lifts and drops its hand . . .

p. 1934

SPECULATION

By marking off this footstep from that
And various other efficiencies of the day
One can easily dismiss the mind's insistence
As to direction, one can protect
The suspicious eye by diversion from the
Horizon's symmetrical doom, its carefully
Draped clouds, patterned stain, the rain
Coming in curtains of downward arrows, not
Yet felt upon the skin.

                          Though one must hear
Distant thunder, when the alert attention
Is drawn away from its visible manifesto
That can mean not omen, not cannon.
Can mean bold perhaps music or heavy
Traffic of increased commerce or crass
Stupid bodies' collapse of those we loathed.
Shortly the arriving rain will lay a chill
Finger on the unprepared skin, then up-
ward focused eye, annoyed at disturbance will
Appreciate storm's reality, appreciating
Folly past not fully, thinking Here's a
Splendid show, what grandeur Nature in this mood
Displays! gazing around in idiot wonder till
The sudden lightning shatters skulls,
Melts bones, coagulates all blood.

p. 1934

SONNET

Progressing forward to the backward gates
With frequent conquests followed by despairs,
Divided thus and so the Soul repairs
Not to the tabernacle carved with dates
And stuffy with death-quiet, where there waits
Some chance of rediffusion, where a hand
Rises in blessing over this fast land,
But to null vacuum, as the wind states.

Or are there pastures somewhere off the track
Patterned with light of *This* and shade of *That*
Where pain and pleasure both alike fall flat . . .
The pilgrimage is weary and the heart
Ticks not so fast as at the giddy start.
Has not the hour arrived for turning back?

p. 1934

THEY SPOKE OF A NEW CITY

And they spoke of a new city, a new order
And as it were a new race of men who
Shared all one with another and thought
The same thoughts, to live there where
There was a new architecture which meant
Clean buildings light and ribbed strongly with
Steel, for theirs was the steel age, the age
Of machines (day and night throbbing and
Electricity always burning). One could
Imagine the muscular bare arms of the men
Moving like pistons, and the strange lights and
The streets and the marching, the plain food,
The stone vistas. One could imagine it all
Clear as a film when they spoke of
Revolution and the proletariat and of
Russia. To them the words of Lenin were
More beautiful than any poem. And they had
An incorrigible dialectic to bind together their
Images of flags and tools and workers' unions. But

It seemed that this new city they spoke of
(Using an image) was to them only a
Utopia, or an escape for their minds from the
Dirty fly-blown offices where they worked,
The grey towns and the hard set faces
Of their ordinary neighbours, from the hard
Times and the narrow ways, because it was
Sordid to them to be working for only
Wages.

      These young have the power, though, driven
By desperation and disgust, to carve upon the
Future that lies like an untouched jewel before them,
As a triumphant insignia marking the commencement
Of an epoch, the realisation of their dream.

p. 1934

THE ROOTS OF EVIL

The roots of evil in the depths of silence
The silently boiling sea dissolves the rocks
And a depraved star takes root
On the foreheads of those whose days are numbered
Out of the black sack leaps the livid crime
A boneless cudgel with a blinding eye.

The roots of evil in the swollen landscape
The bright landscape of fountains and green dresses
Penetrating the rich sod of fallen fruit
Where foaming monsters gorge in the succulent mire
Poison the source of the sources and springs
The web of sweet waters enclosing its fields.

Pluck the roots from the flaming carapace
Pluck the hotel's roots from the burglar's alarum
Pluck the androgynous calumny from the midst of the tuppeny crabs
And the water will boil in the frozen jungle
The brainless acolyte will rush into the jungle
And the herds will come home.

p. 1934

GERMINAL

In a manner of speaking
>I should in that manner indicate
>That which has processed through my skull
>Yesterday entering at the eyes and ears
>Issuing tomorrow from the mouth

>The marvellous is yet unborn
>In the Manor of the Tongue
>Seed fallen until now on stony ground

>Spoken then
>An announcement of future marvels.

p. 1935

GNU OPAQUE

No more resistance
>No letters this morning
>Tomorrow will be a fine day

>Screeds of such blossomings
>Should fill each lenten interval
>Lobster-clawed love should diminish
>On the roads leading to all countries
>Famine veers away

>They said maritime provinces
>N or M
>It isn't easy to see in this light
>And night writes no replies

p. 1934

MARROW

O talisman and all the rest
Where is the teeming myriad gone
I seem to see a mushroom growing upon the globe
Women are often spectral
They often walk down the street like banjos
Their eyes are often no more than mere scraps of paper

Incandescent mutability
Decrees that emotion goes early to bed
Metallic starshine of the mood
Indicates losing breath
Losing head and heart
In the shopwindows of the wind
Like watercress

Until I wear the close chaplet
There will be no more time for tears.

p. 1935

BAPTISM

Have had enough barbarity
But enough too of illusion
Dreams of peace

Walking in the water
Or upon it
With wet fingers on the brow
And sombre eyes turned upwards
No longer expectant but prepared
Have had enough of was . . .

Statement:
If you are with us you are red.

p. 1935

FUTURE REFERENCE

The roof-garden was full of strangled flowers
Full of stones like feet and feet like fronds
There was a still pool in the garden's eye
But now there is no more time to see
How in the unanimously carried vote of censure
There could be even a vestige of saltpetre
How could there be a voice talking in the annexe
How could there be a machine to reproduce trees
And if all these questions remain unanswered
It is not the fault of the cheese-mites
Those dainty creatures with fleur-de-lys on their breasts
No it is not my fault if the ovens get cold
Nor yours if the blades of the swords get warm
My little dog has folds of skin round his arse
That worry him all day long
My little Jesus my little Jesus what pretty curls you've got
What pretty pansies you wear in your seething hair
And if the oppressive odour of gelatine gets too much for you
Under your eyes will appear a whole hornets' nest
To tickle your weeping glands.
But stay but stay you have not yet learnt to fly
You cannot climb stairs without chains round your knees
Nor will the sky descend to kiss you
Till every aquarium under the sun is broken
And duets are danced no more in the holes in the sand
For colossal fruits are about to fall from the trees
And every child in the world will be able to bite their pink flesh
A colossal thigh covered with veins
Is the monument to be raised on the seaswept shore
To all who have lost their lives in pursuit of a dream.

w.1935, p.1985

MAN'S LIFE IS THIS MEAT
(1936)

THE CHARIOT

At sound of heaven cracking, stars collide.
From trembling atmosphere such forms condense
As earth has never gazed upon before:
A chariot with horses, wheels immense.

The hills declare a prodigy, amazed
They wreathe the charioteer with omens proud.
He rushes through them utt'ring wildest cries,
Spurs on the horses, drives into a cloud.

The sea envisages huge wheels of flame,
Engulfs the mariner who only craves
Such vision of a violent sudden death.
The chariot crashes on between the waves.

In vain the firmament postpones its doom:
Its orbs disintegrate with hollow roar,
The chariot grinds their debris into dust
And rides into the infinite once more.

c. 1936

THE COLD RENUNCIATORY BEAUTY

The cold renunciatory beauty of those who would die
to hide their love from scornful fingers of the drab
is not that which glistens like wing or leaf in eyes
of erotic statues standing breast to chest
on high and open mountainside.

Complex draws tighter like a steel wire mesh
about the awkward bodies of those born under shame,
striping the tender flesh with blood like tears
flowing; their love they dare not name;
Each is divided by desire and fear.

The young sons of the hopeless blind shall strike
matches in the marble corridor and find
their bodies cool and white as the stone walls,
and shall embrace, emerging like mingled springs
on to the height to face the fearless sun.

c. 1936

LIGHT OF THE SUN OVER ARCTIC REGIONS

Light of the sun over arctic regions
Presides, striking the sides of icebergs
With slanting oblique rays, setting
The opaque snow translucently aglow,
Illumining blocks sedate in indigo depths.

There the unending fields of frost are blown
Upon by the harsh desolate blast;
The sun lacks warmth; alone at last
With wind from beyond, night from above and below,
Snow's light is negative, white equals black.

On the heart's bitter winter shines love's face.
Breaking, a berg groans response;
A facet's radiance, a moment's melting
Are answer. Soon gone is the sun.
The frigid heart feels death's wind only.

p. 1934

MORNING DISSERTATION

Wakening, peering through eye-windows, uncurious, not amazed,
Balance the day, know you lie there, think: I'm on earth.
Remember death walks in the daylight, and life still through filter
  seeps,
While you will remain unchanged, perhaps, throughout the day.
Time like an urgent finger moves across the chart,
But you are you, Time is not yours alone,
You are but one dot on the complex diagram.

Then are you a star, a nucleus, centre of moving points?
Are you a rock-crumb, broken from cliff, alone?
Or are you the point of a greater star, moving in unison?
If you are isolate, only a self, then petrify there where you stand;
Destinies crumble and bodies run down, the single sconces burn
   out,
But you are complete if without you completion is lacking,
Then you burn with the perfect light and are Time's bodyman.

p. 1933

THE UNATTAINED

On the evening of a day on the threshold of Summer,
Before the full blast of vertiginous Summer, I flung
This foursquare body down upon the crumpled ground,
Moist with a dew-like sweat; and on all sides heard
The ceaseless clicking and fret of insect swarms;
I felt energy drain from these limbs spread cruciform,
Dribble away like sap from crushed bracken's veins;
Felt this my heaviness upon acid-green grass and sand,
Under the passive sky, becoming magnetic as stone;
And my lids slid down over eyes fanned by coloured winds.

And fierce desires swelled up from out my quiet:
To pierce through this flesh outwards, to embrace
The eternal blue, against my nostrils to smother
The fragrant cotton of the clouds; to feel beneath
Impatient soles of feet the grinding grit
Of gravel, the sharp sides of stones; and without end
Against the eyeballs' skin to press fresh images,
To lave in the swift stream of forms these avid eyes:
By passion suspended, hands stretched out, gnawed
From within, O how and to where could I pass?

Not within facile grasp swings that unattainable globe:
Though to catch an echo of the spheres' music these ears strain
And nostrils yearn for the rich scent of flame and of blood,
Hands strive clumsily phantom's ambiguous flesh to caress,
In vain the inward divinity batters against the gates,
Kicking against the pricks until the urgent spirit breaks.

Hourly the ocean, World's clock, smashes against the cliffs;
And savage relentless Time shreds onwards through the skull,
Whispers: 'Come home, only Death burns out there'. And I know
That this is my body, my cell, and I am alone and prone.

p. 1934

REINTEGRATION

After a plenitude of defeat, a load of sorrow.
Forget your coward victories, your crown of thorns,
And send the sulky eye-witness away;
Block out that solitary figure, the proud
Indomitable one. Hack down the heavy black
Statue. And because you can only remember
The darkest days of defeat, your weariness,
Because you can see but death's sinister finger
Always pointing to the shadowed wall,
Raise no more gloomy monuments, or build
A more transparent wall.
                        And listen
To the rich voice like flute-voice breaking
Suddenly from the white marble larynx;
Sunlight breaking suddenly upon the naked torso
Like the rustling down of a flimsy dress.
Listening, join proud singing with the voice,
As the sound of an inland sea now freed,
Smashing its winter cage of ice and rushing
With liquid arms and hands of foam uplifted
Across the frozen lands toward the outer seas.

p. 1934

NO SOLUTION

Above and below
The roll of days spread out like a cloth
Days engraved on everyone's forehead
Yesterday folding Tomorrow opening
Today like a horse without a rider
Today a drop of water falling into a lake
Today a white light above and below

A fan of days held in a virgin hand
A burning taper burning paper
And you can turn back no longer
No longer stand still
The words of poems curling among the ashes
Hieroglyphics of larger despairs than ours.

c. 1936

DIRECT RESPONSE

The four elements are sitting at the table
There is a shipwreck on the sands
A warm hand in the mist
Flowers turn colour in the mist
Without moving

Sensitive needle at the extremity of breathing
What can you etch upon the eyes' quick web?
Up to your middle in the dewy grass
Whose profile can you sketch upon their filmy screen?

I have long forgotten why I am young
A bird's blue shadow trembles on my breasts
A bird's song blossoms from the water
Till my neck bends back in a curve like stone
And I am neither white nor warm nor cold

c. 1936

THE LAST HEAD

In the warm sand-coloured room at the end of the watery road
I saw the last head with its fingers plaited in curls
And its sides ridged and smooth, worn by runnels of light.
The obvious table supported a map of the moon.
The faces in trees must be stopped, and the towers
And peninsular madness and gems
The canals are all stopped with a white-flowering weed
The beetle conspires to bring doom to the bridge
The night air is salt on the tongue. The white shields
In the stable fall clattering down from the walls.

But the last head is safe in its vegetable dome:
The last head is wrapped in its oiled silk sheath,
While the pale tepid flame of its ichorous brain
Consumes all its body's dry shells.

c. 1936

PURIFIED DISGUST

An impure sky
A heartless and impure breathing
The fevered breath of logic
And a great bird broke loose
Flapping into the silence with strident cries
A great bird with cruel claws

Beyond that savage pretence of knowledge
Beyond that posture of oblivious dream
Into the divided terrain of anguish
Where one walks with bound hands
Where one walks with knotted hair
With eyes searching the zenith
Where one walks like Sebastian

Heavy flesh invokes the voice of penitence
Seated at the stone tables
Seated at a banquet of the carnal lusts
Behind our putrid masks we snicker

Our men's heads behind our masks
Twisted from innocence to insolence

And there the pointing finger says and there
The pointing finger demonstrates
The accuser struggles with his accusation
The accused writhes and blusters
The finger points to the chosen victim
The victim embraces his victimization
The accused belches defiance

How could we touch that carrion?
A sudden spasm saves us
A pure disgust illumines us
The music of the spheres is silent
Our hands lie still upon the counterpane
And the herds come home.

p. 1935

CHARITY WEEK

To Max Ernst

Have presented the lion with medals of mud
One for each day of the week
One for each beast in this sombre menagerie
Shipwrecked among the clouds
Shattered by the violently closed eyelids

Garments of the seminary
Worn by the nocturnal expedition
By all the chimeras
Climbing in at the window

With lice in their hair
Noughts in their crosses
Ice in their eyes

Hysteria upon the staircase
Hair torn out by the roots
Lace handkerchiefs torn to shreds
And stained by tears of blood
Their fragments strewn upon the waters

These are the phenomena of zero
Invisible men on the pavement
Spittle in the yellow grass
The distant roar of disaster
And the great bursting womb of desire.

p. 1935

REFLECTED VEHEMENCE

Umbilically detached, of sorrowful mien and at the same time decked out in cobwebs – these vanquished ones, whose breathings propagate violence and fear. Their padded fingers point uselessly to the stars of their own eloquence. It is just the same as ever in the outgrown pavilions of vegetable matter. As though St Valentine had smudged the last letters of a secret pact with the powdered antennae of a forgotten fly. As though flying itself were only circular.

But here where the graphite byways meet, there is bound to be always fresh water. See how the ruched waterfalls reply with shaking heads to the invitations of the warrior-like foliage. They seem to vanish in thin air, gasping for a more fluid means of expression. The tinkling belfries glide away of their own volition. Eggs break during the fencing lesson. Masonry, tightly clamped to the nape of the ritual, buries itself in an indulgently frothing explosion of the head, whereby the closed gates are breathed upon anew by the breezes of loyalty and honour. Thus clouds are born.

In my hand lies the same whispering, nail-headed dude, ever imploring the benefice of a hippograph.

c. 1936

THE END IS NEAR THE BEGINNING

Yes you have said enough for the time being
There will be plenty of lace later on
Plenty of electric wool
And you will forget the eglantine
Growing around the edge of the green lake
And if you forget the colour of my hands
You will remember the wheels of the chair
In which the wax figure resembling you sat

Several men are standing on the pier
Unloading the sea
The device on the trolley says MOTHER'S MEAT
Which means *Until the end*.

p. 1935

LOST WISDOM

In the first morning
A cry above the unborn roofs
Of solitude and pain
A faint odour of vegetable matter
Fringing the violet lids of night
And hanging from the water's eyes
The simulacrum of the damned

Disturbance in the weather makes me see
The little angels without wings
The brittle needles in the sand
The ropy veins of polypi
And all the seamless seams

And now and then
From every abandoned mouth
An unstanched stream must flow
And then as now

The graves were opened once
And gold was melted by the snow
Like lilies sown in sifted stone
And gathered once for all.

p. 1935

UNSPOKEN

Words spoken leave no time for regret
Yet regret
The unviolated silence and
White sanctuses of sleep
Under the heaped veils
The inexorably prolonged vigils
Speech flowing away like water
With its undertow of violence and darkness
Carrying with it forever
All those formless vessels
Abandoned palaces
Tottering under the strain of being
Full-blossoming hysterias
Lavishly scattering their stained veined petals

In sleep there are places places
Places overlap
Yellow sleep in the afternoon sunlight
Coming invisibly in through the pinewood door
White sleep wrapped warm in the midwinter
Inhaling the tepid snow
And sleeping in April at night is sleeping in
Shadow as shallow as water and articulate with pain

Recurrent words
Slipping between the cracks
With the face of memory and the sound of its voice
More intimate than sweat at the roots of the hair
Frozen stiff in a moment and then melted
Swifter than air between the lips
Swifter to vanish than enormous buildings
Seen for a moment from the corners of the eyes

Travelling through man's enormous continent
No two roads the same
Nor ever the same names to places
Migrating towns and fluid boundaries
There are no settlers here there are
No solid stones

Travelling through man's unspoken continent
Among the unspeaking mountains
The dumb lakes and the deafened valleys
Illumined by paroxysms of vision
Clear waves of soundless sight
Lapping out of the heart of darkness
Flowing endless over buried speech
Drowning the words and words

And here I am caught up among the glistenings of
Bodies proud with the opulence of flesh
The silent limbs of beings lying across the light
Silken at the hips and pinched between two fingers
Their thirsty faces turned upwards towards breaking
Their long legs shifting slanting turning
In a parade of unknown virtues
Beginning again and beginning
Again

Till unspoken is unseen
Until unknown
Descending from knowledge to knowledge
A dim world uttering a voiceless cry
Spinning helpless between sleep and waking
A blossom scattered by a motionless wind
A wheel of fortune turning in the fog
Predicting the lucid moment
Casting the bodiless body from its hub
Back into the cycle of return and change
Breathing the mottled petals
Out across the circling seas
And foaming oceans of disintegration
Where navigate our daylight vessels
Following certain routes to uncertain lands

p. 1935

YVES TANGUY

The worlds are breaking in my head
Blown by the brainless wind
That comes from afar
Swollen with dusk and dust
And hysterical rain

The fading cries of the light
Awaken the endless desert
Engrossed in its tropical slumber
Enclosed by the dead grey oceans
Enclasped by the arms of the night

The worlds are breaking in my head
Their fragments are crumbs of despair
The food of the solitary damned
Who await the gross tumult of turbulent
Days bringing change without end.

The worlds are breaking in my head
The fuming future sleeps no more
For their seeds are beginning to grow
To creep and to cry midst the
Rocks of the deserts to come

Planetary seed
Sown by the grotesque wind
Whose head is so swollen with rumours
Whose hands are so urgent with tumours
Whose feet are so deep in the sand.

c. 1936

'THE TRUTH IS BLIND'

The light fell from the window and the day was
    done
Another day of thinking and distractions
Love wrapped in its wings passed by and coal-black Hate
Paused on the edge of the cliff and dropped a stone
From which the night grew like a savage plant
With daggers for its leaves and scarlet hearts
For flowers – then the bed
Rose clocklike from the ground and spread its sheets
Across the shifting sands

Autumnal breath of mornings far from here
A star veiled in grey mist
A living man:

The snapping of a dry twig was his only announcement. The two men, who had tied their boat to a branch that grew out over the water's edge, and were now moving up through the rank tropical vegetation, turned sharply.

He raised his eyes and saw the river's source
Between their legs – he saw the flaming sun
He saw the buildings in between the leaves
Behind their heads that were as large as globes
He heard their voices indistinct as rain
As faint as feathers falling
    And he fell

The boat sailed on
The masts were made of straw
The sails were made of finest silken thread
And out of holes on either side the prow
Gushed endless streams of water and of flame
In which the passengers saw curious things:

The conjuror, we are told, 'took out of his bag a silken thread, and so projected it upwards that it stuck fast in a certain cloud of air. Out of the same receptacle he pulled a hare, that ran away up along the thread; a little beagle, which when it was slipped at the hare pursued it in full cry; last of all a small dogboy, whom he commanded to follow both hare and hound up the thread. From another bag that he had he extracted a winsome young woman, at all points well adorned, and instructed her to follow after hound and dogboy.'

> She laughed to see them gazing after her
> She clapped her hands and vanished in thin air
> To reappear upon the other bank
> Among the restless traffic of the quays
> Her silhouette against the dusty sky
> Her shadow falling on the hungry stones
> Where sat the pilot dressed in mud-stained rags
>
> He knocked the fragile statue down
> And ate her sugar head
> And then the witnesses all gathered round
> And pointed at the chasm at his feet:

Clouds of blue smoke, sometimes mixed with black, were being emitted from the exhaust pipe. The smoke was of sufficient density to be an annoyance to the driver following the vehicle or to pedestrians.

> The whispering of unseen flames
> A sharp taste in the mouth.

p. 1935

THE CAGE

> In the waking night
> The forests have stopped growing
> The shells are listening
> The shadows in the pools turn grey
> The pearls dissolve in the shadow
> And I return to you
>
> Your face is marked upon the clockface
> My hands are beneath your hair
> And if the time you mark sets free the birds
> And if they fly away towards the forest
> The hour will no longer be ours

58

Ours is the ornate birdcage
The brimming cup of water
The preface to the book
And all the clocks are ticking
All the dark rooms are moving
All the air's nerves are bare.

Once flown
The feathered hour will not return
And I shall have gone away.

c. 1936

EDUCATIVE PROCESS

1

What though the weather changes?
What though you do not sleep?
Now that at last we've arrived
(Forget the wasteproducts of love)
Whiteness envelops houses
To prepare to begin to prepare
And snow on the roofs,
Your horror of snow!

2

The month's pocket holds many days
The paraphernalia of seeing and hearing.

3

The feathers fledged from your flesh meet mine
And ardent haloes meet like plates above our heads

You are not gentle.

4

Crescendo of flames, the steps
Of stone that lead into the swamp
Where wanderings begin and the first birds

The last birds, the sun's bicycle racing,
Our eyes lose one another, autumn splutters
On the sidewalks houses eat the afternoon
Soft outline of the leaves upon the wall
Foliage blown by the wind
Streams into the memory of hair.

5

Wire twisted back bites into the cheek
The gardens of neurosis.

6

Swift algebra of love pretends
That barriers must fall
To gourmandize the warriors of sleep
To sacrifice the carrion
To call home lightnings wandering in the fields
To live life twice.

7

A drop of dew sings psalms upon the hill
Anatomies of wonder opened at the first page
The last page showing the number 3 like a silken knot.

Rockets open the sky like keys
And your breath is warning
Warning the footsteps of Truth
Not to wander too far away
For clutching hands and agonized eyes
Move with their shadows upon the imaginary screen.

8

Hooped foliage, tired antimony,
Blossoms of crumbling columns beneath our feet
Journeys stretch far away and there is the sea
The sea is as salt as health with its marble veins.

9

The glass on the table is empty and so are your eyes.
Footsteps. The shadow just outside the door.
And do you suppose that forgetting
Is as easy as air?

The flowers' voice is evil, the caves
Are asleep. In the grass
Children playing take fear at the clouds carved like skulls.

10

I had forgotten to watch the wind
The wind playing with boats the wind
Shuffling the sands like cards –
But we cannot change now that daylight is here

Negotiations with the infinite
Upon the empty beach.

c. 1936

ANTENNAE

1

A river of perfumed silk
A final glimpse of content
The girls are alone on the highroad.

2

In the evening there is a cry of despair
Silence begins spawning its myriad
Shifting away from the restless neon auras
Disturbed by the menacing gestures of starvation
The unchanging programme of its manoeuvres
Its rasping grasping claws.

3

The sun bursts through its skin
The last smooth man emerges from the tunnel
And flags burst into song along the streets
The morning's garlands pull themselves to pieces
And fly away in flocks

The sea is a bubble in a cup of salt
The earth is a grain of sand in a nutshell
The earth is blue.

4

Truth, fickle monster, gazed in at the open window
Longing to eat of the fruit of the poisoned tree
Longing to eat from the plates on our lozenge-shaped
 table
Fearing the truth

And the peaceful star of the vigil fell from the sky
And spilt its amazing fluids across the mosaic floor.

5

The timeless sleepers tangled in the bed
In the midst of the sonorous island, alone

The tongue between the teeth
The river between the sands

Love in my hand like lace
Your hand enlaced with mine.

6

A delicate breath a wisp of smoke
Floating between our eyes
The rainbow-coloured barque of pleasure
Brushing the fluid foliage aside
Derision's flimsy feathers

Between our eyes
The shadow of a smile.

7

The full breasts of eternity awaiting tender hands.

8

Not wholly unprepared
Nor entirely unafraid
Vigilant
Watching the colours

Discovered by morning:
Dispensation of doubtful benefits.

9

At least alone at last
When gone the body's warmth
The incisiveness of glances
The unwinding crimson thread
The given flower

Forgotten mouths forget.

10

For now we are suspended above life
There are a great many questions to be answered
A great many debts to be paid

So evanescent that which binds us
That more is meant, regret is absent . . .
Our burning possession of each other
Held in both hands because it is all we have.

c. 1936

LOZANNE

It was seven, it was nine o'clock, the doors were closing, the windows were screaming. You bent over the shadow that lay on the floor and saw its eyes dissolving. The band about your forehead began to turn. The band of fever.

The armchair turned into a palace, the carpet became a bank of withered flowers, *and then it was time to go.* Every semblance of that which had gone before became the means by which you ascended the great staircase. And took your place among the stars.

For it is significant, is it not, that the *blemish* about which you were so insistent was nothing less than that interminable voice which haunted you in your dreams, saying 'I love you' over and over again. And the panelling of the room where they asked you questions was made of exactly the same wood as the mallet which you had to hate.

The dusty and ashen residue of a passion that now raged elsewhere, but still raged, rose slowly upwards to the surface of the lake as your blood sank slowly through it. And the other returned to ice. Oh, I can see through your eyes now and I can see what flame it was that melted everything before it! (Though the obstinate sod refused to become softened by the rain of thaw.) But you were spared passing through that black box where a masked man kisses his victim before her death. I ask the glass again: Who gave the victims right to refuse life to those who refuse to be victimized?

Those who damned shall be damned.

c. 1936

SALVADOR DALÍ

The face of the precipice is black with lovers;
The sun above them is a bag of nails; the spring's
First rivers hide among their hair.
Goliath plunges his hand into the poisoned well
And bows his head and feels my feet walk through his brain.
The children chasing butterflies turn round and see him there
With his hand in the well and my body growing from his head,
And are afraid. They drop their nets and walk into the wall like smoke.

The smooth plain with its mirrors listens to the cliff
Like a basilisk eating flowers.
And the children, lost in the shadows of the catacombs,
Call to the mirrors for help:
'Strong-bow of salt, cutlass of memory,
Write on my map the name of every river.'

A flock of banners fight their way through the telescoped forest
And fly away like birds towards the sound of roasting meat.
Sand falls into the boiling rivers through the telescopes' mouths
And forms clear drops of acid with petals of whirling flame.
Heraldic animals wade through the asphyxia of planets,
Butterflies burst from their skins and grow long tongues like plants,
The plants play games with a suit of mail like a cloud.

Mirrors write Goliath's name upon my forehead,
While the children are killed in the smoke of the catacombs
And lovers float down from the cliffs like rain.

p. 1934

THE DIABOLICAL PRINCIPLE

The red dew of autumn clings to winter's curtains
And when the curtain rises the landscape is as empty as a board
Empty except for a broken bottle and a torso broken like a bottle
And when the curtain falls the palace of cards will fall
The card-castle on the table will topple without a sound

An eye winks from the shadow of the gallows
A tumbled bed slides upwards from the shadow
A suicide with mittened hands stumbles out of the lake
And writes a poem on the tablets of a dead man's heart
The last man but one climbs the scaffold and fades into the mist

The marine sceptre is splintered like an anvil
Its spine crackles with electric nerves
While eagle pinions thunder through the darkness
While swords and breastplates clatter in the darkness
And the storm falls across the bed like a thrice-doomed tree.

★

    A basket of poisoned arrows
    Severing seawrack, ships' tracks
    Leadentipped darts of disaster
    A unicorn champs at the waves
    The waves are green branches singing
    The cry of a foal at daybreak
    A broken mouth at sunset
    A broken lamp among the clouds' draperies

    A sound drops into the water and the water boils
    The sound of disastrous waves
    Waves flood the room when the door opens
    A white horse stamps upon the liquid floor
    The sunlight is tiring to our opened eyes
    And the sand is dead
    Feet in the sand make patterns
    Patterns flow like rivers in the distant sky
    Rippling shells like careful signatures
    A tangled skein of blood

In fumigated emptiness revolves the mind
The light laughs like an unposted letter
Railways rush into the hills.

★

A worm slithers from the earth and the shell is broken
A giant mazed misery tears the veil to shreds
Stop it tormentor stop the angry planet before it breaks the sky

Having shattered the untapped barrel
Having given up hope for water
Having shaken the chosen words in a hat
History opened its head like a wallet
And folded itself inside.

c. 1936

THE RITES OF HYSTERIA

In the midst of the flickering sonorous islands
The islands with liquid gullets full of mistletoe-suffering
Where untold truths are hidden in fibrous baskets
And the cold mist of decayed psychologies stifles the sun
An arrow hastening through the zone of basaltic honey
An arrow choked by suppressed fidgetings and smokey spasms
An arrow with lips of cheese was caught by a floating hair

The perfumed lenses whose tongues were tied up with wire
The boxes of tears and the bicycles coated with stains
Swam out of their false-bottomed nests into clouds of dismay
Where the gleams and the moth-bitten monsters the puddles of soot
And a half-strangled gibbet all cut off an archangel's wings
The flatfooted heart of a memory opened its solitary eye
Till the freak in the showcase was smothered in mucus and sweat

A cluster of insane massacres turns green upon the highroad
Green as the nadir of a mystery in the closet of a dream
And a wild growth of lascivious pamphlets became a beehive
The afternoon scrambles like an asylum out of its hovel
The afternoon swallows a bucketful of chemical sorrows

And the owners of rubber pitchforks bake all their illusions
In an oven of dirty globes and weedgrown stupors

Now the beckoning nudity of diseases putrifies the saloon
The severed limbs of the galaxy wriggle like chambermaids
The sewing-machine on the pillar condenses the windmill's halo
Which poisoned the last infanta by placing a tooth in her ear
When the creeping groans of the cellar's anemone vanished
The nightmare spun on the roof a chain-armour of handcuffs
And the ashtray balanced a ribbon upon a syringe

An opaque whisper flies across the forest
Shaking its trailing sleeves like a steaming spook
Till the icicle stabs at the breast with the bleeding nipple
And bristling pot-hooks slit open the garden's fan
In the midst of the flickering sonorous hemlocks
A screen of hysteria blots out the folded hemlocks
And feathery eyelids conceal the volcano's mouth.

c. 1936

AND THE SEVENTH DREAM IS THE DREAM OF ISIS

1

white curtains of infinite fatigue
dominating the starborn heritage of the colonies of St Francis
white curtains of tortured destinies
inheriting the calamities of the plagues of the desert
encourage the waistlines of women to expand
and the eyes of men to enlarge like pocket-cameras
teach children to sin at the age of five
to cut out the eyes of their sisters with nail-scissors
to run into the streets and offer themselves to unfrocked priests
teach insects to invade the deathbeds of rich spinsters
and to engrave the foreheads of their footmen with purple signs
for the year is open the year is complete
the year is full of unforeseen happenings
and the time of earthquakes is at hand

today is the day when the streets are full of hearses
and when women cover their ring fingers with pieces of silk

when the doors fall off their hinges in ruined cathedrals
when hosts of white birds fly across the ocean from america
and make their nests in the trees of public gardens
the pavements of cities are covered with needles
the reservoirs are full of human hair
fumes of sulphur envelop the houses of ill-fame
out of which bloodred lilies appear.

across the square where crowds are dying in thousands
a man is walking a tightrope covered with moths

2

there is an explosion of geraniums in the ballroom of the hotel
there is an extremely unpleasant odour of decaying meat
arising from the depetalled flower growing out of her ear
her arms are like pieces of sandpaper
or wings of leprous birds in taxis
and when she sings her hair stands on end
and lights itself with a million little lamps like glow-worms
you must always write the last two letters of her christian name
upside down with a blue pencil
she was standing at the window clothed only in a ribbon
she was burning the eyes of snails in a candle
she was eating the excrement of dogs and horses
she was writing a letter to the president of france

3

the edges of leaves must be examined through microscopes
in order to see the stains made by dying flies
at the other end of the tube is a woman bathing her husband
and a box of newspapers covered with handwriting
when an angel writes the word TOBACCO across the sky
the sea becomes covered with patches of dandruff
the trunks of trees bust open to release streams of milk
little girls stick photographs of genitals to the windows of their
    homes
prayerbooks in churches open themselves at the death service
and virgins cover their parents' beds with tealeaves
there is an extraordinary epidemic of tuberculosis in yorkshire
where medical dictionaries are banned from public libraries
and salt turns a pale violet colour every day at seven o'clock

when the hearts of troubadours unfold like soaked mattresses
when the leaven of the gruesome slum-visitors
and the wings of private airplanes look like shoeleather
shoeleather on which pentagrams have been drawn
shoeleather covered with vomitings of hedgehogs
shoeleather used for decorating wedding-cakes
and the gums of queens like glass marbles
queens whose wrists are chained to the walls of houses
and whose fingernails are covered with little drawings of flowers
we rejoice to receive the blessing of criminals
and we illuminate the roofs of convents when they are hung
we look through a telescope on which the lord's prayer has been
    written
and we see an old woman making a scarecrow
on a mountain near a village in the middle of spain
we see an elephant killing a stag-beetle
by letting hot tears fall onto the small of its back
we see a large cocoa-tin full of shapeless lumps of wax
there is a horrible dentist walking out of a ship's funnel
and leaving behind him footsteps which make noises
on account of his accent he was discharged from the sanatorium
and sent to examine the methods of cannibals
so that wreaths of passion-flowers were floating in the darkness
giving terrible illnesses to the possessors of pistols
so that large quantities of rats disguised as pigeons
were sold to various customers from neighbouring towns
who were adepts at painting gothic letters on screens
and at tying up parcels with pieces of grass
we told them to cut off the buttons on their trousers
but they swore in our faces and took off their shoes
whereupon the whole place was stifled with vast clouds of smoke
and with theatres and eggshells and droppings of eagles
and the drums of the hospitals were broken like glass
and glass were the faces in the last looking-glass.

p. 1933

SURREALIST AND OTHER POEMS

(1936–1938)

A SUDDEN SQUALL

After some days of heat
Withering leaf and bloom
Like pebbles falls the hail,
Like chips of stone the sleet
Out of the sudden gloom
Across the peaceful vale
Just now so bright.

While we are waiting for
The sulky storm to stop
Hour after hour,
Watching the garden lake
Toss the toy ship,
The orchard fast falls dark
And bruised fruits drop.

Birds are all flown;
Rabbits in holes
Wait for the sun's return;
At sea great whales
Send up their fountains
As they drive taciturn
Through waves like mountains.

Green becomes sodden grey
And across the fields
At death of day
Mist draws its chilly sheets,
And darkness wields
Its eerie power, night's
Creatures begin to cry.

This weather's change is blind.
His hopes grow dimmer
Who thought that summer
Might have no end;
Would have good reason
To resign his mind
To a rainy season.

p. 1936

COMPETITION

The ultimate perfection of wisdom is undesirable
And more so especially since the tongue-twister started to reign
And the calloused trestles proclaimed their destinations
And over the whole of Utopia there was a thick white blanket
Which muffled the horrible sound of colliding trains
And out of the national rivers came swarms of bees
Which mumbled inaudible fragments of ancient lore
Hurrying past the surrounding palace of water
Which stood on its feet to wave them a last good-bye
When the door of the closet opened
Disclosing an endless vista of swollen gems
Turning incessantly upon their pinprick navels
Displaying their undersides to the curious eyes of the thieves
Their lambskin vests to the fatuous undertakers
And all their embroidered fins to the end of the world
So the captain said this has nothing to do with the earthquake
This is awfully brave of the woman I'll give her a bone
And turned in his bed which was folded in half down the middle
And covered with pieces of eight
And announced to the night that a prize would be given for beauty
And another for wearing a wig.

p. 1936

'THE ENTRANCE TO THAT VALLEY STANDS ALONE'

The entrance to that valley stands alone
Bulked boulders strewn where no wind penetrates
And all is quiet as a falling leaf; you would believe,
Almost, that you had died, and this was after-sleep; -
And down the ashy hills on either side
The lava-beds are dead which show where once there flowed
The love which being loveless had to overflow
Into the stillness, and to be turned to stone
As formless as an unloved woman's sigh.

If a voice speaks, it is your voice which speaks;
There are no others here. You hear
Your other self, whose accents cold, in pity

Breaking or in pleading torn, implore, placate
The endless finite silence; and the single dead
Echo of that one voice, a pebble dropped
Into the black depths of a well, will not
Receive another answer, though your wish may be
To have to speak no longer, nor to hear.

The formless clouds swell round the broken peaks;
In all directions are their vapours blown,
Empty and white and substanceless as thought,
And without aim. – Not without time, for time's
The valley's one-way street which guides you on,
Without desire, towards what lies beyond.
What lies beyond? The question's dead
Before it leaves the tongue: Death's violence robbed
Of triumph, grief of majesty, and all illusion gone.

The eye cannot delight in stones or clouds
For long, moves restless on, without desire,
By nervous reflex action, waiting for
A new unknown to break the further sky.
The feet are fixed in dull mechanical trudge;
No destination, always straight ahead.
You cannot die; and sitting still is worse
Than stumbling forward in obedience to
The senseless law of motion and of time.

Take this bone: it is life and death reflected
                              in the movements of the stars
Take this knife: it is my brain
Take this sheet of darkness spread over the fountains of hearts
                              that have stopped too soon
In the rhythmical heat of the dusk,
In the untethered veins of a handful of soil
Thrown down into the radiance of melting snow
It is the heat generated by the prodigious efforts of calm
To efface the salt water that stains the tall brows of the sun
Enclasped in the arms of space

Where the limits of creation lose their claims
And approach the last moments of shattering the formless
                              eardrums of the darkness

To release the definition of a body white with birth
Upsurging from the half-extinguished fires
The rubbish heaps that burn along the delta
In the world beyond the rocks

The slow death of the furnaces does not affect their heat
Bitumen tumbles in the laughter of its excrescences
And a nine-pointed star grows out of man's belief
Which sand has choked back into emotion's twisted coat
Where lice are red in the perpetual rain
And daylight's finger has become caught in the hinges of shells.

w. 1936, p. 2001

PHENOMENA

It was during a heatwave. Someone whose dress seemed to have forgotten who was wearing it appeared to me at the end of a pause in the conversation. She was so adorable that I had to forbid her to pass across my footstool again. Without warning, changing from blue to purple, the night-sky suffered countless meteoric bombardments from the other side of the curtain, and the portcullis fell like an eyelid.

The milk had turned sour in its effort to avoid the centrifugal attraction of a blemish on its own skin. Everything was mounting to the surface. My last hope was to diminish the barometric pressure at least enough to enable me to get out from beneath it alive.

In the end, I remembered that she would not have to make the decision herself, as her own fate was sufficient justification for the hostility of the elements. I turned the page. Nothing could have been more baffling than the way in which the words rose from the places where they had been printed, hovered in the air at a distance of about six inches from my face and finally, without having much more than disturbed my impression of their habitual immobility, dissolved into the growing darkness. As I have said, it was during a heatwave, and the lightning had well nigh worn itself out in trying to attain the limit of its incandescence. I suddenly forgot what I was supposed to be doing, and the soil beneath my feet loosened itself from the hold of the force of gravity and began to slide gradually downwards, with the sound of a distant explosion.

p. 1936

THE LIGHT OF THE LION'S MANE

If I had a candle I would bite it in half, avid with spite and angry greed. Why is it that candles give no light unless they are wrapped in oak-leaves that have been pressed between the pages of books illuminated by ancient monks? I hate to see them melting away like that, losing first their heads and then their tails, and balancing what remains of them as a fishmonger balances his wares on top of a pile of wicker baskets. It would be better to send for a pound of butter on a chafing-dish. Butter is far better, for it does not bite the tongue.

The violet light thrown by the lamp strapped on to the miner's forehead falls gently on to the surface of a subterranean river. Eagles have made their nests along the banks, and the fossilized claws of the neolithic tiger are to be found in the rusty sand of the river's bed. I often sleep there, and when I wake up it always seems as though a procession of foreign tourists had passed by that way during the night, gesticulating with their arms and making lengthy speeches at every turn of the twilit tunnel. I should never have been able to explain to them why the tattered curtains are alive with toads, or why the spectacular staircase is in ruins. It is a long time since I spat into so deep a hole; I have never seen such pilgrims, with their bells, their books, their baskets . . .

But let us pause to consider the cause of the disturbance that is taking place at the far end of this corridor. The waves have thrown up the remains of a small vessel on to the sanded floor and among the shattered casks and the crumbs of the ship's biscuits one can see a dissevered head that is trying to speak to the assembled multitude. The muscular effort made by its jaw is equal to ten times the strength of a derrick trying to break away from the crane to which it is tethered. It is covered with sunspots and will undoubtedly burst into flame at the end of a quarter of an hour or so. Lay your hand on the massive forehead and you will feel the gradual movement of the birds that are imprisoned underneath. Each bird carries a leather glove in its beak, and the fingers of each glove are packed with gunpowder. The final explosion has been timed to coincide with the demolition of the plaster-of-paris monument that has been set up in the middle of the park to commemorate the victims of a savage watchdog who wrought great ravages in these parts towards the end of the nineteenth century.

Heads such as these do not speak as clearly as the heads of missionaries. Let us set up a temple for the Alpine mission, and let us weave a great carpet at the foot of every mountain in the Alps, to express our penitence and our desire to make amends for the broken glaciers and the training clouds of glory. Our whole childhood was spent in the shadow of these great heights, so is it not only right that we should decorate them now with dazzling garments stained with our own blood? I have often expressed a desire to lie down on the floor of a cave, and it seems that my wish is at last about to be granted. Have I put on my head-dress straight?

Looming out of the gloomy shadows of the further chamber there comes a great catafalque drawn by a pair of milk-white does and decked with plumes of lilies and clustering branches of tiger-lilies that look like sword-lilies. It has almost the appearance of a November bonfire set alight in the public square because of a plot that failed. The lights are turned on one by one, the leaves of the candelabrum-trees are shining like buttered gold, the foam of the Gulf Stream glitters like corn in the sun, and the whole effect is one of heat, drums and fireworks. The monster Egg that forms the centrepiece of these celebrations now bursts open, and a living Archangel leaps out. Nine months ago she was but an atom whirling through the wastes of outer space, and now her robe is bright with sweat and all eyes are turned towards her. She blows one blast on her vast brass trumpet shaped like an oar, and the whole brilliant pageant falls to dust.

But who has tied a bandage round my eyes so that I can no longer see what is happening? A bandage saturated with the scent of crushed laurel-leaves, which is used by butterfly-hunters. I have the sensation of being driven away in a rickshaw, I could swear that I heard footsteps behind me, the wheels of the conveyance bump loudly down the stairs. Clusters of sharp little shells are growing beneath my eyelids, ants' eggs to throw to the fishes, chrysalises lying quietly in the dust beneath the feet of the marching tyrants, who will all fall down with fatigue in the end, and bury their arrogant faces in the mire.

p. 1936

THE GREAT DAY

When I woke up it was indeed very beautiful. The banisters were shining intensely and the stairs were coming up towards me. I was well aware that my eyes were no longer clinkers. I sat on the edge of the bed with my feet in the sand and watched the ambulances going past the window. What carnage, what thunderbolts and, indeed, what pascal lambs!

But I'm afraid you will hardly believe me when I tell you that at the hour when the night-bird should have flown, at the hour when all the matrons no longer able to have children should have entered the room, precisely at the hour of the one-o'clock séances and balloon-course meetings, it was one o'clock. I went out as the cock was crowing and held my head above the basin which I thought was full of water but it was full of cream and ashes. This, of course, brought on one of my fainting fits, but I soon recovered, and there, to my infinite surprise, sitting upon the left-hand flap of the little linoleum wigwam which looks like a forge-bellows, was she upon whom my heart had been set ever since that marvellous sunset long long years ago when my heart was still a captive beating its pitiful wings in the great silence of all the empty rooms and the dining-rooms and the cellars and all the wine-cellars. Without a moment's hesitation I went straight up to her and caught hold of her icy hand, I can tell you, and her mouth was like a beautiful garden full of flowers and full of bronze flowers and beautiful flowers like medals. My adoration knew no bounds and the sound of my kisses on the air was like the flapping of sheets, I know what I am saying, it was like the bottling of new wine. But what was my amazement and despair when she told me she could never be mine for she was married to a leper, imagine it, what could I do to prevent my heart from bursting into a million little pieces like diamonds and emeralds and rubies, yes real ones, not imitation glass ones, never, I have never stooped to that. She tore her hands and feet away and a great pain shot through me like a shaking spear, for it was she who had taught me all those wonderful words, it was she whose blood I had wanted to feel pulsing beneath mine own, and now she refused to open her veins for me! My passion was so frightful that I might have spat right in her face, but fortunately I was able to restrain myself and she passed away like the great wave after the earthquake of Messalina.

When everything was once more as clear and as peaceful as the falling rain and the terrible burden of my sighing had lifted itself from my poor ravaged breast, I was able to see all the dear little children playing at blind hands' muff on the mantelpiece. I took out my great burnished watch that sings like a bird and whose very hands are like feathers and whose face is divided into four sections that are the four seasons all coloured like the rainbow. I even went so far as to open it for them and show them all the needlebones and chalcedonies going round and round in its chemical inside. I take a great delight in mechanisms of all kinds, especially those that repeat themselves like the famous reproduction of the great hunting-horn that hangs on the wall in my family ward.

And then it was at last time for the operation. Were I to describe to you all the details of what took place on that memorable occasion it would take me ten times as many books as there are stars in the universe and in any case my pen would have turned to dust long before I got to the last astonishing page where I should sign my name in letters of flame and of gold and in letters of flaming gold.

First of all it was like **drinking oxygen**. I had the gentle maternal pigeon on the one side of me and the symbol of the crossed keys on the other, so I felt perfectly safe. It was like looking at that picture of a girl climbing a rope which hangs on the wall in the warden's room, it was like woollen buttons and angel's skin. It kept changing all the time, of course, so that one minute you saw the pattern of the minutes coming and going and the next you saw the sort of sawdust that they throw down on the floor if you look at it hard enough. I stretched out my hands and they went sliding far away out over the multitudinous seas whose voices came to me like the sound of chariots and firearms roaring and terrible chariots grinding the limbs of the helpless Christians to powder. Then the bed started to go up and down but it wasn't a bed it was a sort of automatic pianola and it began to gallop away with me on its back right into the middle of the forest where the chimneys were all smoking away like fury because the silly things thought it was the middle of the night. But I knew better, of course, so I sat up there and then and told them that I wasn't going to stand any more of it and I smote the ridiculous creature with the wooden leg a terrific blow across the backside, and they were all absolutely terrified of my voice like hundreds of railways thundering and my face like a red indian's.

But what am I saying? They thought they could scratch me with their tigers' claws and their eagles' talons, the wretches, they thought they could scratch my eyes out, but they weren't going to get away with it so easily. I lifted my imperious iron hand, I whose hands and feet are the very seal of all that is powerful and triumphant in this miserable world where the flowers only grow to please me, I lifted my iron hand and it became a sword and sceptre against all the wicked and unruly tongues that were clacking in the caverns in the valley of the shadow of death. My breathing became like the wind of the great tempest and I felt my body growing to stupendous size and the blinding light was like organs playing. What noble pity surged into my melting soul and how I knew everything that had been forgotten down the centuries by the mages and the saviours and the nobility of all European countries! For that was easily the greatest moment of all, when all the candles were being burnt for me and all the banquets were being given in my honour and all the assembled nations were singing songs in which my name was mentioned at least once, I think I might even say without boasting that it was mentioned ten times, in every verse.

After that, as you will well understand, it was not so difficult for me to come back into the daylight. The room was just the same as before except that the window seemed to have lost something of its original transparency and the table had been replaced by a milk-float. Nobody seemed to notice any particular change in my appearance, but if they had looked closely enough they could not have helped seeing the little snow-white footprints on my eyelids and the little black stars on my lips. In any case I took no notice of them, for I despise all men who have not the words LOVE AND DEATH inscribed on their banners, and when I went out in the evening I met my mother walking in the garden. She was wearing one of my most cherished hats and I told her of all my recent experiences, ending up by explaining how I had been awarded the Nobel Peace Prize for my exploits among the redskins. She smiled gently and, lifting her veil, began to talk about the time when she went to tea with George Sand. Then we went to choose the flowers for the wreath. And the phosphorescent night began to fall.

Night, yes indeed it was the night that fell, for I distinctly saw its columns dissolving one into the other and its arches falling and its great **aqueducts** falling down like the very symptoms of a weak heart after taking belladonna. I knew it was soon going to be very beautiful again and I was just as sure that, after what had been revealed to me and to me alone, I should never fall down. Two very massive and indestructible shoulders support this noble and imposing head of mine, this head which is so full of gorgeous pictures of the wonderful palaces, castles, fortresses and great endless glittering palaces that are my inheritance and where I shall at last rest these weary bones of mine, far from the stupid creatures I despise, far from the snaggle-toothed turnip-heads and the heartless women whom I still adore although they have made my life such a misery, far, I say, from the turnip-tops and the butterflies' hearts and the rascally curly-locked gas-meters

And now it is time for me to end, or rather, since I never really **end**, shall I say **come to** an end before saying good night to you and a downright sentimental journey.

p. 1936

THE VERY IMAGE

To René Magritte

An image of my grandmother
her head appearing upside-down upon a cloud
the cloud transfixed on the steeple
of a deserted railway station
far away

An image of an aqueduct
with a dead crow hanging from the first arch
a modern-style chair from the second
a fir tree lodged in the third
and the whole scene sprinkled with snow

An image of the piano tuner
with a basket of prawns on his shoulder
and a firescreen under his arm
his moustache made of clay-clotted twigs
and his cheeks daubed with wine

An image of an aeroplane
the propeller is rashers of bacon
the wings are of reinforced lard
the tail is made of paperclips
the pilot is a wasp

An image of the painter
with his left hand in a bucket
and his right hand stroking a cat
as he lies in bed
with a stone beneath his head

And all these images
and many others
are arranged like waxworks
in model birdcages
about six inches high.

p. 1936

THE CUBICAL DOMES

Indeed indeed it is growing very sultry
The Indian feather pots are scrambling out of the room
The slow voice of the tobacconist is like a circle
Drawn on the floor in chalk and containing ants
And indeed there is a shoe upon the table
And indeed it is as regular as clockwork
Demonstrating the variability of the weather
Or denying the existence of manu altogether
For after all why should love resemble a cushion
Why should the stumbling-block float up towards the ceiling
And in our attic it is always said
That this is a sombre country the wettest place on earth
And then there is the problem of living to be considered
With its vast pink parachutes full of underdone mutton
Its tableaux of the archbishops dressed in their underwear
Have you ever paused to consider why grass is green
Yes greener at least it is said than the man in the moon
Which is why
The linen of flat countries basks in the tropical sun
And the light of the stars is attracted by transparent flowers
And at last is forgotten by both man and beast
By helmet and capstan and mesmerised nun
For the bounds of my kingdom are truly unknown
And its factories work all night long
Producing the strongest canonical wastepaper-baskets

And ant-eaters' skiing-shoes
Which follow the glistening murders as far as the pond
And then light a magnificent bonfire of old rusty nails
And indeed they are paid by the state for their crimes
There is room for them all in the conjuror's musical-box
There is still enough room for even the hardest of faces
For faces are needed to stick on the emperor's walls
To roll down the stairs like a party of seafaring christians
Whose hearts are on fire in the snow.

p. 1936

THE SYMPTOMATIC WORLD

I

At the age of nine months I entered the world
As an automatic apprentice
My wages were divided
By the comparison between fire and water
My muscles were contracted
By the song and the wedding-ring
By the man in the front room smoking a cigar
And my eyes were especially opalescent
In that I gave them tears to drink each morning
Tears of warm milk in which flies were seen to float
Tears of cold amber in which miracles appeared
So that I seemed to see through them a world of metal
A world of intrinsic gestures and straight lines
I might even say a world in which there was no absence
And no unknown degrees
In which the pale green torture of the mountains
Appeared to consist of feathers sprouting from maps
And where the only women
Were negresses with breasts like collar-bones
And heads like violins played on by lightning
A world at last as empty as my mirror
Yet full of coach-horses and sails of ships
And vocal clocks all calling:
This way home.

II

Following an arrow
To the boundaries of sense-confusion
Like the crooked flight of a bird
The glass-lidded coffins are full of light
They displace the earth like the weight of stones
Eating and ravaging the earth like moths
Which follow the arrow
In a shower of freshly variegated sparkles
Confusing the issue of the arrow's flight
Till its feathers are all worn out
And the trees are all on fire
The pillow-case is bursting
The feathers are blown across the roofs
The room is falling from the window
And O where did that woman come from
Who chases the muleteer across the pampas
And covers her flaming face with the huge shadows of her hands?

III

The pinecone falls from the sailor's sleeve
The latchkey turns in the lock
And the light is broken
By the angry shadow of the knave of spades
Kneeling to dig in the sand with his coal-black hands
His hair is a kite to fly in the dangerous winds
That come from the central sea
He is searching for buried anvils
For the lost lamps of Syracuse
And behind him stands
The spectre whose lips are frozen
Unwinding the threads of her heart
From their luminous spool
She is stone and mortar
And tar and feather
Her errand is often obscure
But she comes to sit down in the glow of the rocks
She comes with a star in her mouth
And her words
Are rock-crystal molten by thunder
Meteors crushed by the birds.

IV

Intelligence resides in the sparrow's beak
And the seat of the will is the wing of the wasp
I am here I am there and my mind is in the middle
I hold in my hands the knob of the door of sleep
I stand on my feet on the rock of the principle
And my eyes are on top of my head
They see all that happens in the sky
The horse that bears his master in his mouth
And is ridden by the girl with red plush breasts
My ears grow out of my feet
And they hear all the sounds underground
The ringing of bells in the caves
And the whisper of wandering roots
The intellect resides in the mineral's neck
And the seat of the soul is the mouth of the stone
Which is why the earth's veins are so stopped up with sand
And the sea is so full of green flame
For the earth is a kiss on the mouth of the sky
And the sky is a fan in the hand of the sun

V

This is my world this is your realm of clay
Our dreams have all come true
The ash of sleep is deeper than dust on the stairs
Of this mine-shaft brimmed with gold
The sunken garden of a fugitive
Cold with black rain that stains the soil like ink
Enigma like a skull with petrol eyes
A sprouting head of plumes of silver grass
That haunts the sanded paths
The booming caves are full of birds
With silken wings and beaks of solid stone
Who pass the time away
With burning feathers from their tails
In the flaming waterfall
This is my world this is your garden gate
Our vistas stretch a thousand leagues from here
As far as forests full of moving trees
As far as fingers holding tigers' skins
As far as bushes on the window-sill

As far as castles with unlicensed towers
As far as caskets full of human hair
As far as clouds on fire and dying swans
On lakes that swallow beds as fast as tigers swallow hands.

VI

On the sidewalks of New York
There are women who pass to and fro with napkins wrapped round their heads
So that no one can see their eyes
And machines lean out of the windows to record the number of their footsteps
A record is made of the sound of falling coins
That cover the streets with silver and cause fruit to ripen in bowls
And the lift-boys chant:
The sea comes once too often up the street
And the wind goes once too seldom down the sky,
And their song goes on till morning
When the inhabitants put logs outside their doors
For the children to make fires in all the gutters
Which awakens the town to the sound of derailed trains
While baskets of boot-buttons light up the distant hills.

VII

Undoubtedly the sun has burnt his hands
Undoubtedly the corn has grown too high
And when this is done
The first-class trains will stop running every afternoon at five o'clock
And the passengers next morning will alight
In a ditch of frozen milk
Their thoughts will return with regret to their twice-locked trunks
Full of borrowed dresses and discarded wedding-rings
They will groan with dismay at the thought of the coming day
Full of empty bags and crumbs of stalest bread
From house to house the frost will spread its warnings
And weathercocks fall from the roofs.

VIII

The needle glitters inch by inch
And the sound of its stitches reaches the sea
Where bombs explode in every other wave
And the beaches are paler than curd
I return there every other night
Wearing the same clothes, breathing the same air
And the weasels only laugh at me but it is not my fault
I can hardly help it if the lines of the meridian resemble fish
That fly away
To where the heat softens the equator
With hair growing out of its ears
And birds' nests in its hair to keep the rain off
The rain that whispers in decrepit castles
Great clots of clay and the effigies falling to dust
Preserve us from the singing towers
And the chapter which turns the page of its own accord
For fear of reading its own history there.

p. 1936

THE SUPPOSED BEING

Supposing the mouth
The hard lips crowned with bright flowers
A bursting foam of petals
And each gold stamen an anxious arrow
As each firm finger a signal
Pointing to fire and water's junction
Whose furious fumes would stifle the passers-by
With their startled eyes
With their nervous hands and faces
Whose language is black whose language has
Never been ours.

Supposing the eyes
Luscious in lashes and deep stained with sleep
The eyes in the forehead like pools in the rocks
And the turbulent sea approaching
Shivering ravenous venomous scarred

By the sharp-taloned claws of its waves
As eyes by their ravaging lids
As their lids by the richly veined hands
That are burnt by the light of the sun
And the stones are on fire
And the pupils of eyes are glazed by the
Heat of their flames.

Supposing the hands
With their nails and their delicate bones
Like the frail limbs of birds
And their tips like the pink tips of buds
That probe the cold curious air
And discover the blood neath the skin
And the surface of stones.

Supposing the breasts
Like shells on the oceanless shore
At the end of the world
Like furious thrusts of a single knife
Like bread to be broken by hands
Supposing the breasts still untouched by desires
Still unsuckled by thirsts
And motionless still
Breasts violently still and enisled in the
Night and afraid both of love and of death.

Supposing the sex
A cruelty and dead in the thighs
A gaping and blackness – a charred
Trace of feverish flames
The sex like an X
As the sign and the imprint of all that has gone before
As a torch
To enlighten the forest of gloom and the
Mountains of unattained night.

And supposing the being entire
The tangible body standing
The visible limbs existing
And moving across the daylight
Or motionless in the darkness

A stone on the torrent's bed
Or a torrent above the stones –
And at last

Such a being escapes from the sight of my visible eyes
From the touch of my tangible hand
For she only exists
Where all contradictions exist
Where darkness is light and the real is unreal and the
World is a dream in a dream.

p. 1936

EAU SIFFLÉE

La tête d'épines vertes
Cache de son ombre
Un sac – de quoi ?
Pourquoi ? Mais dites :
Les vieillards tombent de haut en bas
Comme des clous – mousse – lard
(Le mur est fendu)
N'est-ce pas ?
Nids de pâté
Dont les oiseaux s'en sont volés
Se cacher sous les ponts.

Et tout le temps
Immobiles et le plancher et le plafond,
Immobiles et rouges.

w. 1936

GOÛT DU JOUR

Today there is fur on the tongue of the wakening light
There is dust in the darkening streets
Whose tongue is brick dissolved in lime
The sound of sight
Reduced to ashes by the height of the bloom's decay
In the caverns of the smell
Where moth-balls leap like mole-hills in the pocket of grey fowls
Thin grey fowls with leather gullets
And with claws of too much rain
Too much anthracite in pain
In the cities of the plain
Although anthrax is the secret of the way to find your way
From the paling of the pillars to the breaking of the bars
Where the breezy bellows stand in bright array
And the castanets are forming little holes in women's sleeves
In order to allow their sound to breathe.

w. 1936, p. 1996

CAFARD

Sickness and charity like death's heads tied to the mast
Return to the bottomless sea from whence they came
Where islands of snow sink like holes into the heart
And the revenge of death is remembered no more
By those whom the firmament betrayed
Life's nebulous champagne is forgotten before it is drunk
For each of its bubbles is a brief lapse of its blood
Of the somnolent clay whose arms embrace the sleeper
And whose veins are of lead – life's bouquet
Has lost all its scent for those who plucked it
Their senses are tied to the battlecry's torn floating web
And the landscape's oblivious light is
Where islands of snow sink like holes into the heart.

w. 1936, p. 1996

RÉCUPÉRATION

The gradual emergence of the
Instincts the hard sharp
Laughter of the sudden daylight
And out of the sleepy funnel
Of the waking mouth
Breath
Merges again with the waiting
Whiteness of what is to be.

w. 1936, p. 1996

FOOL'S PARADISE

The man dressed in armour
joins his hands and feet
and his body forms a ring
which spins round the chain that hangs from the torso of
    a racehorse
unseen by the crowd
who are busily building a tent
in the glare of a Bengal light
a tent that will soon be a ship
if it could but float
though that consideration is of no importance
what is important is that beans are getting sleepy
and will soon fall right off the plate
onto a fork made of soap
which will then sing the national anthem
through its nose
which is always a danger-signal to the ants
who will immediately cease work
form fives
and march through the streets to the house of the mayor
    of the town
who will stand on a chair
to deliver this speech to the world.

w. 1936, p. 1996

SYMPTOMATIC WORLD

The resinous globes of your sweat the moist hair
Of your savage tongue tying your head
To the branches that grow from your bed
Invite me to wrap you in sheets
Of precaution and cover your feet
Will beware of the wolves' padded howl
The thin ghostly love of the planets the wool
And the rock of the tetanous scream
Of the half-melting needles
Your eyes
Your eyes like burnt leaves are beginning to fade
And the last rain will wash them away
Like the colour of sleet and the odour of putrified hay.

w. 1936, p. 1996

ELEGIAC STANZAS IN MEMORY OF ALBAN BERG

First draft

I

When a rich (sick) rose falls in flakes from its thorn-spiked
    stem
Its petals stain the dark eroded soil;
So tears fall heavily to stain the heart's stone floor
A grief akin to madness sets its sudden springs
To leap without a cause from out our sleep
Our (jarring) nervous dreams
Until we shake with sorrow that we cannot name.

The rain with turbid drops adorns the leaves
Of rose-bushes that grow among the rocks
And stifle with their scent the chilly air.
It is the hour when disembodied heads,
The faces of the lost, glide, pensively
Across (Along/Among) the misty twilight (shadows) of this
    distant place, –
Cimmeria, the refuge of the shades.

On high
Striations of white light amaze the sky;
While round the staring lead-eyed pool below
A dull wind stirs the agony of reeds
Concentric ripples strike the water's rim
Like echoes of a desperate final cry,
And (While) arrow-headed birds fly fast away.

II

The snake-like roads that writhe across the plains
The agonized cities and towns
The valleys of melting snow
And the cruel mountain heights
By day lie exposed to the blows of the sun
Are oppressed under darkness by night
And have never repose

Or monotonous colourless skies
Weigh down the appalling /dreadful streets
Where human misery seems too great to bear –
Thugs trained to beat the poor to death
Neurotics groping in distress; –
Or fear-distended eyes through windows see
The glare of gasworks bursting on the outskirts of the town.
Lying tired and silent in a darkened room
One hears the trains rush by across the viaduct
Raucously hastening to attain the heart of Europe
And one lies wondering:
Where can all the trains be going?
Why is it all the trains are crashing
In my head?

III

[Dream, desire, death, all told,
The present's pain,
Centreless, all-pervading,
Drowns in its daft white glare
The dissolving world retracts
Its image from our eyes]

The world dissolves, retracts
Its image from the eye's
Dissolving glare. The present's pain
(Dream, desire, death all told)
Centreless, (ever-present) pervading all,
Drowns in its daft white glare
The mind as music drowns

Us, listening on the . . . verge
Of virgin silence, that last
Comfort of the battered, and it seems
Its sense is stronger than the eye's;
No words, no passionate description
Can move us more than these:
'*Les sons d'une musique enervante et calme.*

Semblable au cri lontain de l'humaine douleur,'
Too complicated to explain,
Too like a wound (cruelly true) to bear for long
Before the wind rises again at last.
Blowing the hair back from our heads,
And snatching away the music in our ears
To lose it in the vast sky's sombre waste

[*The stanza below is written on a separate page under the heading* **IV**]

[A man's life now, like the wind
That passes, the winds above us,
No longer fixed nor separate in itself
But with all the others merging,
As where a lonely column melts
Into the distance and the breast of doves
Are seen a moment as they cross the brow,]

Elegiac Stanzas IV

As the wind strikes light from the sides
Of waves and silver from their crests
Though of no Southern Ocean but the couch
Of gloom and icebergs, as the wind
[That passes in its passing wrests

(A transitory smile) from (the) rock
Grinds one more grain of sand
From rock]
That passes in its passing wrests
A transitory smile from utter rock
And stirs the sleep of sand,
As where a single column melts
Into the distance and the wings (breasts) of doves
Whirl for a moment past the gazer's eyes,
As smoke climbs up behind a hill
To tell of towns or tents beyond,
And as these vaguer images
Merge one by one into a waking dream,

A man's life passes, is not fixed or one,
But is not substanceless as (things)
In all the loud apocalypse of time,
One man or millions, (each is set)
from which no-one escapes
The place and date. Man's present state
How fearful, and how real.

V

A sombre script in half-light read
Text of an ancient or some sage
Transfigured by a sudden inward ray
That floods the meditative page
Instructs the bewildered heart:
Death is not only death nor yet
Shall life prevail if death should die

Whose is the memory we mourn?
But countless memories, innumerable stones,
Each spark that the dark defeated
And at last shall kindle in a blinding
Blaze, make mourning seem
A child's misapprehending weakness, when
Flame leaps from the very urn.

An ancient text – but we do not look back
But forward out of meditation rear

A dustless and determined clear
Inscription like a fervent pointing hand:
We lived this time and saw
Ruin and death at work on every side –
We also saw your light who burn/shine ahead
(But never doubted)

★   ★   ★

Elegiac Stanzas in Memory of Alban Berg
Second draft

I

When a rich rose falls in flakes from a thorn-spiked stem
Its petals stain the dark eroded soil;
So tears fall heavily to stain the heart's stone floor.
A grief near madness sets its sudden springs
To leap without a cause from out our sleep,
Our jarring nervous dreams,
Until we shake with sorrow that we cannot name.
The rain with turbid drops adorns the leaves
Of rose-bushes that grow among the rocks
And stifle with their scent the chilly air.
It is the hour when disembodied heads,
The faces of the lost, glide pensively
Across the twilight of this distant place, –
Cimmeria, the refuge of the shades.

On high
Striations of white light amaze the sky;
While round the staring lead-eyed pool below
A dull wind stirs the agony of reeds,
Concentric ripples strike the water's rim
Like echoes of a desperate final cry;
And arrow-headed birds fly fast away.

II

The roads that writhe across the plains
The harrowed upland fields
The valleys of melting snow
And the cruel mountain heights

By day lie exposed to the blows of the sun
Are oppressed under darkness by night
And have never repose

Our monotonous colourless skies
Weigh down the appalling streets
Where human misery seems too great to bear:
Thugs trained to beat the poor to death
Neurotics gasping in distress
Or fear-distended eyes through windows see
The glare of gasworks bursting on the outskirts of the
   town.

Lying tired and silent in a darkened room
One hears the trains rush by across the viaduct
Raucously hastening to attain the heart of Europe;
And one lies wondering:
Where can all the trains be going?
Why is it all the trains are crashing
In my head?

w. 1936, p. 2007

CHORUS

Is this the final coast
Between the dark land and tomorrow's sea
Home friends and lover lost
Is this the cost
Wandering aimlessly
And questions asked
Unlock the monster's jaws at last

Now he has come
Into a foreign hall
Which is not home at all
Now he is here
The cross-word puzzle fan
Looks up but does not hear
Or answer our lost man.

In the unfriendly street
Wings of the pavement beat
About the bright bowed head
No questions answered no
Encouragement, and so
Best beat a swift retreat
Before the signals change from green to red

And now the answer's plain
Stand and stare down again
Where water flows
Biting the town in half –
Unlock death's easy jaws
Fall like a stone
And disregard the frown

But men conspire
The desperate to cheat
Street after street
Our wanderer
Seeks for a lock to try
He wants to die
But does not dare

Here will he hear
Another's angry voice
Teaching the crowd to fear
God and the State –
Hurl then the heavy mace
Although it may fly too far
And fall too late

Away again away
The phrase repeat
Day after day
Follows these weary streets
Searching forgotten joy
No stone commemorates
Who did not dare to die

Till the town's furthest bound
Cements its bond

With lonely ruined fields
Desolate acres spanned
By a forbidding wall
Whose shadow shields
No-one at all

But this old clumsy clown
Last remnant of the past
See how his beard falls down
See on the ground
His unknown captive squirm –
Fear an old fool at last
And the silk worm

Now a familiar face
Appears when all hope seemed lost
Joy with a summer grace
Come like a welcome ghost
To save what mattered most
Lovers embrace
Making the past a jest

If out of sight be out of mind
Then leave this place
If love be blind
Happy then not to see the clown's grimace
Together advance once more
Along the wall set out to find
The certain door

Though landscapes lie beyond
Tragic as those once passed
Now they go hand in hand
The terrors still ahead
Seem but their journey's last
Warning lest too great a speed
Should rob them of their land.

w. 1936, p. 1998

MOON OVER LONDON

Last night a woman's veil
Above the city drifting like a bat
Or some lost wing of smoke
By hateful influences was rent in twain
Predicting ruin for the denizens below

Out of its house of cerulean shell
The twin-breasted eclipse
Released its venom on the world
And poured its quick-tongued vapours
   on our sleep
While dire hounds howled on Hampstead Hill.

Then sighed the half-extinguished torch:
'Aversion of the violence foretold
Is in the courage of the weak
To brace the breaking rock
And cut adrift the tethered keel of Time.'

w. 1937, p. 1996

AN UNFINISHED, UNPUBLISHED POST-AUDEN PRE-WAR PROEM

For J.S.

The nervous bats are twitching through the dusk.
    The lamp's honey-coloured light
      Upon the page, the early rose
Stuck in the one-time inkwell on the desk,
At the garden-window the wireless playing Mozart's
    Soothing but earnest voice:

Harbour the meditation: upon you and the endless world
    About which you reflect;
      In which we live; which swings
The mere wind into the daze and ache of void;
The object of every greed, which hourly sets
    Writhing a thousand pens.

In all this peace (a man walks a dog down the road,
        The wireless softly sings,
        Night concentrates its blue),
I think of you, and long with fascinated dread
For all the noise and punishment of Facts:
        All that we could or could not know.

But think: have we filled in our map, have we drawn
        An extensive plan?
        Are we really aware
Of all the precise implications of having been born?
You and I, are we really so knowing that we can avoid
        The ubiquitous fear?

This is what we must cast out, we are agreed.
        But we are alone
        And all our courage – (null)
If they still go on fearing whom we arrogantly called
'The small', pretending that we were privileged
        To be – (ill)

Consider the chicken and the egg and which was first.
        Outer or inner?
        The world of loves
And hates, of the intimate one and two; and just as vast
And complicated, implicating us, the world
        Of human lives.

w. 1937, p. 1996

THREE VERBAL OBJECTS

In Memory of Humphrey Jennings

I

The poet is dead; and it is in the people that we must seek to find what remains of the mysterious radiation of his soul: – birthpangs of a series of images stretching away into infinity; crystallization of the movements of impulsion and repulsion; from the hermit's cave to the broken shell of the great roc, a trail of bones and other fragments.

In the centre of the arc is fixed a hunter's bow and arrow, festooned with deadly flowers. This is the node of animal magnetism and of all dreams of hate and fear. The people have secretly proclaimed their love for those who haunt them.

Over the marshes, in the summer air, there hang invisible monsoons which, if the human eye could register them, would have the form of funnels. Into their mouths pass the warm breath of sinking creatures and the emanations of defeated warriors, whose shields and armour glitter strangely in the green light of the setting sun. Some representative of a distant tribe is seated passive on the bank, occasionally beating an idle note upon his drum. There will be no more thunder for at least another month.

The people love the warrior; and even as he lies sinking in the marsh, they deck his image with a thousand lethal flowers. They cannot see his wounds.

To the warrior, war; to the lover, love. And the lower species also shall give instances of their passion: in the twilight crevices, silent bubbles, swelling and deflating like the lungs. Smoke rises out of the eyes, distorting the labyrinthine perspective. This is sleep. Its oscillations only serve to aggravate the decay of the outer ramparts. There, our projected bodies parade themselves, clad in all the amazing appearance of the illusions which, without knowing it, we can entertain about them in the night.

Violent is the falsehood with which we have clothed our desires. To eat, to kill and to make love. Magic, the clotted valve, intoxication, cold invading the pores, the syren-call of giddiness falling from North to South. The ocean does not cease to lacerate the shore; nor the blood to circulate through the channels of the brain.

II

It is well-nigh impossible to describe in words the natural beauties of this country. The hills are bathed in a glow of the most subliminal tranquillity, like that which is given out by the innocent eyes of children, milky and diffuse. The shadows cast by the further ranges eat into the plain like acid. There are only a few houses round the edge of the lakes, dwelling-places of fakirs and water-diviners, untroubled spirits who appear on their thresholds only at evening, when the sun throws an additional lustre upon the bismuth grottoes which adorn the shores. Who would not envy them, who pass their days in the ecstatic contemplation of the death of Time? To the North, there stand the remains of one or two deserted villages. These were once inhabited by an outlandish race, wearing skins and communicating with one another in a speech most closely resembling that of birds, shrill yet guttural. Their wells ran dry, or became salt, and they migrated, we know not where. In their abandoned huts, which were hewn from volcanic stone, a few pots and other utensils have been discovered, bearing curious ornamentations which are supposed to illustrate the myths of the lost tribe.

Foremost among these legendary representations is the Wheel. Sometimes this fantasy is expressed as a chain of limbs of animals and of men entwined. Some vessels, again, are covered with what appear to be crudely drawn bands of flowers. Certain monoliths, also, which have recently been discovered among the petrified Western forests, where the ground is frequently shaken by seismic tremors, are ornamented, totem-like, by circular constellations of five eyes.

The phenomenon of the wheel of eyes is said to have been frequently observed in this part of the country by watchers on the hills at dawn. The last occasion on which it was reported to have been seen was when a band of scientifically-minded explorers were making their way into the extreme fastnesses of the nether mountains, not so many years ago. They were emerging from their tents, at about five o'clock in the morning, when their guides drew their attention to a curious patch of light in the sky just above their heads. A few moments later, it became quite clear that this light was being given out not, as they had at first imagined, by a cluster of stars, but by five enormous and distinctly outlined eyes, which hovered gravely, motionless and without blinking in the sky for about ten minutes, holding the spectators spell-bound with silent awe and wonder, and then faded away like cloud.

The phenomenon was accompanied by a distant grinding, ringing sound. It is supposed that this mirage, or optical illusion, is due to the peculiar reflective properties of the mica rocks with which the region is encumbered; and that it was this appearance which originally gave rise, in association with the other and more obvious symbols of perpetual recurrence, to the legend of the Wheel.

III

Vast expanses of devastated territory, jagged skyline, wooden scaffoldings 140 foot high and blazing like giant torches – young women and little old children lying murdered in disordered heaps – abandoned gun-carriages, drifts of snow lying melting in the sun here and there among the ruins . . .

Everything was in order. Our leader called a halt. He turned his face towards us, away from the shattered landscape, and we saw that he was smiling through his tears. When the last trace of the old world is cleared away, comrades, he cried, we shall build our city here.

And one of our number planted the standard on top of a hillock of refuse. We set to work with diligence in the fresh morning smell. Everything is in order, we repeated to ourselves, looking up now and then to observe the destruction of a last altar, or a prison wall.

From the tower of a quietly blazing mansion whirled a flock of doves, and the smell of their half-scorched feathers became confused with the scent of the countless damp and trampled plants that lay a-rotting on the terraces. And the sky flung a column of wind like a wide-flung scarf into the distance, where the earth was turning on its never-ending hinge.

p. 1937

TRANSPARENCY OF THE VEGETABLE WORLD SEEN FROM THREE PACES AWAY BY THE THREE FACES OF A FACTORY

then fawn is in the litigation of its repeatable tower
which is as clear as malt the spider of the glass dance
the dangerous glass dance of domes surmounted by smiles
and branching out towards the suns of oval fame
in tubes of nacre and of lipsalved iron
importunate as doves
but even the colossal egresses could not contend
        with the stone bed of the marriage settlement
the stone bed in which the fiery boa lowered its hood in
        order to see through the rent in the ceiling
through which poured the Thames

bastard is the thin imagery of the rickshaw's cotton-wool
                                                                             eyebath
it goes backwards and forwards like a dog
trying to unwind the binding of its malefic tail
and only succeeding in awakening the chorus of the buckets
        in the yard of the hotel
where the flies which wear stays have burnt holes in
        all the mangled heaps of spontaneous
            combustion which so magnificently attains the summit of
        the green yawning-mixture
the grey hoops of method and mild liturgy
the little soiled eggs which inhabit the hairdresser's mouth
in the jug's pierced heart the beehive is burning like a sceptre
and the vine-covered wall is enjoying the Princess's foot
while the intermission regains the frequent equilibrium between
spraying the thorny surface of the vision with the
        wild trace of a thousand confusions and a thousand
        interplanetary speedboats' echoes
and the gloved shock of a woven light-wave's path
through the thicket of a swan's coiled neck
before the day breaks upon China and removes the other swans
from their vapour-baths and holds them upside down above
                                            the mountains

meanwhile the antipodes of the crystal break down into their
                                            respective elements

which are
the night of the log palace
the calm of the medusa's hair-net
the beetle of the western plains which breaks the lock of
                                              rockplants' wings
the flame-coloured fruit surmounting the debris of the
   necrophological ruin of Christ
the sap in the sex of the brain
and the beast with two toes whose music is like that
           of the slow turning of eyes from side to side in the
             great wind which blows out of the empty mansions on
the tops of the hills
the great wind which will blow down the last of the gallows of
   pride.

w. 1937–38, p. 1996

PHANTASMAGORIA

For Margaret W.

The wind has stopped at last
in that little black town on the edge of a violet sea
where a man in an upstairs-room of the empty house
which stands overlooking the yard of the Sodium Works
is sitting blindfold on the draughty floor
trying to hear the feeble groans of the North Pole inside his skull
and thinking of the iron teeth of Death
thinking of the rusty police-whistle chained to so many necks
of the last Act of *Faust*
of the cherry-coloured gown his mistress wore on that fatal night
    when she lost her head so irretrievably while sailing in a gondola
and of the incomparably curvilinear and seductive effect to be
    obtained
by writing one's name in water
with the white of one's own glass eye . . .
In this poor blackened town on the edge of a violet sea
the wind has left stray locks of hair behind
in almost every street –
locks which appear like loosely-knotted strands of twilight sleep
or fragments of Opal-tree bark

preserved in wine
and left all night to dry upon the steps of a Russian church . . .
These scattered tresses make the passers-by turn pale
then hurry home to disinfect their wells
They glitter faintly like the dust of poisoned stars
and hypnotize the gaze of the last birds still to remain
in that seaside town as black as a burnt cake
where the dead are sitting propped-up in the windows robed in
    flags
of all the nations – where the homeless night
is kept awake by Autumn's chill aurora in the sky
and silence lolls like smoke along the disused harbour-quays . . .
And in this little town like a charred bun beside a sea
which stains its shores with blackberry-juice ink
the crowds continue playing their quaint melancholy games
in street and market-place although dense clouds of smoke
are pouring from the windows of the Luxury Hotel
in which the foreign guest in Room 13
swathed in red bandages from head to foot
lies thinking of the monkey's-paw of Death
thinking of the frozen music in the eyes of statues
of the brutal naked beauty of a surgical machine
of his father's raincoat gleaming in the twilight long ago
and of the fungus growing on the tree-trunk of Desire . . .
In that charcoal-black town on the edge of a vein-coloured sea
where shadow smoulders in the cave-like shops
and copper bells toll slowly all day long
the wheels of a great lacquered Rolls-Royce car
left lying in the middle of the main street upside-down
are to be seen months later still continuing to spin
in the tensely sensational glare of the naphtha torch
left burning there by the authorities to mark the fatal spot –
continuing still to spin like a soul in pain
like a tin-plate sent whirling out without a word through the
    window-bars of a condemned man's cell
or like the breasts of Destiny revolving night and day . . .
And now that the day's white wind has stopped at last
the hoofs of dusk go trampling through the hollow clouds on high
from beneath their rocks the scorpions of the darkness soon creep
    out
and faintly in the distance on all sides is to be heard
the dread hyena-laughter of the prehistoric Night . . .

Meanwhile through narrow twilit streets flock jostling throngs of
    masks –
red oblong leather faces stuck with clusters of tiny shells
faces of cheese with green protruding fangs
faces like pillows wet with tears and moulting feathers through the
    torn holes of their eyes
and snarling hairy faces like the hindquarters of apes
and sickly faces weak as greasy smudges left by flies
and hungry faces gaping like raw muddy graves in Spring . . .
The thoroughfares of Evening swarm with rapid shifting scenes
and everywhere the lamps of lust and terror thrust their beams
to scour the countless cage-like haunts of men with scorching light
while waves of sound roll out across the rooftops overhead –
waves swollen with dreamy cries and rumbling words
with the last thick sobs of harlots stabbed to death
and with that unbearably heart-rending melody which the blind old
    men who live alone in freezing garrets are forever playing to
    themselves upon their broken violins . . .
See! here is a ring of dancers round a blazing marriage-bed
and here is a bunch of bearded dwarfs dangling chained by their
    heels from the top of a convent-wall
and here are the bones of a Saint which calmly float
upon the silken surface of a swimming-pool hewn from the heart of
    an amethyst-rock
in a glass-panelled coffin of cork lit-up inside on the stroke of
    midnight by a magnesium-flare . . .
Here is the Theatre standing open to the sky
in which dead flowers and moonlight perform ballets once an
    hour
and there the Children's Home stands on the hill behind the town
where hidden in steep gardens among shadows and blue shrubs
an orphan whose huge head lolls like a glass-eyed hirsute globe
squats weeping in the dew-chilled herb of dreams
and thrusting the blade of his pen-knife ever deeper into his thigh
And here is the swift silhouette of a sphinx on a screen in the sky
Here is the abandoned saw-mill with its broken windows' haggard
    gaze
and see! here the pair of superb nocturnal swans
each of which has been saddled with a mirror and firmly trussed to
    the back of a mule
and the mules stationed as sentries on either side the harbour's
    mouth

where every now and then they are washed gently from side to side
    by the changing tide . . .
And here among the dunes are strewn the battered hulks of wrecks
which ere the hour is far advanced abruptly rise into the air
and like a furtive school of whales go lunging inland through the
    night
to make their clumsy nests on the most lofty towers and domes;
while here upon the beach is the vast ballroom with invisible glass
    walls
across the luminous floor of which a hundred pairs of invisible
    slippers are picking their way among numberless pools of
    invisible blood . . .
And O how pungent is the firedamp's musty fragrance in the hollow
    of each wave
that falls on the shore by that small black-eyed town on the edge of a
    heliotrope sea
where a man in a brilliantly illumined subterranean padded-cell
concealed at a depth of about 69 feet below the level of the ground –
(a man wearing a mask designed to resemble the head of a
    Paradise-bird
with a diamond-encrusted beak of solid gold
and clad in a sky-blue satin tunic across the front of which are
    embroidered in silver thread
the words SPITTOON – OSMOSIS – SINGAPORE) –
sits swinging regularly to and fro upon a platinum trapeze
and thinking of the iridescent and immobile nipples of Death
thinking of the vivid short-lived blossoms which are seen to sprout
    occasionally from the mouths of pregnant women
of how the midnight-sun drapes the landscapes of Arabia with
    invertebrate question-marks like plumes snatched from an ailing
    eagle's tail
of the colourless abyss of idle days
of Mary calling home the cattle across the sands of Dee
and of the end of Summer with its interminable showers of salt and
    of soot . . .
But now that the great water-spouts of midnight have subsided out
    at sea
and that those barbaric cortèges of clouds swaying dangerously from
    side to side across the steeps of heaven
like sodden hayricks in a sudden storm
have finally all vanished one by one into the fuming workhouse-
    chimneys of the East –

now that the cavernous yawn of the lonely female Titan lying
    sleeping on the softly gleaming sands
has at last swallowed-up every starfish in sight –
the livid wind once more begins to lift,
stealthily weaving its fine-spun shawls in writhing swathes around
the radius of that small black seaside town
through which by now down each long soundless street
swarms of somnambulistic barefoot children creep
by slow degrees, still sealed by spell of dream,
towards where soon the spume-besilvered waves shall shine and
    seethe
as a new Sun soars like song out of the silence of the sea.

w. 1938, p. 1941

From **HÖLDERLIN'S MADNESS**
(1938)

HÖLDERLIN'S MADNESS

FIGURE IN A LANDSCAPE

The verdant valleys full of rivers
Sang a fresh song to the thirsty hills.
The rivers sang:
'Our mother is the Night, into the Day we flow. The mills
Which toil our waters have no thirst. We flow
Like light.'

      And the great birds
Which dwell among the rocks, flew down
Into the dales to drink, and their dark wings
Threw flying shades across the pastures green.

At dawn the rivers flowed into the sea.
The mountain birds
Rose out of sleep like a winged cloud, a single fleet
And flew into a newly-risen sun.

– Anger of the sun: the deadly blood-red rays which strike oblique
Through olive branches on the slopes and kill the kine.
– Tears of the sun: the summer evening rains which hang grey veils
Between the earth and sky, and soak the corn, and brim the lakes.
– Dream of the sun: the mists which swim down from the icy heights
And hide the gods who wander on the mountainsides at noon.

The sun was anguished, and the sea
Threw up its crested arms and cried aloud out of the depths;
And the white horses of the waves raced the black horses of the
    clouds;
The rocky peaks clawed at the sky like gnarled imploring hands;
And the black cypresses strained upwards like the sex of a hanged man.

★

Across the agonizing land there fled
Among the landscape's limbs (the limbs
Of a vast denuded body torn and vanquished from within)
The chaste white road,
Prolonged into the distance like a plaint.

Between the opposition of the night and day
Between the opposition of the earth and sky
Between the opposition of the sea and land
Between the opposition of the landscape and the road
A traveller came
                    Whose only nudity his armour was
Against the whirlwind and the weapon, the undoing wound,

And met himself half-way.

Spectre as white as salt in the crude light of the sky
Spectre confronted by flesh, the present and past
Meet timelessly upon the endless road,
Merge timelessly in time and pass away,
Dreamed face away from stricken face into the bourn
Of the unborn, and the real face of age into the fastnesses of death.

Infinitely small among the infinitely huge,
Drunk with the rising fluids of his breast, his boiling heart,
Exposed and naked as the skeleton – upon the knees
Like some tormented desert saint – he flung
The last curse of regret against Omnipotence.
And the lightning struck his face.

*

After the blow, the bruised earth blooms again,
The storm-wrack, wrack of the cloudy sea
Dissolve, the rocks relax,
As the pallid phallus sinks in the clear dawn
Of a new day, and the wild eyes melt and close,
And the eye of the sun is no more blind –

Clear milk of love, O lave the devastated vale,
And peace of high-noon, soothe the traveller's pain
Whose hands still grope and clutch, whose head
Thrown back entreats the guerison
And music of your light!

The valley rivers irrigate the land, the mills
Revolve, the hills are fecund with the cypress and the vine,
And the great eagles guard the mountain heights.

Above the peaks in mystery there sit
The Presences, the Unseen in the sky,
Inscrutable, whose influences like rays
Descend upon him, pass through and again
Like golden bees the hive of his lost head.

p. 1938

ORPHEUS IN THE UNDERWORLD

Curtains of rock
And tears of stone,
Wet leaves in a high crevice of the sky:
From side to side the draperies
Drawn back by rigid hands.

And he came carrying the shattered lyre,
And wearing the blue robes of a king,
And looking through eyes like holes torn in a screen;
And the distant sea was faintly heard,
From time to time, in the suddenly rising wind,
Like broken song.

Out of his sleep, from time to time,
From between half-open lips,
Escaped the bewildered words which try to tell
The tale of his bright night
And his wing-shadowed day
The soaring flights of thought beneath the sun
Above the islands of the seas
And all the deserts, all the pastures, all the plains
Of the distracting foreign land.

He sleeps with the broken lyre between his hands,
And round his slumber are drawn back
The rigid draperies, the tears and wet leaves,
Cold curtains of rock concealing the bottomless sky.

p. 1938

TENEBRAE

Brown darkness on the gazing face
In the cavern of candlelight reflects
The passing of the immaterial world in the deep eyes.

The granite organ in the crypt
Resounds with rising thunder through the blood,
With daylight song, unearthly song that floods
The brain with bursting suns:
Yet it is night.

It is the endless night, whose every star
Is in the spirit like the snow of dawn,
Whose meteors are the brilliance of summer,
And whose wind and rain
Are all the halcyon freshness of the valley rivers,
Where the swans,
White, white in the light of dream,
Still dip their heads.

Clear night!
He has no need of candles who can see
A longer, more celestial day than ours.

c. 1938

EPILOGUE

This severed artery
The sand-obliterated face
Amazed eyes high above catastrophe
Distributed – Is this the man's remains
Who walked the lap of lands, and sang?

Explosions of every dimension
Directions run away
Towards the sun
The bitter sunset, or
Who knows, where all things rise and fall,
Revolve, and meet themselves again?

This is the man of matted hair
And music, whom a wanderer
Had scented a long way off, by reason of
The salt blood in his heart,
The black sun in his blood,
The gestures of his skeleton, simplicity
Of white bones worn away
Like rock by milk of love.

Dissolve and meet themselves again
All things; the sandy artery
The severed head
Limbs strewn across the rocks
Like broken boats:
So shall their widespread body rise
And march, and marching sing.

c. 1938

POEMS 1937–42

(1943)

MISERERE

> 'Le désespoir a des ailes
> L'amour a pour aile nacré
> Le désespoir
> Les sociétés peuvent changer.'
>   PIERRE JEAN JOUVE

TENEBRAE

'*It is finished.*' The last nail
Has consummated the inhuman pattern, and the veil
Is torn. God's wounds are numbered.
All is now withdrawn: void yawns
The rock-hewn tomb. There is no more
Regeneration in the stricken sun,
The hope of faith no more,
No height no depth no sign
And no more history.

Thus may it be: and worse.
And may we know Thy perfect darkness.
And may we into Hell descend with Thee.

p. 1939

PIETÀ

Stark in the pasture on the skull-shaped hill,
In swollen aura of disaster shrunken and
Unsheltered by the ruin of the sky,
Intensely concentrated in themselves the banded
Saints abandoned kneel.

And under the unburdened tree
Great in their midst, the rigid folds
Of a blue cloak upholding as a text
Her grief-scrawled face for the ensuing world to read,
The Mother, whose dead Son's dear head

Weighs like a precious blood-encrusted stone
On her unfathomable breast:

Holds Him God has forsaken, Word made flesh
Made ransom, to the slow smoulder of her heart
Till the catharsis of the race shall be complete.

p. 1939

DE PROFUNDIS

Out of these depths:

Where footsteps wander in the marsh of death and an
Intense infernal glare is on our faces facing down:

Out of these depths, what shamefaced cry
Half choked in the dry throat, as though a stone
Were our confounded tongue, can ever rise:
Because the mind has been struck blind
And may no more conceive
Thy Throne . . .

Because the depths
Are clear with only death's
Marsh-light, because the rock of grief
Is clearly too extreme for us to breach:
Deepen our depths,

And aid our unbelief.

p. 1939

KYRIE

Is man's destructive lust insatiable? There is
Grief in the blow that shatters the innocent face.
Pain blots out clearer sense. And pleasure suffers
The trial thrust of death in even the bride's embrace.

The black catastrophe that can lay waste our worlds
May be unconsciously desired. Fear masks our face;
And tears as warm and cruelly wrung as blood
Are tumbling even in the mouth of our grimace.

How can our hope ring true? Fatality of guilt
And complicated anguish confounds time and place;
While from the tottering ancestral house an angry voice
Resounds in prophecy. Grant us extraordinary grace,

O spirit hidden in the dark in us and deep,
And bring to light the dream out of our sleep.

p. 1938

LACHRYMAE

Slow are the years of light:
        and more immense
Than the imagination. And the years return
Until the Unity is filled. And heavy are
The lengths of Time with the slow weight of tears.
Since Thou didst weep, on a remote hill-side
Beneath the olive-trees, fires of unnumbered stars
Have burnt the years away, until we see them now:
Since Thou didst weep, as many tears
Have flowed like hourglass sand.
Thy tears were all.
And when our secret face
Is blind because of the mysterious
Surging of tears wrung by our most profound
Presentiment of evil in man's fate, our cruellest wounds
Become Thy stigmata. They are Thy tears which fall.

p. 1939

EX NIHILO

Here am I now cast down
Beneath the black glare of a netherworld's
Dead suns, dust in my mouth, among
Dun tiers no tears refresh: am cast
Down by a lofty hand,

Hand that I love! Lord Light,
How dark is Thy arm's will and ironlike
Thy ruler's finger that has sent me here!
Far from Thy face I nothing understand,
But kiss the Hand that has consigned

Me to these latter years where I must learn
The revelation of despair, and find
Among the debris of all certainties
The hardest stone on which to found
Altar and shelter for Eternity.

p. 1939

SANCTUS

Incomprehensible –
O Master – fate and mystery
And message and long promised
Revelation! Murmur of the leaves
Of life's prolific tree in the dark haze
Of Midsummer: and inspiration of the blood
In the ecstatic secret bed: and bare
Inscription on a prison wall, 'For thou shalt persevere
In thine identity . . .': a momentary glimpsed
Escape into the golden dance of dust
Beyond the window. These are all.

Uncomprehending. But to understand
Is to endure, withstand the withering blight
Of winter night's long desperation, war,
Confusion, till at the dense core

Of this existence all the spirit's force
Becomes acceptance of blind eyes
To see no more. Then they may see at last;
And all they see their vision sanctifies.

p. 1942

ECCE HOMO

Whose is this horrifying face,
This putrid flesh, discoloured, flayed,
Fed on by flies, scorched by the sun?
Whose are these hollow red-filmed eyes
And thorn-spiked head and spear-stuck side?
Behold the Man: He is Man's Son.

Forget the legend, tear the decent veil
That cowardice or interest devised
To make their mortal enemy a friend,
To hide the bitter truth all His wounds tell,
Lest the great scandal be no more disguised:
He is in agony till the world's end,

And we must never sleep during that time!
He is suspended on the cross-tree now
And we are onlookers at the crime,
Callous contemporaries of the slow
Torture of God. Here is the hill
Made ghastly by His spattered blood

Whereon He hangs and suffers still:
See, the centurions wear riding-boots,
Black shirts and badges and peaked caps,
Greet one another with raised-arm salutes;
They have cold eyes, unsmiling lips;
Yet these His brothers know not what they do.

And on his either side hang dead
A labourer and a factory hand,
Or one is maybe a lynched Jew
And one a Negro or a Red,
Coolie or Ethiopian, Irishman,
Spaniard or German democrat.

Behind His lolling head the sky
Glares like a fiery cataract
Red with the murders of two thousand years
Committed in His name and by
Crusaders, Christian warriors
Defending faith and property.

Amid the plain beneath His transfixed hands,
Exuding darkness as indelible
As guilty stains, fanned by funereal
And lurid airs, besieged by drifting sands
And clefted landslides our about-to-be
Bombed and abandoned cities stand.

He who wept for Jerusalem
Now sees His prophecy extend
Across the greatest cities of the world,
A guilty panic reason cannot stem
Rising to raze them all as He foretold;
And He must watch this drama to the end.

Though often named, He is unknown
To the dark kingdoms at His feet
Where everything disparages His words,
And each man bears the common guilt alone
And goes blindfolded to his fate,
And fear and greed are sovereign lords.

The turning point of history
Must come. Yet the complacent and the proud
And who exploit and kill, may be denied –
Christ of Revolution and of Poetry –
The resurrection and the life
Wrought by your spirit's blood.

Involved in their own sophistry
The black priest and the upright man
Faced by subversive truth shall be struck dumb,
Christ of Revolution and of Poetry,
While the rejected and condemned become
Agents of the divine.

Not from a monstrance silver-wrought
But from the tree of human pain
Redeem our sterile misery,
Christ of Revolution and of Poetry,
That man's long journey through the night
May not have been in vain.

p. 1940

METAPHYSICAL POEMS

'Without cease and forever there is celebrated the
Mystery of the Open Tomb, the Resurrection of Osiris-Ra,
the Increated Light.'

The Book of the Dead

'Therefore it is said: And the deeper secret within the secret: the
land that is nowhere, that is the true home.'

The Secret of the Golden Flower

CONCERT OF ANGELS

To Kay Boyle

I

Wind! Out of the night of desolate
negation that we suffer in the waste
of time and impotence of thought,
rise in the mind and out of stupor stir
the hidden hearing with deep
echoes from the spirit host of
angels! Their intensely rapt,
almost inhuman faces luminous
with utmost concentration, the incisive bows
held in their long keen hands – enchanted swords
to slay the earth-binding ear and so release
the lost celestial sense – carving broad curves
across the nerve-taut strings, and like invisible
irradiations of sheer light, like resonance
of huge cathedral bell-notes hovering
over the earth in rings of fiery mist,
their clear cathartic music welling out
into infinity's unfathomed well.

II

While from the sonorous black well
emerge and palely fade and form again
white disembodied hands like drifting flames,

buds, tender leaves and tendrils shaped like hands,
and vision-clouded faces cloudily
impending on the air, with hidden eyes
and hungry mouths like mouths distraught with prayer.

Darkness's mouth, which opens in us now
in the most secret place, is over-brimmed
with straining hymns, with stars
like fountains burning upwards with the impetus
of flying gothic buttresses whose rainbow-arc
both aspiration and sustaining force contains.

III

Here is the transcendental source
of every human cry, replenished by
the deepest chords of death, by shrill
destruction's laughter, by the thrilling
arias of love, so lofty none can tell
or human or divine; and shock-torn sobs
of rape and copulation, exiled sighs,
corrupted beauty's ravishing lament, the long
nostalgic call that answers skylines, transference
from mortal sound into eternal song!

Let there be praise, praise and
praise, organic orchestra and cloudy choir,
to the great incandescent power
of sublimation, vitalizing clay,
with sacred fire consuming the grey dross
of sleep and sickness, balancing
in perfect tension between dark and light
the horrid depth, the spiritual height.

w. 1937–8, p. 1946

ELSEWHERE

La vraie vie est ailleurs . . .

        RIMBAUD

Profound is inexistence on this earth
   Among our human kind:
                   Profound
The weight of absence on the sleeping heart
That all war's detonations cannot rouse:
Rumour of selfless hordes with eyes
Red-rimmed and haggard, swarming through the dirt
Of ruined palaces: the roar
Of cannon-mouths, of sawtoothed mouths, the mouths
Of printing-presses, megaphonic maws
Of the possessed and the psychotic: and the pounding waves
Of automatic labour on the daily shore:
Rocked by this deep
And oil-black ocean's tidal pulse
The stunned soul sleeps,
Profoundly absent from its body's condemned house.

The taste of pleasure's now like sand between the teeth;
Worn-out, the nerves are numb; and Death's
Most sumptuous music strikes the ear like wind
Forced dumbly out of emptiness.
                   The sun
Strikes cold upon our nakedness, and shines
With rays of shadow through the diffuse light
Of interstellar space;
While over the last phase of night
The dead face of the moon hangs like a curse.
Deep in our empty sky hangs like a moon
The curse of inexistence; while the spirit sleeps
Profoundly absent from the earth.
                   But on
Negation's further shore, the yonder side
Of sleep and absence, dazzling is the sheer
Rockface set like an ice-barred gate
Beneath that nether tableland's pure height:

Whose sky is the negation of our sky,
Where all earth's ruins are rebuilt

Of stone that sings, and cold fire burns
The scentless incense of the air:
Where time and number are once more atoned
And to its true existence the Unnamed returns.

w. by 1939, p. 1946

WORLD WITHOUT END

See how across the seas of azure milk
Transpire the changing tranquil cloudy forms
Which image us below. The other eyes
Profoundly sunken in us, brim
With such refractions and mysterious
Broken light-webs from the depths
Or inward heights.
                        And without cease
The spirit's upward exhalation stirs
Susurrus and whirled currents of the central flame
Which burns relentlessly away
The lower body and the crystal skull
To carbon purity, and shines
Intense as daybreak down the rocky shafts
Into the world beyond.

p. 1938

INFERNO

One evening like the years that shut us in,
Roofed by dark-blooded and convulsive cloud,
Led onward by the scarlet and black flag
Of anger and despondency, my self:
My searcher and destroyer: wandering
Through unnamed streets of a great nameless town,
As in a syncope, sudden, absolute,
Was shown the Void that undermines the world:

For all that eye can claim is impotent –
Sky, solid brick of buildings, masks of flesh –
Against the splintering of that screen which shields
Man's puny consciousness from hell: over the edge
Of a thin inch's fraction lie in wait for him

    Bottomless depths of roaring emptiness.

p. 1941

LOWLAND

Heavy with rain and dense stagnating green
Of old trees guarding tombs these gardens
Sink in the dark and drown. The wet fields run
Together in the middle of the plain. And there are heard
Stampeding herds of horses and a cry,
More long and lamentable as the rains increase,
From out of the beyond.
                O dionysian
Desire breaking that voice, released
By fear and torment, out of our lowland rear
A lofty, savage and enduring monument!

p. 1938

MOUNTAINS

Pure peaks thrust upward out of mines of energy
To scar the sky with symbols of ascent,
Out of an innermost catastrophe –
Schismatic shock and rupture of earth's core –
Were grimly born.
                O elemental statuary
And rock-hewn monuments, whose shadow we
Lie low and wasting in, a prey to inner void:
Preach to us with great avalanches, tell
How new worlds surge from chaos to the light;
And starbound snowfields, fortify
With the stern silence of your white
Our weak hearts dulled by the intolerably loud
Commotion of this tragic century.

c. 1943

WINTER GARDEN

The season's anguish, crashing whirlwind, ice,
Have passed, and cleansed the trodden paths
That silent gardeners have strewn with ash.

The iron circles of the sky
Are worn away by tempest;
Yet in this garden there is no more strife:
The Winter's knife is buried in the earth.
Pure music is the cry that tears
The birdless branches in the wind.
No blossom is reborn. The blue
Stare of the pond is blind.

And no one sees
A restless stranger through the morning stray
Across the sodden lawn, whose eyes
Are tired of weeping, in whose breast
A savage sun consumes its hidden day.

p. 1939

THE WALL

At first my territory was a Wood:
Tanglewood, tattering tendrils, trees
Whose Grimm's-tale shadow terrified but made
A place to hide in: among traps and towers
The path I kept to had free right-of-way.

But centred later round an ambushed Well,
Reputed bottomless; and night and day
My gaze hung in the depths beneath the real
And sought the secret source of nothingness;
Until I tired of its Circean spell.

Returning to the narrow onward road
I find it leads me only to the Wall
Of Interdiction. But if my despair
Is strong enough, my spirit truly hard,
No wall shall break my will: To persevere.

c. 1943

THE FORTRESS

The socket-free lone visionary eye,
Soaring reflectively
Through regions sealed from macrocosmic light
By inner sky's impenetrable shell,
Often is able to descry:
Beyond the abdominal range's hairless hills
And lunar chasms of the porphyry
Mines; and beyond the forest whose each branch
Bears a lit candle, and the nine
Zigzagging paths which lead into the mind's
Most dangerous far reach; beyond
The calm lymphatic sea
Laving the wound of birth, and the
Red dunes of rot upon its further shore:

A heaving fortress built up like a breast,
Exposed like a huge breast high on its rock,
Streaming with milky brightness, the domed top
Wreathed in irradiant rainbow cloud.
        The shock
Of visions stuns the hovering eye, which cannot see
What caverns of deep blood those white walls hide,
Concealing ever rampant underneath
The dark chimera Death-in-life
Defending Life from death.

w. 1938, c. 1943

DICHTERSLEBEN

Lodged in a corner of his breast
Like a black hole torn by the loss
Of an ancestral treasure, like a thorn
Implanted ineradicably by his first
Sharp realization of the world, or like a cross
To which his life was to be nailed, he bore
Always the ache of an anxiety, a grief
Which nothing could explain, but which some nights
Would make him cry that he could fight no more.

Time ploughed its way through him; and change
Immersed him in disorder and decay.
Only the strange
Interior ray of the bleak flame
Which charred his heart's core could illuminate
The hidden unity of his life's theme.

He knew how the extremity of night
Can sterilize the final germ of faith;
Appearance crushed him with its steady weight;
Futility discoloured with its breath
His tragic vision. All his strength was spent
In holding to some sense from day to day . . .
Slowly he fell towards dismemberment.

Yet when he lay
At last exhausted under his stilled blood's
Thick cover and eyes' earth-stained lids,
The constant burden of his breast
(Long work of yeast) arose with joy
Into its first full freedom, metamorphosised, released.

c. 1943

I.M. BENJAMIN FONDANE

(1898–1944)

This is the osseous and uncertain desert
And valley of death's shadow, where the desired
Sweet spiritual spring is sought for
But unfound. It is beyond
And far, and lost in the essential blue
Of space, among the rock and snow, the locked
Domain the instinct asks for. They who wait
Without the great thirst of despair are cursed;
And they who quench their thirst in death
Shall fall asleep among the mirages. But the
Inspired and the unchained and the endowed of desperate grace
Shall break through the last gate, by violence take
God's Kingdom, and attain the certain State.

p. 1938

MOZART: SURSUM CORDA

For Priaulx Rainier

Filters the sunlight from the knife-bright wind
And rarifies the rumour-burdened air,
The heart's receptive chalice in pure hands upheld
Towards the sostenuto of the sky

Supernal voices flood the ear of clay
And transpierce the dense skull: Reveal
The immaterial world concealed
By mortal deafness and the screen of sense,

World of transparency and last release
And world within the world. Beyond our speech
To tell what equinoxes of the infinite
The spirit ranges in its rare utmost flight.

p. 1939

CAVATINA

Now we must bear the final real
Convulsion of the breast, for the sublime
Relief of the catharsis; and the cruel
Clear grief; the dear redemption from the crime,
The sublimation of the evil dream.

Beneath, all is confused, dense and impure;
Extraordinary shiftings of a nameless mass
From plane to plane, then some obscure
Catastrophe:
          The shattered Cross
High on its storm-lit hill, the searchlight eyes
Whose lines divide the black dome of the skies,
Are implicated; and the Universe of Death –
Gold, excrement and flesh, the spirit's malady,
A secret animal's hot breath . . .

Yet through disaster a faint melody
Insists; and the interior suffering like a silver wire
Enduring and resplendent, strongly plied
By genius' hands into the searching fire
At last emerges and is purified.

Its force like violins in pure lament
Persists, sending ascending stairs
Across the far wastes of the firmament
To carry starwards all our weight of tears.

p. 1938

ARTIST

Caught in a web, and crushed within a vice;
Watched by an Eye, but out of sight;
By a brand burnt, and wounded by
More keen a rustless blade than ever cut
This earth's black veins. – The voice
Of prophecy destroys the speaker. Bleak
As a scraped bone, the stony tablelands
On which he stands. – He cannot kill
The serpent of the blood: but his ghost shall.
Though armies of his enemy extend
In coiling ranks around his feet, still yet
Shall he transcend defeat, if his great wound
Be kept from healing. – ARTIST! hold that host
Once more at bay by offering your flesh
As sacrifice to the Void's mouth in your own breast!

w. 1939

INSURRECTION

Turbulence, uproar, echo of a War
Beyond our frontier: burning, blood and black
Impenetrable smoke that only blast
Of Archangelic trumpet could transpierce!
What savagery
And what inhuman crime,
What odour of hot iron, nocturnal flesh
Of sexual animal these uncouth cries invoke!
Till round the naked hill of rearing rock
With roaring torches suddenly emerge,
Shaking archaic instruments of strife,
Infernal armies sent us to avenge
The too-long-suffered tyranny and
Celebrated scandal of man's life!

w. 1938

LEGENDARY FRAGMENT

Below, in the dark midst, the opened thighs
Gave up their mystery. Myrrh, cassia
And spikenard obscurely emanated from
The inmost blackness. As from all around
There rose a heavy sighing and a troubled light:
Reverberated in the ears and eyes
And stunned the senses.
                      Thus the harlot queen
Was vanquished, while the outmost walls
Of that great town still echoed with her praise.

p. 1940–1

EVE

Profound the radiance issuing
From the all-inhaling mouth among
The blonde and stifling hair which falls
In heavy rivers from the high-crowned head,
While in the tension of her heat and light
The upward creeping blood whispers her name:
Insurgent, wounded and avenging one,
In whose black sex
Our ancient culpability like a pearl is set.

p. 1938

VENUS ANDROGYNE

With gaze impaired by heavy haze of sense
And sleep-dust, see: the blasphemy of flesh!
The breast is female, groin and fist are male,
But the red sphinx is hidden underneath the
Weed-rank hair: muscle and grain
Of man inextricably twined
With woman's beauty.

Stand up, thorn
Of double anguish born, and pierce
The gentle athlete flank, that fierce pain
May merge like honey with the spirit's blood,
Purging desire: with agony atone
For such abhorrent heresy of seed,
And weld twin contradictions in a single fire!

p. 1938

POST-MORTEM

O mercury-green glare, grey flesh, black hair,
Harsh, frigid spasm, the spilt pool and spreading stain,
Mixed in the spirit, sharply printed there
By nightly pressures, between web-like sheets,
Such horrifying sheets as cling in dreams:
How can timebound a memory escape
From so much detritus
And humus of the depths?
Yet the bespittled hidden face,
Vile and reviled
Emerges out of life as from a sleep,
The complex hatred and long-implicating lie
At last released that heavy skein unwound.

w. 1937, rev. 1940, p. 2007

AMOR FATI

Beloved enemy, preparer of my death,
When there's no longer any garment left
To lessen the clenched impact of our limbs,
When there is mutual drought in our swift breath
And twin tongues struggle for the brim
Of swollen flood – an aching undertow
Sucking us inward – when the blood's
Lust has attained its whitest glow
And the convulsion comes in quickening gusts,
Speaking is fatal: Do not break

That vacuum out of which our silence speaks
Of its sad speechless fury to the star
Whose glitter scars
The heavy heaven under which we lie
And injure one another O incurably!

p. 1940

SIGNS

There fell down on the shadowed sand
Like dead birds from an evil nest
Across a livid space of sky:
A writhing hand,
The pale globe of a breast
And a dismembered thigh.

But from the dark's most secret place
Across the curtains of the air
There presently began to rise
A dream-transfigured face
With lips exhaling prayer
And lambent eyes.

p. 1938

THE HERO

The laurelled profile with the Caesar's nose and lip
Beneath the garlanded triumphal arch
Is not the Hero, for he has no face
But is as featureless as light.
Only the hands,
Stretched out before him in unending process of
Possessing all, are human as hands are: only
The hands, the heart
Which turns from side to side like searchlight rays,
Unresting, through the night, proclaim him man,
Because the man has died.

He is unknown in death. He brings
No music with him. But he seems
Still listening to the moment of the vast
Explosion which has snatched him out of life,
So hugely deafening that it cannot end
But is forever everywhere,
As the dust of a lost glory fills
Even the crevices of furthest stars.

p. 1938

THE FAULT

To live, and to respire
And to aspire, to feel the fire
Urge upward through the mortal part and gain
Through burnt-out veins still higher!
But who has lived an hour
In the condemned condition of our blood
And not known how a wound like a black flower,
Exquisite and irreparable, can break
Apart in the immortal in us, or not felt
An intimation of the fault: to be alive!

p. 1938

THE DESCENT

Where everything sinks down,
Is petrified in its descent, as still as vast
Perspectives full of ragged mountain and
Black forest of mortality
And azure air,
Sink swollen slowly downward frozen tears.

All is reflected in that Angel's eye
Who sees beyond the inward depth
Into the glittering schist of the far floor.

Naked the beautiful remembered limbs
And downward clustering hung
And mirrored in the dark encircling floods;
Suspended like a wreath and tremulous
In the mysterious wind of their blind flight and fall:

Unnumbered wings: and Ah! voluminous
The cloudy chasm like a gasping mouth
From whence the last deep cry so throughly torn
Unseals the Sepulchre of holy rock.

p. 1939

THE OPEN TOMB

Vibrant with silence is the last sealed room
That fever-quickened breathing cannot break:
Magnetic silence and unshakably doomed breath
Hung like a screen of ice
Between the cavern and the closing eyes,
Between the last day and the final scene
Of death, unwitnessed save by one:

By Omega! the angel whose dark wind
Of wings and trumpet lips
Stirs with disruptive storm the clinging folds
Of stalagmatic foliage lachrymose
Hung from the lofty crypt, where endlessly
The phalanx passes, two by three, with all
The hypnotizing fall of stairs.

Their faces are unraised as yet from sleep;
The pace is slow, and down the steep descent
Their carried candles eddy like a stream;
While on each side, through window in the rock,
Beyond the tunnelled grottoes there are seen
Serene the sunless but how dazzling plains
Where like a sea resounds our open tomb.

p. 1939

THE PLUMMET HEART

In Memory of Hart Crane

  Down, Hart, you fell down sound-
 lessly, as though through shaft of lift,
leaving the roar of birth's wind-parted rift
 around the topmost floor, no ground

  beneath, no wreath of rock
 to crown your exit from this crux;
and as you dropped through the restricted flux
 of such duration as the clock

  controls, on swift walls shone
 in mirrors as you hurtled by
the scripture chiselled by your heart: until
the sea received you, azure antiphon
 whose octave answer is the sky
  where your wrecked smile drifts still.

w. 1939, p. 1941

THE THREE STARS

A Prophecy

The night was Time:
The phases of the moon,
Dynamic influence, controller of the tides,
Its changing face and cycle of quick shades,
Were History, which seemed unending. Then
Occurred the prophesied and the to be
Recounted hour when the reflection ceased
To flow like unseen life-blood in between
The night's tenebral mirror and the lunar light,
Exchanging meaning. Anguish like a crack
Ran with its ruin from the fulfilled Past
Toward's the Future's emptiness; and *black*,
Invading all the prism, became absolute.

Black was the No-time at the heart
Of Time (the frameless mirror's back),
But still the Anguish shook
As though with memory and with anticipation: till
Its terror's trembling broke
By an unhoped-for miracle Negation's spell:
Death died and Birth was born with one great cry
And out of some uncharted spaceless sky
Into the new-born night three white stars fell.

And were suspended there a while for all
To see and understand (though none may tell
The inmost meaning of this Mystery).

The first star has a name which stands
For many names of all things that begin
And all first thoughts of undivided minds;
The second star
Is nameless and shines bleakly like the pain
Of an existence conscious only of its end,
And inarticulate, alone
And blind. Immeasurably far
Each from the other first and second spin;
Yet to us at this moment they appear
So close to one another that their rays
In one blurred conflagration intertwine:
So that the third seems born
Of their embracing: till the outer pair
Are separate seen again
Fixed in their true extremes; and in between
These two gleams' hemispheres, unseen
But shining everywhere
The third star balanced shall henceforward burn
Through all dark still to come, serene,
Ubiquitous, immaculately clear;
A magnet in the middle of the maze, to draw us on
Towards that Bethlehem beyond despair
Where from the womb of Nothing shall be born
A Son.

w. 1939, p. 1942

EPODE

Then
The great Face turned away in silence, veiled and slow,
Resigned and imperturbable: the brow
A grave dome drastic in its upthrust, and the eyes'
Unquenched blue fires of grief sealed and concealed
Beneath lids of irrevocable flint. It turned
Away; and as the shaft below began to slant
Towards its headlong fall into unknown
Futurity, the sacred Mouth enshrined
Like a sarcophagus within its midst revealed
During that moment's timeless flash
The wordless Meaning of the Whole
(Which may be spoken by no man)
Through the unearthly brilliance of its smile . . .

While the old world's last bonfires turned to ash.

w. 1939, p. 1941

PERSONAL POEMS

SONNET: FROM MORN TO MOURNING

Morning. Full Chorus of the birds. A Sun
Of nascent ardour in the sapphire dome.
Now Memnon's massive kings with mouths of stone
Chant their aubade. Now down the valleys come
Innocent minstrels in whose unstained eyes
Vision unfolds vibrating like a flower:
Yggdrasil spreads above them; Jordan flows
About their feet; they hear the magic lyre
Of Orpheus echo from the Underworld . . .
All Earth's calm landscape shimmers; rainbows dance
Above the mountain meadows wherein Love's
Flocks graze . . . But what chill shadow, not of cloud,
Is this that darkens noonday's crystal? Whence
Comes that far wail of mourning through the groves?

p. 1943

THE FABULOUS GLASS

For Blanche Reverchon-Jouve

In my deep Mirror's blindest heart
A Cone I planted there to sprout.
Sprang up a Tree tall as a cloud
And each branch bore a loud-voiced load
Of Birds as bright as their own song;
But when a distant death-knell rang
My Tree fell down, and where it lay
A Centipede disgustingly
Swarmed its quick length across the ground!
Thick shadows fell inside my mind;
Until an Alcove rose to view
In which, obscure at first, there now
Appeared a Virgin and her Child;
But it was horrid to behold
How she consumed that Infant's Face
With her voracious Mouth. Her Dress

Was Black, and blotted all out. Then
A phosphorescent Triple Chain
Of Pearls against the darkness hung
Like a Temptation; but ere long
They vanished, leaving in their place
A Peacock, which lit up the glass
By opening his Fan of Eyes:
And thus closed down my Self-regarding Gaze.

c. 1943

CAMERA OBSCURA

When Summer sifts its first dusts through the mesh
Of twig and tendril that the Spring has spun, again
Splashing with verjuice stains the lanes and avenues down which
The annual lovers stroll towards their bliss;
And when along banks and beaches warming waves
Throw up wet limbs like ingots for the wind to wipe
Dry, the sun's fervid kissing to ignite; when high-
Charged and bruise-coloured clouds, like tight
Emotion-swollen bosoms rising, brew
Intoxicating storm-broth for the night:

Desire's beams, breaking through a furtive aperture
Into the *camera obscura* of my dream,
Flash on that secret and uncensored screen
Flagrant fast-changing frescoes filled
With rearing torso-monoliths, strong tender lines
Of thew and tendon carved in bas-relief, gunmetal shine
Like mist from neck to thighs: unflawed anatomies
Of nakedness too dizzying to envisage long:
Marlowe's Leander, Michaelangelic gods, that young
High-diving Mercury I once cut from a sports-page . . .

Their dark or sparkling heads just out of reach
Of my outstretched and empty questing palm, have faces
Hidden or turned away, unclear or with glass eyes
Impersonal and cryptic as a fortune-teller's orb;
And so that other quarry that Desire
Projects alternately inside my sight's closed lids:

The fragile natural heroines with submissive fard-sweet lips
But icebound opal eyes that my male fires must melt
Into admiring mirrors: female cherubim, are all
Like disembodied birds or beauteous busts on plinths of air.

How can the Janus gaze, pinned living to twin poles,
Like a rare moth with one white wing one black,
Fly ever to the act's clear candle-flame?
Rely on memory to back these makeshift shades
With Love's hard-won diplomas of accomplishment? Regret
For lost accomplices of other Summer nights, whose hands
Articulated more than all their voices (restless winds
Around what clandestine hotels: O moonlit hells!), blows back
With long-held burning breath through eyeholes bored
By image-laden rays, into my isolation-cell . . .

Touch cannot undivide the pinioned heart
Foaming with helpless fury that could not be shared
Or lessened by acceptance; nor can speech mean more
Than tired preliminaries to farewell: which leaves when said
A slow deep-rooted sting. Then let these briefly bared
Bright simulacra starving need brings forth
Out of the void between two wounds unwind
Designs of pure lubricity, and people the short peace
Of celibacy with myths' lucid smiling flesh;
And wraithlike vanish, leaving no scar behind.

w. 1940, p. 1941

APOLOGIA

'Poète et non honnête homme.'
PASCAL

1

It's not the Age,
Disease, or accident, but sheer
Perversity (or so one must suppose),
That pins me to the singularly bare

Boards of this trestle-stage
That I have mounted to adopt the pose
Of a demented wrestler, with gorge full
Of phlegm, eyes bleared with salt, and knees
Knocking like ninepins: a most furious fool!

2

Fixed by the nib
Of an inept pen to a bleak page
Before the glassy gaze of a ghost mob,
I stand once more to face the silent rage
Of my unseen Opponent, and begin
The same old struggle for the doubtful prize:
Each stanza is a round, and every line
A blow aimed at the too elusive chin
Of that Oblivion which cannot fail to win.

3

Before I fall
Down silent finally, I want to make
One last attempt at utterance, and tell
How my absurd desire was to compose
A single poem with my mental eyes
Wide open, and without even one lapse
From that most scrupulous Truth which I pursue
When not pursuing Poetry. – Perhaps
Only the poem I can never write is *true*.

c. 1943

THE WRITER'S HAND

What is your want, perpetual invalid
Whose fist is always beating on my breast's
Bone wall, incurable dictator of my house
And breaker of its peace? What is your will,
Obscure uneasy sprite: where must I run,
What must I seize, to win
A brief respite from your repining cries?

Is it a star, the passionate short spark
Produced by friction with another's flesh?
You ache more darkly after. Is it power:
To snap restriction's leash, to leap
Like bloodhounds on the enemy? There is no grip
Can crush the fate you fight. Or is it to escape
Into the dream-perspectives maps and speed create?

You never listen, disillusion's dumb
To your unheeding ear. But see my hand,
The only army to enforce your claim
Upon life's hostile land: five pale, effete,
Aesthetic-looking fingers, whose chief feat
Is to trace lines like these across a page:
What small relief can they bring to your siege!

p. 1940

THE SACRED HEARTH

To George Barker

You must have been still sleeping, your wife there
Asleep beside you. All the old oak breathed: while slow,
How slow the intimate Spring night swelled through those depths
Of soundlessness and dew-chill shadow on towards the day.
Yet I, alone awake close by, was summoned suddenly
By distant voice more indistinct though more distinctly clear,
While all inaudible, than any dream's, calling on me to rise
And stumble barefoot down the stairs to seek the air
Outdoors, so sweet and somnolent, not cold, and at that hour
Suspending in its glass undrifting milk-strata of mist,
Stilled by the placid beaming of the adolescent moon.
There, blackly outlined in their moss-green light, they stood,
The trees of the small crabbed and weed-grown orchard,
Perfect as part of one of Calvert's idylls. It was then,
Wondering what calm magnet had thus drawn me from my bed,
I wandered out across the briar-bound garden, spellbound. Most
Mysterious and unrecapturable moment, when I stood
There staring back at the dark white nocturnal house,

And saw gleam through the lattices a light more pure than gold
Made sanguine with crushed roses, from the firelight that all night
Stayed flickering about the sacred hearth. As long as dawn
Hung fire behind the branch-hid sky, the strong
Magic of rustic slumber held unbroken; yet a song
Sprang wordless from inertia in my heart, to see how near
A neighbour strangeness ever stands to home. George, in the wood
Of wandering among wood-hiding trees, where poets' art
Is how to whistle in the dark, where pockets all have holes,
All roofs for refugees have rents, we ought to know
That there can be for us no place quite alien and unknown,
No situation wholly hostile, if somewhere there burn
The faithful fire of vision still awaiting our return.

w. 1939–40, p. 1948

TO A CONTEMPORARY

You screwed your heart up to incredible
Rigidity; upon your sleeve it glittered like
A jewelled watch tick-tocking. All your wits
Were tough as wire since you, cut to the quick
By premature cold disabuse,
Had set your face against your inmost face
(Which wept, but which no tears could slake).

Inconsolable one, I watched your eyes
(Which never looked in mine), and saw
How often in those mirrors like the stain
Of some white poison slowly spread,
Making all sanguine colour drain
Out of what they reflected of the world outside,
Your ceaseless sense of the ubiquitous Inane.

And when you pinned up on your mouth that smile
Of purest malice by which you betrayed
Your total lack of trust, how all too well
I recognized its likeness to my own twitch of disgust
With mankind and myself . . . (Had I not made
The same unseeing trek through just such cruel
Subjective labyrinths as your lost feet trod?)

Through even your ignominy one saw at last
That finally despairing pride
From which you drew your courage to endure
The worst self-torments of perversity
(The treadmill of your vice,
The automatic all-dismissing sneer,
The quite deliberate invocation of the Void).

Yours was the courage not to turn away
From knowledge or from Death (whole wiles
And ironies by now surely you know
By heart); and to make unbelief
Your only refuge. You were brave
Enough to bear the seeming truth, could you not dare
To face the last fear, which is that of Love?

c. 1943

AN ELEGY

Roger Roughton 1916–41

Friend, whose unnatural early death
In this year's cold, chaotic Spring
Is like a clumsy wound that will not heal:
What can I say to you, now that your ears
Are stoppered-up with distant soil?
Perhaps to speak at all is false; more true
Simply to sit at times alone and dumb
And with most pure intensity of thought
And concentrated inmost feeling, reach
Towards your shadow on the years' crumbling wall.

I'll not say any word in praise or blame
Of what you ended with the mere turn of a tap;
Nor to explain, deplore nor yet exploit
The latent pathos of your living years –
Hurried, confused and unfulfilled –
That were the shiftless years of both our youths
Spent in the monstrous mountain-shadow of
Catastrophe that chilled you to the bone:

The certain imminence of which always pursued
You from your heritage of fields and sun . . .

I see your face in hostile sunlight, eyes
Wrinkled against its glare, behind the glass
Of a car's windscreen, while you seek to lose
Yourself in swift devouring of white roads
Unwinding across Europe or America;
Taciturn at the wheel, wrapped in a blaze
Of restlessness that no fresh scene can quench;
In cities of brief sojourn that you pass
Through in your quest for respite, heavy drink
Alone enabling you to bear each hotel night.

Sex, Art and Politics: those poor
Expedients! You tried them each in turn,
With the wry inward smile of one resigned
To join in every complicated game
Adults affect to play. Yet girls you found
So prone to sentiment's corruptions; and the joy
Of sensual satisfaction seemed so brief, and left
Only new need. It proved hard to remain
Convinced of the Word's efficacy; or even quite
Certain of World-Salvation through 'the Party Line'. . .

Cased in the careful armour that you wore
Of wit and nonchalance, through which
Few quizzed the concealed countenance of fear,
You waited daily for the sky to fall;
At moments wholly panic-stricken by
A sense of stifling in your brittle shell:
Seeing the world's damnation week by week
Grow more and more inevitable; till
The conflagration broke out with a roar,
And from those flames you fled through whirling smoke,

To end at last in bankrupt exile in
That sordid city, scene of *Ulysses*; and there,
While War sowed all the lands with violent graves,
You finally succumbed to a black, wild
Incomprehensibility of fate that none could share . . .
Yet even in your obscure death I see

The secret candour of that lonely child
Who, lost in the storm-shaken castle-park,
Astride his crippled mastiff's back was borne
Slowly away into the utmost dark.

w. 1941, p. 1941

FROM A DIARY

Imperfections of substance, dross of the day-by-day;
Banality, unlove and disappointment . . . Grey

Webs of attrition, and the trivial tick
Of the nerves' run-down clock – dank skeins of thick

Colourless thought unravelling through the skull, –
This bitter grit of conscience, and the dull

Pulse of internal scars . . . Compression: no
Inscape or scope or space: only the flow

Of stupor's steady muffled fugue. – At night,
While time pursues unwatched its weightless flight,

Blackness lolls on the air, as still as gas
And denser, round each building's lonely mass

Collapsing in the depths of its own dream;
Silence suppresses every pent-up latent scream;

And I lie like a log (as I have lain
How many year-long nights?) and once again

Immobile, mute, locked in my private room,
Hear, ruminating on the unwritten doom

Awaiting all men's hearts in their dumb solitude,
Within me my heart's numb, indifferent blood.

w. 1941, c. 1943

ODEUR DE PENSÉE

Thought has a subtle odour: which is not
Like that which hawthorn after rainfall has;
Nor is it sickly or astringent as
Are some scents which round human bodies float,
Diluting sweat's thick auras. It's not like
Dust's immemorial smells, which lurk
Where spiders nest, in shadows under doors
Of rooms where centuries have died, and rest
In clouds along the blackening cracked floors
Of sties and closets, attics and wrecked tombs . . .
Thought's odour is so pale that in the air
Nostrils inhale, it disappears like fire
Put out by water. Drifting through the coils
Of the involved and sponge-like brain it frets
The fine-veined walls of secret mental cells,
Brushing their fragile fibre as with light
Nostalgic breezes: And it's then we sense
Remote presentiment of some intensely bright
Impending spiritual dawn, of which the pure
Immense illumination seems about to pour
In upon our existence from beyond
The edge of Knowing! But of that obscure
Deep presaging excitement shall remain
Briefly to linger in dry crannies of the brain
Not the least breath when fear-benumbed and frail
Our dying thought within the closely-sealed
Bone casket of the skull has flickered out,
And we've gone down into the odourless black soil.

c. 1943

FÊTE

After long thirst for sky, there was the sky,
That ether lake: vast azure canopy
Intensely stretched between horizons' ends!
Along the quays
The panes of opening windows flashed like wings,
Weaving long rays among the leafless trees;
Sirens of drifting barges sang:
And the whole day
Drank in the fecund flowing of the sky.

And on the outskirts of the town
Where the last house-blocks take their vacant stare
Across the straggling zone, and rusty streams
Among brown squares of threadbare soil
Persist their irrigating ooze, a savage train
Tore through a cutting with triumphant screams,
Releasing streamers of thick whirling breath
Which climbed and were suspended like presentiments on high . . .

Once more the earth, its buried spirit stirred,
Aspired towards the Summer's splendid bursting
And an illustrious death.

w. Paris 1938

CHAMBRE D'HÔTEL

While a sad Sunday's silver light
Slid through the rain of afternoon
    And slimed the town's grey stone,
We side-by-side without a word
Above the cobbled island quays
Round which rolled on the swollen Seine,
    Lay staring at a white
And barren ceiling: till it seemed
We'd lain forever thus entombed
    Deep in unspeaking spleen.

Oh, when at last I tried to take
  Your hand in mine, your stranger's face
      Towards my mouth to bend,
  You sprang up from the bed and went
  Away, across the room, to stand
  And watch, through muslin'd window-glass
      The plane-trees lean to ask
  The river what you too asked then,
  A riddle without answer and
      As old as earth's disgrace.

  w. 1940, p. 1942

JARDIN DU PALAIS ROYAL

To B. Von M.

The sky's a faded blue and taut-stretched flag
Tenting the quadrangle. On three
Sides the arcade (tenebrous lanes
Down which at times patchouli'd ghosts flit by –
Furtive reflections on the filmy panes
Of shops which seem to store only the dusts
And atmospheres of antiquated years, –
Intent on fusty vice), restricts the garden-
Statues' timeless gaze. Here inside this
Shut-off and bygone place, brown urchin birds
Play tag and twitter, jittering around
The central fountain's dance; while children chase
Their ragged shadows round about
The palinged trees, with screams; and iron chairs
With pattern-perforated seats drop their design
Like black lace on the gravel. There we sat
And watched that liquid trembling spire the wind
Made sway and break and spatter a thin spray
Like tears upon our hair and tight-clenched hands . . .
How long? I have forgotten. But you rocked
Backwards and forwards, scraping up small stones,
And never spoke. The day was in July,
Full of a whitish and exhausting glare. And I
Could only stare in silence, trying to see
Into the constantly disintegrating core

Round which the fountain ever climbed again;
Hearing the clack of feet that died away
Down the dim passage, and the unnerving din
Child-voices made behind us. O but then
You turned, and asked me with inconsolable eyes
The meaning of the pain that kept us dumb;
And then we both knew that our pact had been betrayed;
And that cold moment made the garden seem
Too like our lives, abandoned in a wilderness of Time,
Boxed-in by the frustrating and decayed
Walls of the haunted Memory's arcade.

p. 1942

NOCTAMBULES

Hommage à Djuna Barnes

They stand in doorways; then
Step out into the rain
Beneath the lamplight's blue
Aurora; down the street
Towards a blood-red sign
Scrawled swiftly on the wet
Slate of the midnight sky
And then sponged off again . . .
With watchful masks they wait
On stools at bars. I can-
Not see their faces; some
Are weeping; now I hear
A shadow sigh: *The band
Plays recklessly away
Our last hours, one by one* . . .
And then a girl in tulle
With black moths fluttering in
The gold mist of her hair
Enters the hard white pool
Of a great arc-lamp's glare
Revealing, where her face
Should be, a gaping hole!
Their mingling voices roar . . .

Now they have gone again:
The Rue Fontaine is full
Of other shadows; rain
Trickles down postered walls,
Down cafés' plate-glass panes.
Whispers outside the door, –
Words an accordion drowns . . .
Now like the clink of ice
In highball glasses come
Their voices from afar:
Straying from place to place,
Not knowing where we go,
We stumble through our dream
Beneath an evil star . . .
Words the wind's echoes blur,
Lost among tossing trees
Along the Rue Guynemer
Where as the wheezing chimes
Of Ste Sulpice strike three,
In his tight attic high
Above the street, a boy
With a white face which dreams
Have drained of meaning, writes
The last page of a book
Which none will understand:
While down the corridor
Outside the room return
Their faint footsteps again . . .
They wait outside the door;
Their whispers fall like sand
In hour-glasses; I hear
Passionate sobbing; then
A voice that I've heard before
On many a night like this –
Strident with anguish – cries:
Darkness erodes the hearts
Locked in our breasts: the Night
Is gnawing our lives away:
O let Lust deaden without end
This aching void within . . .
And when the voice has died
Away, more cries are heard

Which, merging with the wind
In wordless tumult, blend
In an inconsolable dirge
And desperately press
Onwards in waves across
Acres of wet roofs, on
Across the unseen Seine,
Away beyond the Madeleine
And deep into the gulf that yawns
Behind the Sacré Coeur . . .
The rustling driven rain
Ceases awhile; the air
Hangs numb; Night still wears on.
Now down the desolate wide glade
Of Boulevard Sebastopol,
Beneath the creaking iron boughs
Of shop signs hung along each side,
A young American, intent
On finding a chance bed-fellow,
Pursues a vagrant *matelot's*
Slim likely-looking form . . .
An English drunkard sits alone
In a small *bistro* in Les Halles
And keeps rehearsing the Lord's Prayer
In a mad high-pitched monotone
To the blue empty air.
And in a Left-bank café where
At about half-past four
Exiles are wont to bare
Their souls, a son-and-heir
Of riches and neurosis casts
His frail befuddled blonde
Brutally to the floor
And with despairing fists
Tries to blot out the gaze
Of her wet senseless eyes . . .
One who has wandered long
Through labyrinths of his own brain
More solitary and obscure
Than any maze of stone
Pavements and lamplit walls
Now stops beside the Seine

And leaning down to peer
Into the swirling gloom
Of swollen waters, says:
What day can ever end
The night of those from whom
God turns away his face,
Or what ray's finger pierce
The depths wherein they drown?
Exhaustion brings no peace
To the lost soul . . . But soon
Behind the Eastern slums
A chalky streak of dawn-
Light gradually gleams;
And men from women turn
Away to face the wall,
All lust exhausted, in
Dozens of one-night rooms . . .
Then suddenly a chill
Breath sneaks along the stones
Of narrow streets and makes
The lids of rubbish-bins
To clatter faintly, shakes
The rags and scraps and tins
Strewn in the gutters; and
A rapid shiver runs
Throughout the still, grey, blind
Mass of the city. – Now
As countless times before
I make my roomward way
Across that silent square
Where always as I pass
Them snarling lions stare
At me with stony eyes
From round about the base
Of their dry fountain . . . O!
How derelict is this
Hour of Night's ending: when
The Dark's pale denizens must go
With tales untold and tears
Unwept, – their shrivelled souls
Unsold, unsaved, – back to
The caves of sleep, their worn-

Out beds in lonely holes
Wherein they hide by day.
And climbing the last stair
How timeless seems this time
Of vigil in despair:
Of night by night the same
Weary anabasis
Between two wars, towards
The Future's huge abyss.

p. 1941

SONNET: THE UNCERTAIN BATTLE

Away the horde rode, in a storm of hail
And steel-blue lightning. Hurtled by the wind
Into their eardrums from behind the hill
Came in increasing bursts the startled sound
Of trumpets in the unseen hostile camp. –
Down through a raw black hole in heaven stared
The horror-blanched moon's eye. Across the swamp
Five ravens flapped; and the storm disappeared
Soon afterwards, like them, into that pit
Of Silence which lies waiting to consume
Even the braggart World itself at last . . .
The candle in the hermit's cave burned out
At dawn, as usual. – No one ever came
Back down the hill, to say which side had lost.

w. 1941, p. 1942

LINES

So much to tell: so measurelessly more
Than this poor rusting pen could ever dare
To try to scratch a hint of . . . Words are marks
That flicker through men's minds like quick black dust;
That falling, finally obliterate the faint
Glow their speech emanates. Too soon all sparks
Of vivid meaning are extinguished by
The saturated wadding of Man's tongue . . .
And yet, I lie, I lie:
Can even Omega discount
The startling miracle of human song?

w. 1941, p. 1942

THE ANCHORITE

I   *His departure out of the City.*
II *His Habitation in the Wilderness.*
III *In a Vision He is Assaulted by Demonic Powers and by the Temptation to Surrender to the Void.*
IV *He Addresses himself to God in the Following Psalm.*
V   *His Journey Along the Endless Road resumed.*

★   ★   ★   ★

I. *His Departure out of the City*

In all that city there was not one man who knew
Of his departure; not one eye to watch him go
When he went striding out through the great Eastern Gate
That sunny Lenten day. Only the stern fixed stare
Of a stone lion's head carved jutting from the arch
Followed the progress of his black unswerving back
Away into the out-of-sight, through drifting dusts . . .
Before him rose remotely the blue tooth-like rock
Which masked for him where the real wilderness began;
Above his head, on the high plateaus of the air
The larks released their pale electric ecstasies;
And as he strode along, he laughed, calling to mind

All that he'd left behind him: the great labyrinth
Of the sleep-walking masses, – the dense midnight maze
Of dread, through which they wandered without speech, as though
To name their suffering would be to die of it; –
The city like a time-beleaguered termite-heap,
Swarming with flocks of languishing or fevered masks,
Never a naked face among them; – all night long . . .

II.   *His Habitation in the Wilderness*

III. *In a Vision, He is Assaulted by Demonic Powers and by Temptation to Surrender to the Void*

      . . . Until one night (after indefinite
Succession of long nights) closed in
Around him unfamiliarly, a night
Fraught with some secret sense of change
And danger.
    On the slopes
Of every nearby foothill, strange
Orchards broke into flower and the air
Was stirred with rustling as their
Petals opened, colour of snow, of fire,
Of eyes. A flight of birds
Swept by invisibly, with small swift cries.
And all the darkness throbbed
With premonition.
    A great trembling glow
About the middle of the night appeared
Along the border of the Western sky,
Reflecting some far conflagration;
    In its unreal light
The rocks around like an arena seemed,
Encircling him with watchful tiers;
And music like a faint
Blue mirage streamed about his ears . . .
Out of the distance issued sudden bursts
Of dense machine-gun fire.
Uncertain haze of insubstantiality.
Anxiety and emptiness.
Dim images. A maze
Of muddled intimations in the mind,

A blank expectancy. Quick images again . . .
(A broken arch bridging the desert stream;
Beneath the bridge a breaking wave
Through which a bright fish swam.
A soldier sleeping open-mouthed
Outside the entrance of a mountain-cave,
Caught in a cage, a black misshapen beast,
Half-ox, half-bear, eyes red with rage.
An ancient sword mysteriously thrust
Up to the hilt in the desert's sandy floor.)

IV. *He Addresses a Psalm to God*

V.   *His Return to the Road Without an End*

w. 1940–41, p. 1998

TIME AND PLACE

SNOW IN EUROPE

'Au temps où la douceur
Est cruelle et le désespoir est brilliant.'
        PIERRE JEAN JOUVE

Out of their slumber Europeans spun
Dense dreams: appeasement, miracle, glimpsed flash
Of a new golden era; but could not restrain
The vertical white weight that fell last night
And made their continent a blank.

Hush, says the sameness of the snow,
The Ural and the Jura now rejoin
The furthest Arctic's desolation. All is one;
Sheer monotone: plain, mountain; country, town:
Contours and boundaries no longer show.

The warring flags hang colourless a while;
Now midnight's icy zero feigns a truce
Between the signs and seasons, and fades out
All shots and cries. But when the great thaw comes,
How red shall be the melting snow, how loud the drums!

w. Christmas 1938

ZERO

September, 1939

Who can by now not hear
The hollow and annihilating roar
Of final disillusion; or not know
How our condition is uncertain and obscure
And difficult to bear? Yet through
The blackness of his dungeon there still peer
Man's eyes, unmoving, lit by their desire

To see *the worst,* and yet not die
Of their lucid despair
But in such vision persevere
Through time into Eternity.
For this is Zero-hour
When the most penetrating gaze can see
Only the Void, the emptier than air,
The incoherent *Nada* of the seer:
Who blind is yet not blind, being aware
Of the Negation's double mystery!

Tomb of what was, womb of what is to be.

w. 1939

AN AUTUMN PARK

Dark suffocates the world; but such
Ubiquity of shadow is unequal. Here
At the spiked gates which crown the hill begins
A reign as of suspense within suspense:
Outside our area of sand-bagged mansions and of tense
But inarticulate expectancy of roars,
The unhistoric park
Extends indifference through all its air.

During these present days
None but the lonely and reflective care to walk
Through the unworldly and concealed preserves
Of vegetable integrity (where trees
Though murmurous at least are without words . . .)
For such unsocial ones the park negates
With its consistently non-human peace
All the loud mind-polluted world outside its gates.

When sudden sunrays break the brooding haze
Which makes monotonous these grounds,
Livid the little wind-flaked lakes appear,
Vivid the fever-mottled leaves still bound
By mouldering stalks to idly shaken boughs;
Brief light and breath intensify the scene

With glitter drifting across wet grass wastes
And odour of crushed bracken and raw sand . . .

These acres bordering on plains of brick
And brain and coin and newspaper and noise,
Still store for townsmen such as seek
Remembrance of the simpler earth that was
Our dwelling and contentment once, a chance
Of re-beholding that lost innocence; may show
To those that walk today there to forget, the true
And imminent glory breaking through Man's circumstance.

w. October 1939

THE CONSPIRATORS

PRELUDE TO AN UNFINISHED NARRATIVE

    Here is the Capital.

                          'Observe
How like a microscopic slide whose glass arena holds
Spectacular combat of schizomycetes, these grappling streets
Elucidate with their contrasting quarters the disease
Disintegrating all these fated lives. Lives of the refuse-heap, the
Slum, the rusty dump, packed in a fouled dilapidated bed,
Running with sores for years like washerless taps. The lives
Of eremites, black-coated, in their desert no-man's-land
Of tidy, sterile, separate brick cells, pitched just half-way
Between the catacombs of want and the gilt mansions of big pots.
Lives of the latter, lush as scum on standing water, limply led
Through periods of alternating boredom, frantic spending and
Bewilderment, by an unhappy little race of monsters
Caricatured by Grosz, staring with fascinated eyes
At their own image on the cruel plate-glass their diamonds
Cannot break.'

Thus speaks the voice of the didactic guide
In the intelligentsia-tourist charabanc. But let's remove
Clinical spectacles, look round with naïve gaze: Here slide

The undramatic trams crammed with normality, shop-windows greet
The morning housewife with their pyramid displays, and children
Chase callous hoops among thin legs along the curb. But O
The glamour of the metropolitan sunlight, coffee smells,
Striped awnings, the bright water-dust of fountains! O the
Pigeons, scattering foam of wings! 'Call me a taxi!' 'Midday news!
New Cabinet Formed. All Racing Form.' '. . . We'll meet you in
The Park.' 'The Ritz for cocktails . . .'

                        Surface appeal conceals
With fragrant clouds the city's noisesome heart, as the façades
Of these white buildings flecked with flags and
Flowering window-boxes can divert a strolling eye
With the irrelevance of statues' nudity, so hide
The dramas in their bowels: the Senate House and the
State Hospital. The Institute of Science, where the famous
Flambow lectures.
                  This same afternoon
The National Socialist minority in the Senate rose

Up in a body, shouting: 'Treacherous reds! If we
Resign we shall return in triumph, set this
House in order in the people's name!' Their barking
Met with smiles from liberal benches. When a telephone
Called for a left-wing member, he returned with a white
Face: 'Max Kleinborg, Jewish leader, died in hospital
An hour ago. Mysterious injuries. Unknown
Assailant.' No one smiled again. At the same hour
In a packed lecture-theatre at the Institute
Flambow declared: 'Our highest of ideals
Is to maintain and serve the freedom of research that we
Have won. I do appeal to every student here
Never to sacrifice the human interest to any such demands
As may be made on us by an exterior cause. When I was asked
To aid the government by giving up my time
To the discovery of new poison-gas, explosives and death-rays,
I categorically refused.' Bursting applause
Completed his last words; but from the shadows at the back of
The long hall, an angry cry: 'The Fatherland
Comes before all! Flambow, beware!'
                          Clapping of hands,
Raised voices. Heard down the corridor. Third floor,

First on the right, door 17: the Faculty of
Sociological Studies, where reports from the anonymous
Observer are received and filed (under the supervision of
Jules Hartmann, son of Flambow's greatest friend). Today
A busy afternoon. Piles of thick sheaves whose contents
'Plot on a graph that tortuous nervy line, the mass's
Changing life.'
   Chosen at random:

      'Rose
At half-past five. Argued at breakfast with the wife over the
Pending strike. Quit house at six. Rode through the rain
To work. Outside the gates a Grey-shirt stood distributing
His party's pamphlets (paid for by funds subscribed to by
Our boss). One of my mates went up to him and wrenched
The bundle from his hands. Bit of a scuffle. Later saw,
Lounging at lunch-hour, leaflets in the mud.'

      '. . . to tea
With a professor and his wife in Tower Street. A Madame D.,
A well-dressed, cultured-looking woman, said she thought
That life was meaningless. Professor shrugged. The conversation
 turned
To table-turning and astrology.'

      'One of the girls
In our department came to work today with a framed
Photo of "the Leader", as she calls him, which she stuck
Over her desk.'

      'After the children had gone back
To school, I went up to lie down, as every day, but could
Not rest because of worry over what last night my
Husband said about his job, how he might lose it soon.'

'First came the standard-bearers clothed in tiger-skins, and then
A squad of troopers at salute. The band struck up a fanfare, and
Through curtains stepped the hero of the evening. The crowd's cheers
Were deafening. One woman fainted and was carried out. At last
He raised his hand. "My people!" he began, and then I heard
A man behind me say "Not yet, thank God!" At once
He disappeared beneath a dozen blows.'

                              'As I
Was leaving the Exchange, a fellow said to me that if
The NS party were in power there'd be no unemployment
Benefit. He'd rather die, he said. He used to be
On the same shift with me. We strolled to the disused pithead,
A car was standing there, drove off as we came by.'

'The street was full of people and I saw a van
Loaded with special police arrive, but they were not
Able to make the rioters disperse. Then someone shouted:
"Let them have it, they're his bloody guards!" That started
It. I noticed that a clock said half-past ten. Then I was knocked
Down by the baton charge.'

                    So would a seismograph describe
Its dire parabolas. The scattered records utter all the same
Act, act, to Hartmann's ear. How can one hear them, impotently tied
By scientific objectivity, he urgently inquires. The will of one
To climb upon the roof-top of the Institute, launch a premonitory cry
Like meteoric words of sky-sign smoke across the town
To hang there hugely inescapable, for all to see, subsides
A disillusioned wave in him. 'What can I do
But urge my Father to persuade the leading men of the
Executive to issue an immediate appeal
For unity, to act, to act, throughout
The workers' movement. Soon will be too late.'

But evening takes its coat down from the peg,
Portals are closing, private lives resume
Their homechat-crossword puzzles and the knitting of
Protective woollies: armies evacuate
The daily battlefield, and clad in mufti roam
Through park, arcade and alley whistling gay
Or wistful tunes, not marching-songs. And though
The hour's as heavy as a pear tense on its bough
Awaiting a mere puff to make it drop, a ripened fruit
Swollen with change and danger like a bomb, only a few –
The soothsayer, the seer, the rebel poet – see it there
Suspended in the sunset, ominous.

                    O evening flares
Placard this town and country with perfervid colours! O

Remember, when the coming night is thick and weak the pulse
Of hope and under cover of the dark your freedom's last
Defenders have deserted or been shot, remember this
Dazzling finale! Music in the parks and lights beneath
The trees, where the loudspeakers not yet blare
With only race-hysteria; crimson lakes
Poured out across the heavens that do not as yet
Reflect a nation's blood; on outward roads
Car-fleets that are not freighted yet with loads
Of refugees. In floodlit sapphire pools
Still swim the golden poignant limbs of youths
Unregimented, girls for whom kisses do not seal
A cannon-fodder contract. On the greens
Children play games untouched by creed or badge,
Not yet corrupted by the partisan's
Crude flag.

                              Flambow, returning late across
The City Gardens from laboratory, heard
Their mothers call them home, and sighed, and sought
Not to imagine how those voices might ascend
One day in agonized crescendo, how the blooms
In the neat beds might be replaced by red
Flowers of carnage, and that placid lawn
Be suddenly transformed into a desert waste
Littered with bones and stony fragments. 'Peace
Is our most precious ally to defend: my work
Is unrelenting undestructive war against war's works
And evil allies.' Overhead the air
Condensed the overtones of dusk, and at his door
He turned awhile to gaze up at a star.

The clock says Night. Now the conspirators
Assemble: now in the centre of the town within
The wooden horse of the Grey House the shirted band
Prepare their fatal coup round shaded lamps
Which drop white circles on their charts and black-
Marked lists. Passwords, salutes and codes observe
Their midnight ritual. Assassinations brew
In shady cafés: while in the frank glare
Of chandeliers the Leader drinks champagne,
The guest tonight of patriotic heads

Of certain industries, not slow to recognize
Their Saviour. Trusting to dreams less well-insured
The people plunge into the fogs of sleep
Through which they drift towards tomorrow's rocks.

p. 1939

FAREWELL CHORUS

I

And so! the long black pullman is at last departing, now,
After those undermining years of angry waiting and cold tea;
And all your small grey faces and wet hankies slide away
Backwards into the station's cave of cloud. And so Goodbye
To our home-town, so foreign now its lights no longer show;
And to old lives already indistinct as a dull play
We saw while staying somewhere in the Midlands long ago.

Farewell to the few and to the many; for tonight
Our souls may be required of us; and so we say Adieu
To those who charmed us with their ever ready wit
But could not see the point; to those whose polished hands
And voices could allay a little while our private pain
But could not stay to soothe us when worse bouts began;
To those whose beauties were too brief: Farewell, dear friends.

To you as well whom we could never love, hard though
We tried, because our pity told us you were weak,
And because of pity we abhorred; to you
Whose gauche distress and badly-written postcards made us
    ache
With angrily impatient self-reproach; you who were too
Indelicately tender, whose too soft eyes made us look
(Against our uncourageous wish) swiftly away . . .

To those, too, whom we hardly knew, or could not know;
To the indifferent and the admired; to the once-met
And long-remembered faces: Yes, Goodbye to you
Who made us turn our heads to look again, and wait
For hours in vain at the same place next day;

Who for a moment might have been the lost selves sought
Without avail, and whom we know we never shall find now.

Away, away! Yet now it is no longer in retreat
That we are leaving. All our will is drowned
As by an inner tidal-wave that has washed our regret
And small fears and exhausted implications out of mind.
You can't accompany our journey. Nor may we return
Except in unimpassioned recollections from beyond
That ever-nearer frontier that our fate has drawn.

II

And so let's take a last look round, and say Farewell to all
Events that gave the last decade, which this New Year
Brings to its close, a special pathos. Let us fill
One final fiery glass and quickly drink to 'the Pre-War'
Before we greet 'the Forties', whose unseen sphinx-face
Is staring fixedly upon us from behind its veil;
Drink farewell quickly, ere the Future smash the glass.

Even while underneath the floor are whirling on
The wheels which carry us towards some Time-to-Come,
Let us perform this hasty mental rite (as one
Might cast a few imagined bays into the tomb
Of an unloved but memorable great man);
Soon the still-near will seem remotely far; there's hardly time
For much oration more than mere Goodbye, again:

To the delusive peace of those disintegrating years
Through which burst uncontrollably into our view
Successive and increasingly premonitory flares,
Explosions of the dangerous truth beneath, which no
Steel-plated self-deception could for long withstand . . .
Years through the rising storm of which somehow we grew,
Struggling to keep an anchored heart and open mind,

Too often failing. Years through which none the less
The coaxing of complacency and sleep could still persuade
Kind-hearted Christians of the permanence of Peace,
Increase of common-sense and civic virtue. Years which bade
Less placid conscientious souls indignantly arise

Upon ten thousand platforms to proclaim the system mad
And urge the liquidation of a senile ruling-class.

Years like a prison-wall, frustrating though unsound
On which the brush of History, with quick, neurotic strokes,
Its latest and most awe-inspiring fresco soon outlined:
Spenglerian lowering of the Western skies, red lakes
Of civil bloodshed, free flags flagrantly torn down
By order of macabre puppet orators, the blind
Leading blindfolded followers into the Devil's den . . .

III

And so, Goodbye, grim 'Thirties. These your closing days
Have shown a new light, motionless and far
And clear as ice, to our sore riddled eyes;
And we see certain truths now, which the fear
Aroused by earlier circumstances could but compromise,
Concerning all men's lives. Beyond despair
May we take wise leave of you, knowing disasters' cause.

Having left all false hopes behind, may we move on
At a vertiginous unmeasured speed, beyond, beyond,
Across this unknown Present's bleak and rocky plain;
Through sudden tunnels; in our ears the wind
Echoing unintelligible guns. Mirrored within
Each lonely consciousness, War's world seems without end.
Dumbly we stare up at strange skies with each day's dawn.

Could you but hear our final farewell call, how strained
And hollow it would sound! We are already far
Away, forever leaving further leagues behind
Of this most perilous and incoherent land
We're in. The unseen enemy are near.
Above the cowering capital Death's wings impend.
Rapidly under ink-black seas today's doomed disappear.

We are alone with one another, but our eyes
Meet seldom in the dark. What a relentless roar
Stuffs every ear, as though with wool! The winds that rise
Out of our dereliction's vortex, hour by hour,
To bring us word of the incessant wordless guns,

Tirades of the insane, thick hum of planes, the rage of fire,
Eruptions, waves: all end in utmost silence in our brains.

'The silence after the viaticum.' So silent is the ray
Of naked radiance that lights our actual scene,
Leading the gaze into those nameless and unknown
Extremes of our existence where fear's armour falls away
And lamentation and defeat and pain
Are all transfigured by acceptance; where men see
The tragic splendour of their final destiny.

w. New Year 1940, p. 1941

SPRING MCMXL

London Bridge is falling down, Rome's burnt, and Babylon
The Great is now but dust; and still Spring must
Swing back through Time's continual arc to earth.
Though every land become as a black field
Dunged with the dead, drenched by the dying's blood,
Still must a punctual goddess waken and ascend
The rocky stairs, up into earth's chilled air,
And pass upon her mission through those carrion ranks,
Picking her way among a maze of broken brick
To quicken with her footsteps the short sooty grass between;
While now once more their futile matchwood empires flare and blaze
And through the smoke men gaze with bloodshot eyes
At the translucent apparition, clad in trembling nascent green,
Of one they can still recognize, though scarcely understand.

p. 1942

A WARTIME DAWN

Dulled by the slow glare of the yellow bulb;
As far from sleep still as at any hour
Since distant midnight; with a hollow skull
In which white vapours seem to reel
Among limp muddles of old thought; till eyes
Collapse into themselves like clams in mud . . .
Hand paws the wall to reach the chilly switch;
Then nerve-shot darkness gradually shakes
Throughout the room. *Lie still* . . . Limbs twitch;
Relapse to immobility's faint ache. And time
A while relaxes; space turns wholly black.

But deep in the velvet crater of the ear
A chip of sound abruptly irritates.
A second, a third chirp; and then another far
Emphatic trill and chirrup shrills in answer; notes
From all directions round pluck at the strings
Of hearing with frail finely-sharpened claws.
And in an instant, every wakened bird
Across surrounding miles of air
Outside, is sowing like a scintillating sand
Its throat's incessantly replenished store
Of tuneless singsong, timeless, aimless, blind.

Draw now with prickling hand the curtains back;
Unpin the blackout-cloth; let in
Grim crack-of-dawn's first glimmer through the glass.
All's yet half sunk in Yesterday's stale death,
Obscurely still beneath a moist-tinged blank
Sky like the inside of a deaf mute's mouth . . .
Nearest within the window's sight, ash-pale
Against a cinder coloured wall, the white
Pear-blossom hovers like a stare; rain-wet
The further housetops weakly shine; and there,
Beyond, hangs flaccidly, a lone barrage-balloon.

An incommunicable desolation weighs
Like depths of stagnant water on this break of day. –
Long meditation without thought. – Until a breeze

From some pure Nowhere straying, stirs
A pang of poignant odour from the earth, an unheard sigh
Pregnant with sap's sweet tang and raw soil's fine
Aroma, smell of stone, and acrid breath
Of gravel puddles. While the brooding green
Of nearby gardens' grass and trees, and quiet flat
Blue leaves, the distant lilac mirages, are made
Clear by increasing daylight, and intensified.

Now head sinks into pillows in retreat
Before this morning's hovering advance;
(Behind loose lids, in sleep's warm porch, half hears
White hollow clink of bottles, – dragging crunch
Of milk-cart wheels, – and presently a snatch
Of windy whistling as the newsboy's bike winds near,
Distributing to neighbour's peaceful steps
Reports of last-night's battles); at last sleeps.
While early guns on Norway's bitter coast
Where faceless troops are landing, renew fire:
And one more day of War starts everywhere.

w. April 1940, p. 1941

WALKING AT WHITSUN

'La fontaine n'a pas tari
Pas plus que l'or de la paille ne s'est terni
Regardons l'abeille
Et ne songeons pas à l'avenir . . .'
      APOLLINAIRE

. . . Then let the cloth across my back grow warm
Beneath such comforting strong rays! new leaf
Flow everywhere, translucently profuse,
And flagrant weed be tall, the banks of lanes
Sprawl dazed with swarming lion-petalled suns
As with largesse of pollen-coloured wealth
The meadows; and across these vibrant lands
Of Summer-afternoon through which I stroll
Let rapidly gold glazes slide and chase

Away such shades as chill the hillside trees
And make remindful mind turn cold . . .

        The eyes
Of thought stare elsewhere, as though skewer-fixed
To an imagined sky's immense collapse;
Nor can, borne undistracted through this scene
Of festive plant and basking pastorale,
The mind find any calm or light within
The bone walls of the skull; for at its ear
Resound recurrent thunderings of dark
Smoke-towered waves rearing sheer tons to strike
Down through Today's last dyke. Day-long
That far thick roar of fear thuds, on-and-on,
Beneath the floor of sense, and makes
All carefree quodlibet of leaves and larks
And fragile tympani of insects sound
Like Chinese music, mindlessly remote,
Drawing across both sight and thought like gauze
Its unreality's taut haze.

        But light!
O cleanse with widespread flood of rays the brain's
Oppressively still sickroom, wherein brood
Hot festering obsessions, and absolve
My introspection's mirror of such stains
As blot its true reflection of the world!
Let streams of sweetest air dissolve the blight
And poison of the News, which every hour
Contaminates the ether.

        I will pass
On far beyond the village, out of sight
Of human habitation for a while
Grass has an everlasting pristine smell.
On high, sublime in his bronze ark, the sun
Goes cruising across seas of silken sky.
In fields atop the hillside, chestnut trees
Display the splendour of their branches piled
With blazing candle burdens. – Such a May
As this might never come again . . .

                        I tread
The white dust of a weed-bright lane; alone
Upon Time-Present's tranquil outmost rim,
Seeing the sunlight through a lens of dread,
While anguish makes the English landscape seem
Inhuman as the jungle, and unreal
Its peace. And meditating as I pace
The afternoon away, upon the smile
(Like that worn by the dead) which Nature wears
In ignorance of our unnatural tears,
From time to time I think: How such a sun
Must glitter on their helmets! How bright-red
Against this sky's clear screen must ruins burn . . .

How sharply their invading steel must shine!

w. Marshfield, May 1940, p. 1941

OXFORD: A SPRING DAY

For Bill

The air shines with a mild magnificence . . .
Leaves, voices, glitterings . . . And there is also water
Winding in easy ways among much green expanse,

Or lying flat, in small floods, on the grass;
Water which in its widespread crystal holds the whole soft song
Of this swift tremulous instant of rebirth and peace.

Tremulous – yet beneath, how deep its root!
Timelessness of an afternoon! Air's gems, the walls' bland grey,
Slim spires, hope-coloured fields: these belong to no date.

w. 1941

THE GRAVEL-PIT FIELD

Beside the stolid opaque flow
Of rain-gorged Thames; beneath a thin
Layer of early evening light
Which seems to drift, a ragged veil,
Upon the chilly March air's tide:
Upwards in shallow shapeless tiers
A stretch of scurfy pock-marked waste
Sprawls laggardly its acres till
They touch a raw brick-villa'd rim.

Amidst this nondescript terrain
Haphazardly the gravel-pits'
Rough-hewn rust-coloured hollows yawn,
Their steep declivities away
From the field-surface dropping down
Towards the depths below where rain-
Water in turbid pools stagnates
Like scraps of sky decaying in
The sockets of a dead man's stare.

The shabby coat of coarse grass spread
Unevenly across the ruts
And humps of lumpy soil; the bits
Of stick and threads of straw; loose clumps
Of weeds with withered stalks and black
Tatters of leaf and scorched pods: all
These intertwined minutiae
Of Nature's humblest growths persist
In their endurance here like rock.

As with untold intensity
On the far edge of Being, where
Life's last faint forms begin to lose
Name and identity and fade
Away into the Void, endures
The final thin triumphant flame
Of all that's most despoiled and bare:
So these least stones, in the extreme
Of their abasement might appear

Like rare stones such as could have formed
A necklet worn by the dead queen
Of a great Pharaoh, in her tomb . . .
So each abandoned snail-shell strewn
Among these blotched dock-leaves might seem
In the pure ray shed by the loss
Of all man-measured value, like
Some priceless pearl-enamelled toy
Cushioned on green silk under glass.

And who in solitude like this
Can say the unclean mongrel's bones
Which stick out, splintered, through the loose
Side of a gravel-pit, are not
The precious relics of some saint,
Perhaps miraculous? Or that
The lettering on this Woodbine-
Packet's remains ought not to read:
Mene mene tekel upharsin?

Now a breeze gently breathes across
The wilderness's cryptic face;
The meagre grasses scarcely stir;
But when some stranger gust sweeps past,
Seeming as though an unseen swarm
Of sea-birds had disturbed the air
With their strong wings' wide stroke, a gleam
Of freshness hovers everywhere
About the field: and tall weeds shake,

Leaves wave their tiny flags to show
That the wind blown about the brow
Of this poor plot is nothing less
Than the great constant draught the speed
Of Earth's gyrations makes in Space . . .
As I stand musing, overhead
The zenith's stark light thrusts a ray
Down through the dusk's rolling vapours, casts
A last lucidity of day

Across the scene: and in a flash
Of insight I behold the field's

      Apotheosis: No-man's-land
      Between this world and the beyond,
      Remote from men and yet more real
      Than any human dwelling-place:
      A tabernacle where one stands
      As though within the empty space
      Round which revolves the Sage's Wheel.

w. Spring 1941, p. 1941

REQUIEM

'Permets que nous te goûtions d'abord le jour de la mort
Qui est un grand jour de calme d'épousés,
Le monde heureux, les fils réconciliés.'
                              PIERRE JEAN JOUVE

I

[Voice: Recitative]
O hidden Face! O gaze fixed on us from afar
And that we cannot meet: Grant us, who wait
In the great park of crumbling monuments that is
The world, that we may meet at last those eyes
In which black fires burn back to white,
With perfect clearness, and not blurred by fever's heat
Nor in the sudden spasm of disintegrating fear
That rends the breast of beasts and blinds
The blind and undefined: And O instruct
Us how to ripen unto Thee.

[Choir: Sotto Voce]
                        Hearts are unripe
And spirits light as straw that in Thy light
Shall kindle like the straw, and flare away
To nothing in an instant breath of smoke.

[Voice]
Thy light is like a darkness and Thy
Joy is found through grief. And they who search
For Thee shall find Thee not. And hidden in Thy mouth

The blinding benediction of the final phrase
Which shall not fall upon a listening ear.

[Choir]
For they who listen at the secret door
Hear only their own heart beat out its fault.

II

[Voice]
In the great park,
A wanderer at sundown by the weeping falls
Of pallid spume and high prismatic spray
Once saw across the water in the last illusive light
A figure with a gleaming chalice come . . .

[Choir]
But it was not Thy Angel!

[Voice]
              And another heard
A warning echo in a mountain cave,
Reverberant with distance and the undertone of guilt . . .

[Choir]
But it was not Thy voice!

[Voice]
              For silent and invisible
Are all Thy works; and hidden in the depths midway between
Desire and fear. And they who long for Thee and are afraid
Of Life, and they who fear the clear stroke of Thy knife
Obsessed with the pale shadows of themselves, shall lose full sight
And understanding of that final mystery.

III

[Choir]
Tenebral treasure and immortal flower
And flower of immortal Death!
O silent white extent
Of skyless sky, the wingless flight
And the long flawless cry
Of aspiration endlessly!

[Voice]
The seed is buried in us like a memory; the seed
Is hidden from us like the omnipresent Eye; it grows
Within us through Time's flux, both night and day.

[Choir]
Darkness that burns like light, black light
And essence of all radiance!
O depth beyond confusion sunk,
The timeless Nadir at the heart
Of Time, where all creative and
Destructive forces meet!

[Voice]
The seed is nurtured by involuntary tears; by blood
Shed from Love's inmost wounds; its roots are fed
By the concealed corruption of unknown desires.

[Choir]
    We cannot hear or see, nor say
    The name: There is no light
    Or shade, nor place nor time,
    No movement, no repose,
    But only perfect prescience
    Of the Becoming of the Whole.

[Voice]
The seed springs from us into flower; yet none can tell
At what hour late or early those concealed furled leaves
And multifoliate petals shall outgrow their tender shell.

[Choir]
    The hour is unknown:
    The hour endures:
    The hour strikes every hour.

IV

[Voice]
Each hour of life is glorious and vain.
O thirst and glorious unsatisfied
Lamenting cry! How vain the short relief

And unabiding refuge from the tide
That nearer crawls each day across the sands
On which our house is founded! Vanity
Of vanities, all things held by our hands!
Beyond their reach, with diamond-rays, and high
Above the furthest fields of ether lies
The core of glory, only ascertained
By inward opening of Death's deep eye
And outward flight of Spirit long sustained:

[Choir: distantly echoing]
By wings the swift flames of the funeral pile
Are fanned . . . Dead faces guard a secret smile.

w. 1938–40, p. 1956

STROPHES ÉLÉGIAQUES À LA MÉMOIRE D'ALBAN BERG (1885-1935)

The titles of the first, second and fourth parts of the following sequence were taken from Berg's Lyric Suite. *Lines 14 and 15 of the third part are a quotation from a poem in Baudelaire's sequence 'Le Vin', which was set to music by Berg as a cantata. Two earlier versions of these* Strophes *were written in English, but were not satisfactory enough to be printed. The following version, written in 1939, three years after the original impulse, appeared in* Cahiers du Sud *in January 1940.* D.G.

Andante Amoroso

Souvenir d'un musicien: des cordes lyriques
Soulèvent des draps de brume et l'ouïe est entraînée
Parmi des perspectives dissolvantes où son élégie
Fleurit comme une couronne qu'arrosent des pleurs
De sons: orchidées couleur d'ecchymose, et roses
Flétries, fleurs de la passion, une gerbe flottante
Lente à travers la vue des yeux fermés.

Sa musique est une pluie qui rafraîchit
Les cyprès seuls parmis ces rochers gris,
Trouble comme l'amour dans la mémoire les airs

Du soir, à l'heure où la hantise et l'obsession,
Figures du passé, glissent comme des têtes coupées
Sur les courants du crépuscule lointain
De Cimmérie, refuge des ombres perdues.

L'illusion tremble. En haut, aigües
Des lames de lumière crue incisent les cieux;
Et au-dessous, autour d'un lac de plomb
Le vent agite des roseaux dissonants;
Des vagues concentriques frappent le bord de l'eau
Comme les échos d'un cri désespéré.
Très vite s'envolent des oiseaux comme des flèches.

Tenebroso

Les grandes plaines où les routes sont comme des veines,
Les rangs de montagnes et les lacs réfléchissants,
Même les prairies les plus vides ou fleuries
Portent l'ombre énorme du *Zeitgeist*, qui menace
Avec ses nuages noirs de sort solides
Toutes les moissons; les saisons ne font plus
Qu'illustrer les phases des luttes humaines.

Et au-dessûs du chaos des grandes villes
Qui gonfle le continent, la noirceur des ceux pèse
Comme un jugement sur toutes les rues-prisons
Où rôdent encore les peurs de l'ancienne nuit
Avec des uniformes, des bâtons, des fusils,
Et où la folie couve ses fantaisies
De persécutés, d'espions, d'élus de Dieu.

Nous couchés sans sommeil dans nos chambres séparées
Nous écoutons un fracas comme de trains-fantômes
Se précipitant vers le bout de nos souffrances;
Et tandis que leur tonnerre ruine nos rêves on se demande
Quel grand minuit peut être le but de leurs roues chaudes,
Quel signe pourrait empêcher tout espoir comme un train fou
De se dérailler dans la tête de l'homme.

Intermezzo

Tout chant est triomphe et toute plainte
Est réconciliation. Brûle encore,

Brûle, O lyre du larynx, guérisse le tourment
Qui ne sait pas trouver une sortie
Parmi le labyrinthe de la poitrine. Encore
Plongez-vous dans la mélodie, O ailes sonores
A la recherche de repos et de paix.

Toute plainte est réconciliation
Avec le lamentable, et sait résoudre
Les pleurs et les ruines, la maladie
Des empires, dans des arabesques
De cancereuse corruption et de pluie
D'étincelante semence stérile, tels que
'Les sons d'une musique énervante et câline,

'Semblable au cri lointain de l'humaine douleur;'
Et une telle musique peut nous consoler
De la condition damnée, la blessure secrète,
Qui grimpant vers le silence à travers l'oreille
Invisible de l'espace, avec des chants brûlés
Dans les royaumes de l'inouï créé de lointains
Paysages, exaltés et profonds.

Misterioso

Il se hâte vers sa fin, le requiem
Que des événements inconnus doivent interrompre;
Prémonitoires de la rupture les cordes forcées
A travers tous les tons par le vent rude
De l'angoisse! et répétition de pressentiments
Intérieurs: ces fusées d'étoiles rouges et
L'Etoile de la Mort au milieu qui projette

Sur nous la paralysie de ses rayons pénétrants
Jusqu'au recoin le plus secret de l'âme,
Là où coupable le miroir tourne
Sans cesse et ne cesse pas de rendre
Des images deformées de notre détresse: telle la fumée
Qui accompagne la Bête hors de l'abîme, l'agneau
Meurtri, et ces chevaliers aux quatre couleurs criantes . . .

Mais toutes les visions surgies hors du temps
Se fanent enfin; ne peuvent nullement cacher

La révélation de la nudité affreuse
De l'homme tragique divisé en lui-même
Qui maintenant doit monter sur l'échafaud de son trône
Et porter une couronne de feu, et être trahi, tomber
Dans les ténèbres du mythe pour retrouver son Christ.

Epilogue: 1939

Les vrais témoins ne sont plus aujourd'hui
Ecoutés, le silence les cache
(En était un celui qu'on commémore
Ici: en exil son esprit,
Sa ville natale perdue
Aux barbares bruns et noirs, et ses partitions
Verboten comme un scandale dangereux).

Villes glorieuses de la musique, de l'art,
Vienne, Salzburg et Prague, des millepieds
Chaussés de fer ont envahi vos rues,
L'araignée hideuse de la croix gammée
Partout suspend ses toiles; ce sont des rats
Qui font la musique de chambre dans vos chambres;
Et dans vos jardins ombrageux se cachent les loups.

Elle s'agrandit toujours la tache
Flagrante, et déshonore l'histoire.
Les injustes règnent, leurs orateurs perfides
Rendent sourd le peuple tandis que tombent les haches.
Mais hors de l'avenir quel orage effrayant
Va effacer leurs dernières traces avec ses foudres!
Les vrais témoins nous resteront toujours.

w. Eté 1939, p. 1940

A VAGRANT AND OTHER POEMS
(1950)

A VAGRANT

'Mais il n'a point parlé, mais cette année encore
Heure par heure en vain lentement tombera.'
                    ALFRED DE VIGNY

'They're much the same in most ways, these great cities. Of them all,
Speaking of those I've seen, this one's still far the best
Big densely built-up area for a man to wander in
Should he have ceased to find shelter, relief,
Or dream in sanatorium bed; should nothing as yet call
Decisively to him to put an end to brain's
Proliferations round the possibilities that eat
Up adolescence, even years up to the late
Thirtieth birthday; should no one seem to wait
His coming, to pop out at last and bark
Briskly: "A most convenient solution has at last
Been found, after the unavoidable delay due to this spate of wars
That we've been having lately. This is it:
Just fill in (in block letters) on the dotted-line your name
And number. From now on until you die all is
O.K., meaning the clockwork's been adjusted to accommodate
You nicely; all you need's to eat and sleep,
To sleep and eat and eat and laugh and sleep,
And sleep and laugh and wake up every day
Fresh as a raffia daisy!" I already wake each day
Without a bump or too much morning sickness to routine
Which although without order wears the will out just as well
As this job-barker's programme would. His line may in the end
Provide me with a noose with which to hang myself, should I
Discover that the strain of doing nothing is too great
A price to pay for spiritual integrity. The soul
Is said by some to be a bourgeois luxury, which shows
A strange misunderstanding both of soul and bourgeoisie.
The Sermon on the Mount is just as often misconstrued
By Marxists as by wealthy congregations, it would seem.
The "Modern Man in Search of Soul" appears
A comic criminal or an unbalanced bore to those
Whose fear of doing something foolish fools them. *Je m'en fous!*
Blessèd are they, it might be said, who are not of this race
Of settled average citizens secure in their *état
Civil* of snowy guiltlessness and showy high ideals

Permitting them achieve an inexpensive lifelong peace
Of mind, through dogged persistence, frequent aspirin, and bile
Occasionally vented via trivial slander . . . Baa,
Baa, O sleepysickness-rotted sheep, in your nice fold
Are none but marketable fleeces. I my lot
Prefer to cast at once away right in
Among the stone-winning lone wolves whose future cells
Shall make home-founding unworthwhile. Unblessèd let me go
And join the honest tribe of patient prisoners and ex-
Convicts, and all such victims of the guilt
Society dare not admit its own. I would not strike
The pose of one however who might in a chic ballet
Perform an apache role in rags of cleverly-cut silk.
Awkward enough, awake, yet although anxious still just sane,
I stand still in my quasi-dereliction, or but stray
Slowly along the quais towards the ends of afternoons
That lead to evenings empty of engagements, or at night
Lying resigned in cosy-corner crow's-nest, listen long
To sounds of the surrounding city desultorily
Seeking in loud distraction some relief from what its nerves
Are gnawed by: I mean knowledge of its lack of *raison d'être*.
The city's lack and mine are much the same. What, oh what can
A Vagrant hope to find to take the place of what was once
Our expectation of the Human City in which each man might
Morning and evening, every day, lead his own life, and Man's?'

p. 1948

INNOCENCE AND EXPERIENCE

Beneath the well-born weak-lined gentle flesh
Its firmly-moulded bonework did much to sustain
This face's actively upheld nobility. I had the time
To gaze upon a late transmuted beauty
Known none too kindly to the North in our cold time.
Yet I knew warmth was there, where were born both
Her Southern mildness and Repression's bleakest whim,
Which is to spoil the good with greatness, till it do its best
To die in surfeit of a passion lean as sin.
I still knew of her nothing less than this,

She could well have played Portia in Spanish
Making it seem a Terry had conceived
To play the cello to a foreign bard's guitar.
Attentive, I beheld a less premeditated look
Melting the mask till one could see it once had worn
The serene, robust air as of never-rebuked gaiety
That shakes like laughter round a regally-loved child;
And saw her clamber up, her will supported
By the arms of his gold braid-adorned dark dignity,
Till safe in peril perching, from the lofty balustrade
She overlooked a square where waved and roared
In passionate approval of political Papa
The population, it appeared, of the then nascent State.

She'd come down to the mezzanine in person
To welcome us, dismissed the footman, stepped
With lifted dress-train held bunched at the knees
Into the ivory-panelled gilt-grilled lift;
Dismissed her maid on reaching the third floor
And shown us down a quite dark passage, hung
With glass-masked pastels – Redon, Morisot, maybe, –
To her most private salon. One could tell
At once how long she must have sat alone,
Sad lady, with the back of her fauteuil
Turned to the uncommunicative view
Of drear palatial faubourg roofs displayed
Between portentous casement draperies,
There in that room the hotel's master had
But seldom entered, though his youth's collections here
As elsewhere were the source of all that caught
The roving eye: a Degas statuette,
A hand-high Rodin piece; upon the wall
Above the fireplace, a nice Géricault –
Two Turkish ladies, or *baigneuses*; some fine
Old pots, and a miraculously carved
Ivory ball within a ball within a ball
That stood upon the escritoire, still piled
With business correspondence that no secretary
Could have availed much to diminish. 'How
Long it must be now since we last –
When was it? Oh, the Occupation? Yes,
I remained here all the time, I held

The fort. A long grim winter. But Eugène,
Of course, had other things to occupy
In South America his busy mind, than my
Predicament. Nothing changed him; simply we
Became "loyally indifferent"; or I trust I so appeared.'

Under the weight of false presuppositions hanging round
Upon all three of us, the other lady frowned (touched too; too tired) –
Her constant lit cheroot let fall a not entirely
Inappropriate tiny elegy of ash. Three enigmatic masks.

Outside upon the Plaza, the huge crowd still waved and waved!

'God gives us all, yet no one asks
What it is given for . . .'

p. 1950

PHOTOGRAPH

To Philippe Soupault

Whatever you were looking at when Abbott's camera clicked,
It hardly wore the likeness, I suppose, that you wear now;
Yet its reality can hardly have been other than the one
That we both recognize at present, which is made real
By us and all who truly live in it. Your eyes
Are clear, more clear and keen than what they see, and gaze
    through pain,
Frustration and the future of futility. They look
Straight into the hid heart of whatsoever lies ahead, with active
    trust,
With scepticism and with the tried affection that cannot ever be
Made disappointed by its object's failures. You will thus always be
    aware
That what is true is lovable, and you in knowing this
Will have become one in whose love the love of others may find
    rest.

c. 1950

REPORTED MISSING

At the end of the sunny, polished corridor
I opened a door I had not seen before
And stepped into a room in which the air
Had long been undisturbed but was not stale but
Sleepy sweet and half-familiar, half
Reminiscent of another time and life. There were
Bookshelves and two deep basket chairs, that faced
Each other, though the bed was single, spread
With a soft paisley-patterned cloth, no more to be
Unmade. The view from the dormer window, creeper-fringed,
Was the best in the house. Upon the mantelshelf
Stood lonely in its leather frame a photograph I'll not
Forget, I think, although I never met
The sitter, so immediate was the subjugating charm
That struck one from the eyes and features. These
Reported how much he was missing, whom I cannot praise,
Only commemorate in a few unasked-for lines
Which must leave the essential once more all but quite unsaid.

c. 1950

A TOUGH GENERATION

To grow unguided at a time when none
Are sure where they should plant their sprig of trust;
When sunshine has no special mission to endow
With gold the rustic rose, which will run wild
And ramble from the garden to the wood
To train itself to climb the trunks of trees
If the old seedsman die and suburbs care
For sentimental cottage-flowers no more;
To grow up in a wood of rotted trees
In which it is not known which tree will be
First to disturb the silent sultry grove
With crack of doom, dead crackling and dread roar –
Will be infallibly to learn that first
One always owes a duty to oneself;
This much at least is certain: one must live.
And one may reach, without having to search

For much more lore than this, a shrewd maturity,
Equipped with adult aptitude to ape
All customary cant and current camouflage;
Nor be a whit too squeamish where the soul's concerned,
But hold out for the best black market price for it
Should need remind one that one has to live.
Yet just as sweetly, where no markets are,
An unkempt rose may for a season still
Trust its own beauty and disclose its heart
Even to the woodland shade, and as in sacrifice
Renounce its ragged petals one by one.

p. 1950

THE OTHER LARRY

Inwardly corrosive, but to eyes outside most bland,
Chubby and blonde and chuckling: O sardonic friend,
Easily reconciled with, you are sorry after
The black flicked barb has stung
Some tiresome feeble person's too exposed,
Too tender epidermis, though not very and not long:
Exacerbated not yet middle-aged patrician,
Exiled by futile circumstances, ever too well-bred
To make a show of bitterness except in smooth-tongued verse.

Such comment can but seem inept, coming from one
Who's never seen the South of which you sing
But still believes that you will not succeed
In finally convincing all of those
Whom your performance entertains
And makes uncomfortable
That you were meant to grow into a gargoyle
Uttering artful chains of occult smoke-rings
Outside a disbelieved-in anti-god's abode.

c. 1950

EROS ABSCONDITUS

'Wo aber sind die Freunde? Bellarmin
Mit dem Gefahrten . . .'
                    HÖLDERLIN

Not in my lifetime, the love I envisage:
Not in this century, it may be. Nevertheless inevitable.
Having experienced a foretaste of its burning
And of its consolation, although locked in my aloneness
Still, although I know it cannot come to be
Except in reciprocity, I know
That true love is gratuitous, and will race through
The veins of the reborn world's generations, free
And sweet, like, a new kind of electricity.

The love of heroes and of men like gods
Has been for long a strange thing on the earth
And monstrous to the mediocre. They
In whom such love is luminous can but transcend
The squalid inhibitions of those only half alive.
In blind content they breed who never loved a friend.

p. 1949

THE GOOSE-GIRL

She at whose feet I'll finally fall down
With all my niggardly belated offering
Of real emotion, is a lonely silent girl
Who knows no more than I about love's boon
But sits and wonders – feeling at a loss
Among the queens and conquerors who stroll
So poised and pleased about the social scene –
Waiting for no one from an old wives' tale,
But for a childless father and her father's unborn son.

p. 1949

BEWARE BEELZEBUB

Listen, lover of the glistening peril,
The lure lascive and wistful, the sweet pain
Young lacing limbs delight in: the Devil
Will never after smile at you again
When once your easy acquiescence
To his swift-reckoned bargain has put you
Within the power of his swarming lieutenants,
Who lurk in dull disguise the world's mart through
Like fellow fallen men, until the sign
By which the lustless single out a sinner
Bids them to batten, faithful flock of flies,
Dutiful doggers, buzz and drone and whine,
Upon fresh ill-famed flesh for their King's dinner,
Rich-riddled with the worm that never dies.

p. 1949

RONDEL FOR THE FOURTH DECADE

The mind if not the heart turns cold
Seeing the calendar's leaves flying;
Still dare not yet cease trying
To reconcile the heart with growing old.

However often heart's fortune be told
By sceptic mind, the pulse beats on relying
On sanguine heat for hope to hold
Fast to for help when age comes sighing.

But autumn's leaves must cease defying
Grave law and fall like Danae's gold
To stuff blind mouths when, as they turn to mould,
The heart's remains lie still denying
Mind ever knew the truth while dying.

p. 1949

SEPTEMBER SUN: 1947

Magnificent strong sun! in these last days
So prodigally generous of pristine light
That's wasted only by men's sight who will not see
And by self-darkened spirits from whose night
Can rise no longer orison or praise:

Let us consume in fire unfed like yours
And may the quickened gold within me come
To mintage in due season, and not be
Transmuted to no better end than dumb
And self-sufficient usury. These days and years

May bring the sudden call to harvesting,
When if the fields Man labours only yield
Glitter and husks, then with an angrier sun may He
Who first with His gold seed the sightless field
Of Chaos planted, all our trash to cinders bring.

1981

Those days and years! Glitter and husks: what more
Have we to show now that the doomsday clock
Implacably moves onwards to what may
Well prove to be that dreaded final war
So many faithful prophets have foretold? What shock
Can wake to vigil rulers and ruled today?

p. 1949, updated 1983

THE POST-WAR NIGHT

No, nowadays at night the flush of light
Reflected anxiously by urban skies, impresses eyes
In quest of soothing space between the stars, as with a sense
Of guilt, not reassurance. This is Peace,
Our nightly black-out dream; yet back to black skies fly
Our eyes disheartened by futility, to seek
Some sterner strength in the unmoonlit midnight's zenith
Above our heads rebuking light's illusions . . . *In our time*

We have had vision. Now our seeing tries
Not to find blindness everywhere it peers,
Relinquishing belief in any sight surpassing this.
We must see how to justify ourselves
Always. Perhaps indeed that is for ever all
Our eyes are used to look for: We must stand
Justified: – if not before the whole world then before
Ourselves: if not before the candid inmost heart,
Blandly at least before shrewd common-sense
Sole supreme tribunal in this business-driven world,
Still so remote from all the innate sense
Of human destiny that we are born with knows
To be truly our aim on earth: one God-ruled globe,
Finally unified, at peace, free to create! *That sense*
Is dull in all but few today . . . They are not listened to.
They seldom speak. And how absurd they sound
To such as do hear them, how like a child's
Sublime simplicity and sweet ineptitude,
To talk of Brotherhood and of the beautiful
Smooth-running Great Society that might tomorrow mean
Our paradise regained! How well our guilt,
Long versed in all the necessary lies
Required to run the world in practice knows
How always to remain the same calm, sane
Comfortably compromised collusionists, still safe and sound
At least as long as this false peacetime lasts.

p. 1949

DEMOS IN OXFORD STREET

The Ages of the World, since Adam delved
And Eve remained the perfect lady, still
As innocent of culture as her spouse of apron-string,
Having devolved, have brought us the mature
And really average population passing by, away
And onward down this thoroughfare, of all surely the most
Average in any average modern capital. O Sting!
Where is our life? Where is my neighbour, Love?
We have hardened our faces against each other's weariness
Who walk this way; we are not bound to one another

By bomb panic or famine and it is not Christmas Day.
We are aware of Socialists in power at Westminster
Who seem to be making a pretty mess of things: This evening's *Star*
Has bills that tell of Scandal and Enquiry being made
Much in the interest of the Public (i.e. We,
The People) by such as have its interest at heart . . .
We too, while quite disinterested, have of course got hearts.
The latter are as good as most; but who would dare
Risk giving good away each day with maybe no returns?
Besides, we have our families to think of,
And our families have not got too much to spare
Of time or money, tears or trouble. Stare
As boldly as you like into our faces, we'll not turn
Aside out of your way. We're not the Working-Class.

p. 1949

EVENING AGAIN

Evening again.
                              The lurid fuming light
That red sky's smouldering alkali spreads on reflecting stone
Façades of ageing buildings seeming now to slant and strain
Backwards against the leaden East, sheer haggard cliffs
Pitted with windows, baffles with its glare
Those gazing panes. They see nothing but the wrath
Of still prolonged and future conflagrations. With the stain
Of night arising stealthily behind them, fresh leaves shake
Back on their rigid branches, shudder brusquely back and show
How underneath their sparkling green profusion there are hung
Shadows, dull undertone of mourning. Die down, die
Away, brisk wind, let the lit leaves lie still.
Let them with tranquil glitter once more hide
Their secret. Heavy beneath all that is seen
Hangs the forgotten.
                        Heavily night falls.
                                             When shall I desire
No more for rest from restlessness as evening ends?
When no more into silence sinks the sigh that asks for joy.

p. 1949

THREE VENETIAN NOCTURNES

1. BARCAROLLE

Each blue sun-floodlit day floats through a green evening till Night
Releases flows of indigo to stain sea, sky and shore;
And deep into dark velvet folds are absorbed from the air
The orchestrated murmurs of the crowd and bursts of bright
Abruptly ebbing brassy music bruited from the Square.

On the Lagoon drift shreds of serenade from lanterned boats
That bob more quickly like a pulse when from the Lido steers
Close past them the returning *vaporetto*; the heart beats
More quickly for a moment, lifted on a wave of tears
Upwelling but not breaking in the eyes of one who floats

Reclining in a gondola alone and with the tide
Being borne across the Bacino towards where all the stars
In heaven like spilt pearls blur on the black robe Venice wears
Slackly undulating round her when as a nocturnal bride
She mourns her morning glory long drowned in the sea of years.

2. LIDO GALA FIREWORKS

Rockets released tonight rush up to rape the grapebloom sky:
Rainbows of gelid jewellery smashed to flashlit smithereens
And moulting molten-crystal plumes of birds of paradise
Spontaneously splintering their mixed Murano tints
Into a slowly dropping drift of dust of opals, Milky Way
Stained with a long dynasty of fire-peacocks' last blood;
Till all night's spark-sprayed dome is stunned with quick airquakes
    of gold,
Precipitous ephemerae and crepitations, streaked
With shivering scars of wounds stabbed by the rays of soaring stars,
Stars piercing scarlet holes, holes bleeding light,
Light strained through silk, silk blobbed with black,
Black blurred with sea-water, blue . . .

3. ON THE GRAND CANAL

The palaces are sombre cliffs by night;
Some pierced with square-hewn caves,
Grottoes where chandeliers like stalactites
Frosted with electricity blaze dangling in the midst
Of sad high-ceilinged salons' tepid haze;

Or semi-concealed by casement shutter-slats
The twilight velvet cloister-cells of lives
Upon whose intimacy we may gaze
As we slide by, nor stir to any flutter
At solitary privacy intruded on
The page-perusing half-glimpsed inmates' eyes.
Others among these wave-lapped marble fortresses
Within which the patrician past lies passively besieged,
Long before midnight look already left unoccupied
Except by somnolent and unseen soldiery,
As from their blank embrasures only blackness
Broods on the glimmering oracle of the tides
That slowly rise and fall about their feet.
One summer night a passenger upon a steamer, I
While we were floating past before them, tried
To read the mystery of the city's palaces
In the framed scenes and silhouettes displayed
To all that sail down the Canal, and when we paused
A minute at a *stazione* raft, looked up and saw
And seized on instantly, a young girl's head
In a near window, her sweet fresh-coloured face
Vividly lit with eagerness, whose aspect made
Me wonder what it was she held before her
And seemed to read from, what the text and page
Of Goldoni or Shakespeare she rehearsed.
But as the steamer stirred again I saw
It was a fan of playing-cards she held,
A lucky hand, as her expression showed . . .
I wished that lovely face good luck in love,
Though my excitement at the glimpse of her
Swiftly became an elegiac feeling
As the boat's motion swept her from my sight.

p. 1950

BIRTH OF A PRINCE

Many of us remember, too, how very young
And unlike the naïve idea of parents, our own were,
(Though many also may have been less fortunate), when we
Proudly were brought by them into a world of care –
Such genuine gentle care and such brave faith
In the great future which they knew that we should see.
Many also were born within sound of the wind
That can blow no man good, the howling wind of war,
National adversity and Winter. In the historic park
A horn like Herne's was heard; the times were dark;
And the great royal oak creaked in the blast
With grief, its branches cracking, though unshakable it stood.
Another daybreak, and behold with dripping boughs
Uprise after that storm a tree that stands because it stands
For true Peace rooted in the right, from which no wind that blows
Shall shake the many birds whose song is still heard in these lands.
No bird but very bat is he who cannot see
A smile best recognized in solitude
In this momentous birth, nor hear another tongue
Than that of public oratory still speaking through the roar
Of loyal multitudes, asking God grant that we
Give birth to the world's only Prince, *Puer Aeternus*, He
Whose swordlike Word comes not to bring us peace but war
Within forever against falsehood and all fratricidal War.

p. 1949

REX MUNDI

I heard a herald's note announce the coming of a king.

He who came sounding his approach was a small boy;
The household trumpet that he flourished a tin toy.

Then from a bench beneath the boughs that lately Spring
Had hung again with green across the avenue, I rose
To render to the king who came the homage subjects owe.

And as I waited, wondered why it was that such a few
Were standing there with me to see him pass; but understood
As soon as he came into sight, this was a monarch no
Crowds of this world can recognize, to hail him as they should.

He drove past in a carriage that was drawn by a white goat;
King of the world to come where all that shall be now is new,
Calmly he gazed on our pretentious present that is not.

Of morals, classes, business, war, this child
Knew nothing. We were pardoned when he smiled.

If you hear it in the distance, do not scorn the herald's note.

p. 1949

FRAGMENTS TOWARDS A RELIGIO POETAE

'Given that a man has genuine experience of the interior life, then let him boldly drop all outward disciplines, even those practices which thou art vowed to and from which neither pope nor prelate can release thee.'

MEISTER ECKHART

1

The Son of Man is in revolt
Against the god of men.
The Son of God who took the fault
Of men away from them
To lay it in himself on God,
Has nowhere now to lay God's head
But in the heart of human solitude.

2

The way to Life is through the entrance into Night:
The recognition of the Night wherein each man
Must have at first existence: knowing not
The Whole, and yet believing that he knows,
And through such blind belief made blind to Truth.

Truth is that Truth must first remain unknown to me:
That in the unknown dark I feel alone.
In this state only can true being wake
To knowledge of itself through consciousness
Of the non-entity that it is born from and of the desire
For Being, Truth and Light and Human Day.

3

Dear Nameless God, must I say Thee
When I address you? or should I now try
When speaking in close intimacy to friends
To call them Thou, and make sincere and true
What has become archaic in a world of falsity?
An overwhelming contradiction rends
Apart all possibility of our addressing You
Until we have within ourselves made one
The will to self-exist and our desire to be:
To be with God, and not pseudo-divine
Scorn-inspired self-deceivers dreading most to be alone.

4

This world remains 'the World',
An empire under rule
Of a confederacy of lone wolf-hearted birds:
Imperial eagles, each unrecognized
Except by his own world.
No self-reliant haughty bird of prey
Can rule the world wearing an Emperor's crown.

The ancient eyrie-world remains grimly convinced
That no society can thrive without 'religion';
And every now and then duly inaugurates
Another mission drive to raise the same old corpse.

5

That there is Justice in the world
Even the fool who hath said in his heart
There is no God
Would be unlikely wholly to deny:
But if he did, even he would not be such a fool

As the man who declares that there is Justice in the world
And that he can not only see it plainly but must proceed to administer it with perfect justice.
There is no perfectly just man
Because the vision of Justice is the pleasure of God alone.
And that is why the divine part in all men
Longs to see justice and to live by it;
While the enemy of God that is in each of us
Is always trying to make us satisfied with what we can see of Justice without God,
As though He were bound to ratify automatically
Whatever a man-made judge with his own reason decides is just
Provided a sufficiently large number of other men be persuaded to agree with him.

6

There are no harsh laws,
Only laws that in a self-respecting society would be regarded as unnecessary.
There are harsh souls and law-encumbered spirits
Who inflict their conception of decency
On men and half-animals and human beings alike;
Who expect our respect
And would not seriously believe it if told we could feel none for them.

7

Really religious people are rarely looked upon as such
By those to whom religion is secretly something unreal;
And those the world regards as extremely religious people
Are generally people to whom the living God will seem at first an appalling scandal;
Just as Jesus seemed a dangerously subversive Sabbath-breaker
Whom only uneducated fishermen, tavern talkers and a few bluestockings of dubious morals
Were likely after all to take very seriously,
To the most devoutly religious people in Jerusalem in Jesus's day.
Let the dead continue to bury the dead as they did then,
And let the living dead awaken and greet with joy the ever-living.

8

Always, wherever, whatever, however,
When I am able to resist
For once the constant pressure of the failure to exist,
Let me remember
That truly to be man is to be man aware of Thee
And unafraid to be. So help me God.

9

Christ was hung up to die between two thieves;
    And much mirth did the spectacle arouse
    Among the populace who'd heard Him say
    That He was One with God and their true King:
Look at Him now! It's strange that God allows
His Son to come to grief like that, they cried;
All such pretentious scoundrels end that way!
God's Son! Whoever heard of such a thing?
There hangs our King, a thief on either side!

For Christ was executed by the general will,
    Officially and popularly execrated, thrust
    Out of this life in ignominy, put
    To death outside the righteous City's wall:
An unsuccessful outlaw and a grim warning to all
Who would disturb Pax Romana with thought,
With the unmanly doctrine that all men
Should love fraternally their fellow man
Instead of warrior-like despising him.

10

Though towards the suburbs the city becomes wan
And dark with the weariness of the women who have to queue
Outside the horse-butcher's or for the home-bound bus,
On even the busiest days the sun sometimes paints propaganda
For the possibility of the Kingdom of Heaven on earth
Over the prices scrawled in white on the shops' plate-glass,
And the attic window-boxes above the market
Offer tribute of happy beauty to the omniscient Heavenly Eye.

c. 1950

THE SECOND COMING

In the dream theatre, my seat was on the balcony, and the auditorium had been partly converted into an extension of the stage. Several little Italia Conti girls ran forward past my seat from somewhere behind me, and one of them clambered over a ledge and seemed to fall (she must have been suspended by a wire) to the floor below. She gave a small scream: 'God is born!' On a little nest of straw on the ground close to where she had fallen, a baby doll suddenly appeared. At the same moment, a hideous scarecrow-like Svengali-Rasputin figure, mask larger than life-size and painted rather like an evil clown in a Chagall apocalypse, playing an enormous violin which somehow contrived also to suggest the scythe of Father Time, rose upon the circular dais in the centre of the auditorium. I realized at once that he was the personification of Sin and Death. 'When I play my tune, there is not a single one of you all who does not join the dance!' I was most painfully moved by the strident yet cajoling music and by the knowledge that what he had said was nothing less than the truth. Everything then began to move around confusingly. On the darkened stage, thick black gauze curtains had lifted, and one saw a squat black cross outlined against a streak of haggard white storm light across the back-cloth sky. Finally, the stage was full of menacing, jerkily swaying bogies, thick black distorted crucifixes with white slit eyes, covered with newspaper propaganda headlines, advancing towards the audience like a ju-ju ceremonial dance of medicine men. At the very end of the performance, a clearly ringing voice, representing the light which must increasingly prevail against these figures, cried: 'All propaganda that is not true Christian revolutionary propaganda is sickness and falsehood!'

c. 1950

A LITTLE ZODIAC FOR KATHLEEN RAINE

ARIES

Augustly awe-inspiring creature, whose famed Fleece
And cornucopiae-like Mosaic Horns of gold
Foreglimmer from afar the Great Year's harvest of pure peace;

Entangled in the thicket of the World Roof-Tree's dense leaves,
Immortal Ram, like Absalom dangling his slain youth's gold
Caught on an oak bough in the wood, for whom the Father grieves:

Suspended is your splendour in the domed space of the dark,
O scion of the sacred flock, in scripture spelt of gold
The legend of your leap ever recorded in mid-arc.

GEMINI

Each looks towards his brother and sees yet one more than him,
In friendship with each other sealed, they both remain unmet.
Their eyes still gaze towards the misty heights that precede Time;
Whatever one of them looks on, the other will forget.

TAURUS

Lunging Beast,
Bulging hide,
Fatalist
Ruby-eyed,
In coiled maze
Or sordid ring
Blood betrays
Butcher King.

CANCER

This fishy thing that sideways crawls
    But neither swims nor flies,
Elects to dwell in shellac walls
    And has protruding eyes.

About this sign I've nothing more to say.
I'm not born in or near it anyway.

LEO

No smaller than the Sun amidst the mid-day sky,
With oriflamme-spiked ruff of red mane stands
      This calm carnivorous King
     On tufted turf among
  The gentle field-flowers of his wild domain;
        And brands
     With tawny patch of scorch
  The green herbaceous velvet ground on which
The leonine supremacy is thus embroidered plain.

VIRGO

Where waterfalls and willows and interstices
  Of nightblue undissolved by day perform
The offices of backcloth and of trellises
  For briars in bloom to climb upon and swarm
     With emblems white and red
     About her uncoiffed head,
A young lady sequestered and immaculate,
Scarce asking whether any less hermetic state
     Await her, may be seen
     Plaiting a garland green
For Chastity to wear when she is dead.

LIBRA

O unjust man behold
How she must stand blindfold
Who personates the word
Justice, and in one hand
Wield naked sword as wand
Who with the other lets
Two equidistant plates
Dangle, while she forgets
Which yours is, which your fate's.

SCORPIO

    Here is a beastly jewel!
    Its tail can cause to groan.
    If scorned or feared it will
    Lurk under every stone
On the wide avenue towards Success
That seems to lead out of the wilderness.

SAGITTARIUS

I, Father, with my little Bow
Plant my munitions high and low;
Trusting, should they shoot up by night
The buried dragon will not bite.

CAPRICORN

Alone alike elect on heights of prophecy
    And exiled on the darkling plain of Chance,
Trailing the guilt that makes worlds wildernesses, he
    Performs his tragi-comic limping dance.

AQUARIUS

This burly bent, much burdened figure, who
Is he, I wonder, and what does he do?
Old Atlas, is it, staunchly straining still?
Atlas? Oh, no. This man's about to spill
Into some hold from his pot lots of sea.
Of sea? I see. – Unless it's Hippocrene. –
But it's not pink, I think, as that would be.
Perhaps it's just plain drinking-water? – Yes,
That probably would be the wisest guess.

PISCES

    They glitter, but they sing
    Seldom; rather than swim
They slide through that thick element the waves
    Roof in; swing the slow loop

      Of a lassoo through which
      In reflex they can swoop
      And thus with cunning catch
In their own track themselves. And then they sweep
          Down sheerest slopes
          And swerve
          Round sharpest curves
   And leap abruptly up, like swift sea-larks,
To burst through their sky's rolling clouds of foam
And briefly warble, before sinking home,
A stave of bubble-song; to which no sailor harks.

p. 1950

AFTER TWENTY SPRINGS

How vehemently and with what primavernal fire
Has there been voiced the seasonal conviction that new birth,
Aurora, revolution, resurrection from the dead,
Palingenesia, was about to be, was near,
Must surely come. Of course it shall, it must.
The bones shall live, the dust awake and sing.
I hope and trust I shall be there. But seriously,
If it has not already come, and it is we
Who lack the faith to recognize it, if the sun
That shone upon the just and unjust does not shine
This spring upon the risen dead, then what a long
Business this getting born again must be. We dead
Are living, really; and the living are asleep,
Lawrence; and gladly in their sleep they read
The Twentieth Anniversary reprint of your writings, stirred
Fitfully for a while to more impassioned dream.
For many love you now, Redbeard, and wish you had not died
In bitterness, before your time. On dead man's isle,
We who survived you and are struggling still today
(If very feebly and unostentatiously)
For life, more life, new life, fine warm full-blooded life,
Are reconciled with patience, on commemorating you.

p. 1950

LIGHT VERSE

AN UNSAGACIOUS ANIMAL
or THE TRIUMPH OF ART OVER NATURE

The Master of *The Monarch of the Glen*
Was making once a sojourn 'neath the roof
Of an admiring Peer, Lord Rivers, when
Occasion rose which put to sternest proof
That intrepidity and tact which had
Secured for him familiar intercourse
With Nature's greatest gentlemen and made
Him reverenced alike by man and horse.
For while his fellow guests one afternoon
Were raptly gleaning Landseer's dicta, sound
Of lawless canine truculence, which soon
Became intolerable, made him pound
With sudden fist the tea table and cry:
'What insolence of importuning cur,
What rumour as of kennel mutiny
Is this? Shall Man the Master then defer
To a hound's ill-bred fury? Follow me:
Let's to the stable-yard whence these barks come,
And I will prove to you that Art can be
A force more sure than blows to make dogs dumb.
I who not seldom with forbidding gaze
Have known how to persuade huge Highland kine
To emulate the Southern cow's sweet ways
And made whole shaggy herds hang on the line,
Will there, if it amuse you, demonstrate
A sovereign power yet stronger than the eye's:
That of the Human Voice, which is so great
That it can Lions strike dumb with surprise!'
Some of the painter's intimates had been
Already privileged to hear his skill
In imitation of the less obscene
Sounds with which animals are wont to fill
The atmosphere of jungle, swamp and glade
When moved by meal-time longings or by bliss
To self-expression. For some years he'd made
The feat his study, and could bellow, hiss,
Roar, bark, snarl, with a realism which
Was quite astonishing, till in no part
Of all Victoria's realms was known so rich

A repertoire of Imitative Art
As that perfected by the great R.A.
In view of this, it hardly will seem queer
To any that all present there that day
Excitedly accompanied Landseer
Out to the stables, craning and agog,
To watch him stride, masterfully serene,
Towards the kennel out of which the dog
Surveyed defiantly the crowded scene
With jaws aslaver and keen fangs exposed.
Then, not without surprise, they saw him fall
Down on his knees! It was by some supposed
This was in order piously to call
On Providence for aid; but they were wrong.
His aim was to confront the renegade
As man to man (or – dog to dog?). Ere long
That wretched animal's vile din was made
To seem the fretful yap of Pekinese
By an appallingly hyenine bark
Which evidently made the dog's blood freeze,
For his rebellion ceased at once, and stark
Terror replaced the murder in his eye.
The artful mimicry of Landseer proved
So awful that the beast which recently
Had rivalled Cerberus himself, now moved
With such violence away from the advance
Of the superior barker, that his chain
Snapped, and he crossed the yard swift as a glance,
Leaped o'er the wall, and never was again
Seen anywhere on Lord Rivers' estate.
Landseer, on rising, found that only one
Of those who'd watched him still remained to fête
His triumph. 'Twas his host, who breathed: 'What fun!
How good of you to teach them how, dear old
Dog-lover! But come now, your tea's quite cold.'

p. 1949

LE DÉJEUNER SUR L'HERBE: A PASTORAL

LA BELLE-DAME-SANS-MERCERIE:

Thank goodness, *mes chers amis*, that you do not
Object to *negligée*. I was far too hot.
It's such a pleasure to find now and then
Friends who do not just look like gentlemen.

LE DUC DE PROFIL:

Dear *Dame*, we are most flattered by the candour
It pleases you to show towards us and our
Best feelings, I assure you, are excited
By this display of favour. I'm delighted
To find it was not a mistaken hunch
I had about you. Now let's have our lunch.

LE COMTE D'À CÔTÉ:

Let's hope no herd of any kind will pass.
Not only cows, you know, lunch upon grass.

LA DEMOISELLE AU FOND DE LA TOILE:

I should imagine that huge meal they've had'll
Make them too sleepy much to want to paddle.

c. 1950

THE DECAY OF DECENCY

When Man becomes what he calls 'adult' and stops taking himself too seriously
He is apt to get oddly pedantic about the proprieties while even more loose-mouthed than ever
Should anyone foolishly tarnish their honour by calling his into dispute.
A jealous prude, this much (though, alas! unavailingly) chipped blockhead
Is always able to preserve his dignity and our decorum in even the most embarrassing situations
Provided the common law still allow him a remnant of the old apron-cloth with which to camouflage his flyblown shame.
Proud resident of no mean or indecent city, he can be trusted always to think of shielding his neighbour
Who may although bald be still nevertheless immature,
From the horror of being debauched by an unwonted glimpse
Of the unavoidably material source of the carnal life whose too often notorious facts
Are not, when unvarnished, the kind one can mention in public, in verse or to even, of course, one's own wife,
So deep-rooted, apparently, is our innate sense of reverence for whatever must never be spoken of
Till all representatives of the gallant little Sex the Serpent seduced have withdrawn to another room,
Or as resoundingly and full-bloodedly as you like so long as it's only in good clean working-class fun!
Should some contradiction begin to appear in the bourgeois conventions, it can be explained
As due to the obstinate whims of our animal nature, but nowadays not, if you please,
By referring to what we no longer regard as a dogma, our dreadfully common first parents' Fall.
Take away a man's responsibility to our self-respect, and you may rob him of half his charm.

c. 1950

WITH A CORNET OF WINKLES

(VERS DE CIRCONSTANCE)*

O bravo! For a *maladif*, mandarin-miened, mauve melody-man
With a glittering, lissom, pat-prattling lute –
Que c'est beau! as he lo! hums and haws,

And soon again haws, then heigh-ho! how he hums
And whilom most becomingly strums
On his poignantly Quince-flavoured lute!

Ah! what is it, the sensitive rattling of lute-players? What
Is it that makes them persist undeterred by the glees
Of the slums' glum goloshes-clad mummers

Who in average summers become far more raucous than we
Ever dared (my shy mandolin!) be: for much cow-heel and hot
Cake – nothing rare, just plain fare – ever wait

For glee-singers to guzzle as soon as they're through
With their dreary commercial drum-dub rub-a-dub (there's the rub!)
But in Hartford all's mum for a mo

I mean moment: as finicking wryly with *curedent* that one
Still remaining Romanticist who's fully weaned of such pap
(If from involute vocables glibly redundant mayhap

Not so drastically weaned as he might be!), the Great
Gabbo, sole plum among lute-players left
To preserve some bravura or any finesse and who yet

Would never have dreamed of abandoning strumming unless
He'd been vexed (as he has) by the pip of some fruit
Among molars illicitly lingering, – ceases

Perforce to oblige with the teetering tittery-tum
Ti-tumtum titivating of his lacquered lute:
Willy-nilly sit silent. Is not the hush rum?

---

*This tribute to Wallace Stevens was written before he won the Bollingen Prize in 1950.

225

Yet withal scarcely *more* rum, – and rum quite a lot
Will agree it does seem, – than that one should these rum rumin-
Ations style (aptly? or do you think otherwise? Ah!) philosophical:

Though that's what this old-master lute-master opines
That his airy (Hurray! Tipperary for ever!), his endlessly
Varied *echt*-lyrical lute-ditties are! 'Tra-la-la!'

One might here interject, without being inept. I had not,
I confess, ever fully imagined how rum they might be
(Ruminations), if once but a *maladif*, canny, a hey-de-ho whole-

Heartedly cogitatorial *maître-de-luth*
Were to get *un vrai goût* for Philosophy. What as we but
A brief moment ago were about to enquire: What the Hell, O but
   What

Are the, or rather, what *is* (put it plainly) the point
Of this perfectly awful attempt at a parody, piffling without
Doubt to the point of provoking a petulant pout

Of disdainful demur (a mere *moue*, that will do)?
Tootle-loo, Tilly-loo, for no earthly *Poetic What's-What & Who's-
Who* will now ever again deign so much as to look at these too

Caca-caca-cacophonous doodlings of mine
And not think them impudent snook-cocking. Candidly, look you,
   what do
People put up so patiently with them for? Answer: *Nein, nein,*

Far from it, they don't, don't deceive yourself; and what is MORE
'The Corn's Blue!'

p. 1950

THREE CABARET SONGS

1   A BRIEF BALLAD OF THE PARALYSED UPPER LIP

Oh, the Bland Maid of Kensington,
    She Lived there in Sin
With a Bluff Ex-Young Ladies' Man
    With a Permanent Grin.

Oh, the Life that he Led her there
    Was Well-dressed, but so Slow
That she Longed to Abandon him
    Yet could never quite Let go.

Oh, he Grinned at her Frailty,
    She smiled at his Pride!
And Long though this lasted
    They neither of them Died

But Continued in Kensington
    To Adorn every Day
The Saloons of Three Locals
    Well-known to be Gay,

Where her Blandness, his Bluffness
    Continued to the End
To Convince all Acquaintances
    That She was his Friend!

Oh, what really is Dreary
    About all such Brave Pairs
Is that Being Godforsaken
    Is the Least of their Cares.

2   WHAT A WAY TO WALK INTO MY PARLOUR,
    LITTLE MAN!

Ere the hour for aperitif's over
    Take care your tongue doesn't work too loose,
Though if you want wit, you're in clover!
    This young woman, you see, is no blue goose
Nor green-stocking, by Jove!

If you're looking for someone to lie to
   About all the fictitious feelings
You feel you should feel, my reply to
   Your ogling is, I have no dealings
With people unreal.

Keep your labels for people who need them;
   I cannot be pigeonholed neatly.
As for your ideals, I exceed them
   So far, I surpass them completely
Please beat a retreat.

Let me tell you that all this persistence
   Is worse than absurd, and I must say
What I see of your mode of existence
   Inspires in me only disgust. Lay
Off, Less-than-the-dust!

3   SIZZLING SECLUSION: RUMBA

Don't murmur or mut-
Ter: No, no! or: Tut-tut!
I'm deep in the rut
   Your scent rouses.
It's too hot for a hut
Or a bungalow but
I've had such a glut
   of pent-houses.

I could just make do
With a wigwam for two
Though I'm not going to stew
   In a leather one:
One of muslin instead,
Draped around a deep bed,
   A soft feather one . . .

c. 1950

ENCOUNTER WITH SILENCE
POEMS 1950

(1998)

GIVE UP DEAD WORDS

Salt sea can swallow all who thirst
    while our vocabulary
On losing its once saline virtue's not become
    more fresh.
With froth-flecked lips we mouth
    our pithy apothegms and try
Not to put on thereby too great a weight
    for our frail flesh.

w. 1950

STELE

The most enduring final statement
Is the silence we don't hear.
It digests everything.

Silence that's never known this side of death.
Try for a moment to experience it.
You may hear Nothing; but that's not the Silence.

For Nothing just makes its own unquiet noise,
A sort of famished gasping in the eardrums,
An ever-ending syllable of suppressed anguish.

w. 1950

TERMINAL

Poetry? I too dislike it . . .' (M. Moore)

The most enduring massive statement
Is the silence no-one hears.
It sums up everything.

There is no silence on this side of death.
Listen to any muted moment
When all is quiet. You will not hear it.

Yet it is under all and overhead
Not less indubitable than the firmament.
It is itself the Word.

It affords vast relief
To recollect that it is being spoken
Making inept all tongues that would compete.

w. 1950

FRAGMENT FROM AN UNFINISHED/UNPUBLISHED POEM

Among the citizens inhabiting this City,
One hungers, labours, seeks for food and shelter;
One climbs the escalators, waits in queues, one seeks for faces
That are alive (here all wear masks); one fights
Amongst these citizens for life and breath and bread,
One fights with a set face, one fights and falls
Asleep, alone, in a hired room, upon a bed
Uncounted strangers have already slept in – Halt!
There is no way to overthrow this City;
There is no tunnel dug in sleep beneath
This City through which you might find a way
To creep to any Paradise that would not fade
Like rainbow mists transformed to soiled bedcoverings
At stroke of automatic dawn. Yet halt!
Turn, and consider, see yourself a moment, stare
Into the glass I bring you. It reflects
     You. See how fair
The centre of this City lies in summer in the sun
That –

w. 1950

UNTITLED

Mist and damp
Roll down lanes up roads
Dark is day
Sounds all wrapped up [are muffled]
The heart's pain
Knows no remittance
Horizon's bare
Time immobile
I who know no-one
Am turning a stranger
Have long been too silent
Shall stay [keep] silent longer
Whatsoever I say
I remain unexpressed
I believed in meaning
    Who am I?

w. 1950

SATURNALIA

(fragment)

Beneath broad sunlight bent and sweating, chilled
In spite of all our garments by the zero underneath
Upon perdition pondering, rehearsing inwardly
Long rigmaroles of self-defence and calumny, we go
The tortuous hard way towards uncertainty out of
The pit of ages. Harsh is our music. Masks
Like snail-shells are become the smooth and whorled
Concealment we excrete to hide our softness from ourselves.
We shake if silence falls like withered leaves, we fall
A-shaking in mid-winter's silent blast: therefore great noise
We used always to quieten us, crescendo of uproar
To trample down all elegiac echoes, cog-wheels, clogs,
Bad bells and beating blades and drums, drums, bleating tongues
To blend in undertone behind/beneath the screech distorting speech
With falsehood's rising passion for dominion over all

    ★   ★   ★   ★

And reaffirming thus by yearly festival in play
That the whole building of Man's earthly City
Is under rule of powers underneath him
Controlled and armed by the martial law of Pluto.
[Briefed copywriters meanwhile make brisk sales-talk of the tale
Of terror or contempt that each day spills.
With eyes averted from the holy stars, and hands
Clenched tightly round the weapon one must bear
If one would make one's way about this world
We trudge unwillingly the deepworn tracks]
That wind around these walled meadows
Site of what once were annually waged [played] games
Uniting Earth and Hell in common daylight
(And seldom guess what heavy chains we bear)

★   ★   ★   ★

A different version of the bracketed lines [. . .] appears below:

Meanwhile briefed copywriters make brisk sales-talk of the tale
Of terror and contempt that each day tells
And with our eyes averted from the stars,
And hands tight clenched about the weapon one must bear
If one would make one's way about this world
We trudge weary to judgement each on his own winding track

★   ★   ★   ★

Another draft (undated) of the opening 13–14 lines is in the McFarlin Library at the University of Tulsa:

Beneath the sun's rays bent and sweating, cold
Despite thick garments because zero reigns within;
Upon perdition pondering, unwinding without end
The rigmaroles of calumny and self-defence, they go
The tortuous hard way towards uncertainty out of
The pit of ages past, making harsh music. Masks
Are on their faces grown like snailshells, brittle, smooth
Concealment they excrete to hide their softness from themselves.
Should silence fall, they shake like withered leaves,
They fall as tho' blown down by winter's blasts;
                    therefore great noise

Is needed then to quieten them, ~~outbursting uproar~~
~~Crescendo-ing to smother every elegiac echo,~~
                              crescendoing uproar
Alone restores their calm; they crave the crash
~~Of guns, the whirr of wheels~~
Of cannonfire, the whirr of wheels, the blare of brass and bells . . .

w. 1950

THE BOMB-SITE ANCHORITE

Fragment of an abandoned poem

In Homage to Alan Clodd,
Faithful Friend and Publisher

If now to memory's retina his face
Returns to tremble into brief relief
More frequently than most do, that might be
Because of the abnormal evening glare
By which his features were so keenly lit
When first I focused eyes on him, a light
That forced, as though in search of dirt and guilt,
Its way into the least pothole or crack
Of every surface that it fell upon,
Making all that I saw seem as though scoured
By the flushed sky's abrasive radiance
And then on my attentive notice thrust with an
Especially didactic purpose; so that when
He first lurched into view on that canal-bank
Out of the indigo beneath an iron bridge
And then stood looking up to where I sat
Some feet above him on a pile of paving-stones,
It may have seemed to him my eyes beheld him
With an unusual famished zest. He met my gaze
With blank, unyielding imperturbability
Which at once made him an enigma to me . . .

w. 1948–9, p. 1990

A POST-CARD FROM VENICE TO T.S.E.

The pigeons and the floating population fraternize,
Or seem to; though birds get too deep in grain to notice class.
To pose among them Baedeker in hand, with a cigar,
Wishing some Princess predatory as Volupine would pass.
       P. S.
Lucky for B. it was not on the bell-tower
He was together with her in that fell hour.

w. 1950

WHO ARE THE ORTHOSEXUAL?

How unkind are those models of their kind
The heterogeneous orthodox who would forbid
Me to express a warmth springing, not from my mind
But from the blood, and force it to stay hid
Behind a false hard heart like those they wear
Upon their sleeves, as on their chests crêpe hair.

L'HOMME ASSEZ MOYEN (pas très sensuel)

He did not care for too tempestuous cries
Nor for the passions that cause jaws to lather.
He looked upon the world with wry dry eyes
And saw it was not very, nay, but rather.

w. 1950

OTHER POEMS

1950–1956

QU'EST-CE QUE LA DÉCADENCE?

Jeune homme qui n'as peut-être connu que vingt-cinq étés
Entendu tout nu sur l'herbe verte fraîche d'une prairie
Non loin de ces quelques camarades ou plutôt connaissances
Qui ne sont pas tous également beaux mais tout de même
Assez agréables à voir du point de vue du poète
Ordinairement privé de corps
Jeune homme splendidement nu au bord de l'eau dans ce pré tout près
De l'ancienne ville érudite et triviale de plus en plus comblée:
J'aurais dit que de tout ce qu'une civilisation aussi fière que la nôtre
De ses traditions aristocratiques sinon socratiques
Pourrait montrer aujourd'hui encore comme représentatif d'elle
Tu étais un des exemples les plus excellentement beaux.
Si tu n'avais pas ouvert la bouche
Pour causer et ricaner avec tes camarades, je veux dire copains
Qui vous égalent tous dans la grossièreté et l'étroitesse de l'esprit.

p. 1950

YES, YOU!

Stealthy and utterly vain, insane
small nagging voice,
You go on and on, and on, repeating
your wretched obstinate
Unforgivable lies,
Your impotent, impudent accusation
Your little nastinesses and
your filthy imaginings,
On, and on, and on,
Dogged enemy of all truth, and
beauty, and courage of the mind,
and honesty, and the will to
change, and the power to love,
You go on and on with your
stealthy whispering and your
guilty prudent repetition,
Because you are the contemptible
powerless victim
Of a blind raging power by

which you are possessed,
And you go on and on because you
could not even if you would, know
how to stop,
And perhaps in reality, you are
not utterly guilty in the end,
Because you are quite unconscious
of what you are doing, of what
you keep having to say
Over and over and over again,
And quite unconscious of whose
victim it is you are.
Be assured that the silence which
Preceded and follows you is overwhelmingly
vast and deep and just.

w. 1950, p. 2007

UNTITLED

Yes. Thank you. Now I can start the day
Writing this poem. You have shown me the way
I have no longer any gift to give
Yet I must it seems write poems, one has to live.
For a long while I've been piling up a lot
Of things I badly wanted to say but could not.
I've lost my sense of form, I have no style.
No nostalgic melody, no magic, only bile.

w. 1950, p. 2007

REMEMBERING THE DEAD

In the mornings, the day-labourers must set to work once more, and daily tasks be newly undertaken or resumed; and they who work must disregard their usual disillusionment.

'We shall not see a culmination of these labours; our handiwork will not last long nor our success outlive us; our successors taking over what we've done will as like as not disparage it; and if we build houses, they are for strangers to live in for a little while or for the next War to destroy.

'Meanwhile we lose ourselves with a will in what we do today. We tacitly discourage those who would recall too many things or pay too much attention to the future. (All that we cannot see is very small and unimportant). We will put guilt upon them and they shall be silenced.'

And in the mornings, nevertheless, in such a year as this when rain has early in the season put an end to all hope of another extravagant Summer (since a year or two ago an unexpectedly Elysian climate did for once tranform the country with such profusion and intensity of flower-hues and foliage that for the first time many millions were amazed by earth's magnificence); on wet summer mornings, when electric light has to be turned on in the offices in the City, and listlessness and resignation walk the streets, some of the workers (no one knows how many but they may be very numerous) are disturbed by thoughts they have not thought themselves, distracted at their work as though by voices from beneath the chilly ground.

Think, ah! think how vastly they outnumber us by now, the populations of the underworld! How immemorially have they been accumulating there, and how enormous must their number be whom there are none now living to remember. Think how they too may all be working.

I think they think of us – Oh, how incalculably much more than ever we think of them! We scarcely think of them at all; we all prefer soon to forget; if we remember, it is only with regret. They think of us, they think of all of us; they think critically, no doubt, perhaps constructively, with more understanding than we have. Perhaps all day, all night, uninterruptedly.

It may be that only they fully realize that there is no other way of solving the problems of life and death than by thinking about them always.

We do not know the whole Truth; we think we know the Truth. We cannot know it, yet we must. We must seek the Truth we do not know, nor can know while we are still searchers here. Those who have neither curiosity nor doubts are the only real dead.

w. 1950, p. 1959

HAIKU

My own sophistry
Is the dark mistress whose will
Makes me deny her.

w. 1950, p. 1996

Urban Leaves After War
In Holborn leaves float
Down to wild grass among blitzed
Walls from brickdust trees.

w. 1950, p. 1996

Ambiguous Haiku 1
My love's existence
Is mystery. I love him
Through mirror that hides.

w. 1950, p. 1995

Cartesian Haiku 2
I 5 must 7
Tell 5 all in 3 (2 (1))
Ergo: Cogito.

w. 1950, p. 1995

METROPOLIS BY NIGHT

And often I have gone out towards midnight
Through streets of dwelling-houses and apartment blocks
Behind the rows window-squares of which
Numberless tired executives prepared for bed
While past street-corner lamps dogs' pensive escorts
Tugged them on leads along their late patrol;
Through districts full of narrow shady gardens
With strips of black lawn stretching from french windows,
To sooty shrubberies, a seedy tree or two,
Laburnum to o'erhang the pavement pilgrim
When summer has transformed these dormitories
By splashing blossom-sprays across their drabness
For a few weeks each year. And have walked on
Until I came out on an open hillside,
A public park space from which one looks down
Upon the mighty Nocturne of the Capital
Whose twinkling panorama's spread below:
Arena sprawling dazed with concrete gloom,
Freckled with sparks and smeared with arc-lights' gleams
With crawling glares and melancholy glazes,
Slow-sinking monuments and stoic light-houses,
Mile after mile of tenements and terraces,
League after league of palaces and parks.
Here hover hazes of green sick-ward light
And there red neon blurrs flick on and off;
In fixed directions avenues stretch sleekly
To disappear in ultimate uncertainty
In regions where the bottom of the sky
Mingles with fumes that rise from the abyss . . .
Fearful and wonderful, the sleepless monster,
Most Sphinx-like cities Megalometropolis,
Absorbing in its labyrinthine maws
All that has ever been or could be said of it.
The roaring labyrinth enisled upon Night's floor
Teems with such multitudinous noctambulists
That none now fear they'll meet the Minotaur.

p. 1954

NIGHT-WATCHER'S RUMINATIONS

At night, I often sit an hour out thus,
Attentive to a dull insistent roar –
Or not a roar, rather a kind of cry, and yet
No cry, for that would be a sound too clear
And what I hear might come from underground,
It is so thick, and hollow-sounding too,
And yet not resonant at all, but harsh and dead,
If dead is not too definite a word;
And whatsoever this dull urgent rumour be,
It holds me spellbound by the hour and more,
While, I with a great longing to be free
From doubt about what it can signify,
Gaze up through a small skylight's panes and see
Nothing at all of any small still star
That may be burning in the black neglected sky,
See not even that black square the window frames,
As though all sight lay blinded in my ears.

And then, returning suddenly again
To consciousness of my immediate self,
I've had a moment's glimpse into the depths
Of solitary absence through which stray
Our tiring restless bodies and the dead things that are found
Strewn round them on all sides in this unanimated dream:
Dread has distracted us away from what is here
And what we are when faithful to the truth,
And so we suffer hopelessly the sullen apathy
That reigns on a deserted theatre's stage
Where we all night must play out our null roles.

But listen, it begins again, I think.
On many other nights I have heard this,
This sound of distant rioting, the angry voices' sound,
Popular uproar from afar, and crowds from underground
Simmering upwards to invade the city streets
With hell-hoards hoarsely clamouring for blood!
For blood! for justice! for revenge! What is their cry?
Do you not hear some faint far echo of it?

Another Voice:

                    Yes, I hear.
I too have known those ominous night noises. You must not
Be too disturbed by them. Remember fear,
And do not be afraid of it. If you can hear
The echoes of your own anxiety, if you can bear
To listen to that rumour, then you known at least that dread
Of hearing what you fear has not yet deafened you.

Crowd Voice:

Fear, fear, you speak of fear.
What is this fear? The fear we dare not fear,
The fear of fear itself, of others' fears,
That fear which ends in passionate untruth,
Self-justifying falsehood without end; daemonic fear
Of individual guilt, of being caught, of being wrong,
And fear of failure or of being found a fool, and fear
Of anything that might contrast with me
And thus reveal my insufficiency,
My lack, my weakness, my inferiority,
In showing up my difference from itself;
Fear of uncertainty and loss, fear of all change,
Fear of all strangeness and all strangers; and above all else
                                        [the fear
Of Love, of being loved, of being asked for love,
Of being loved and knowing one has no love to return;
Fear of forgiveness –
And the exhausting fear of Death and Mystery,
The huge intolerable Mystery of Everything;
And fear of Nothing,
Nothing, Nothing –

Nothing, fear of Nothing, absolutely Nothing . . .

p. 1954

NIGHT THOUGHTS

1

Night Thoughts. Night Music. Now out of buried labyrinths and caves of the town-dweller's anxious dream, we move away till we emerge into the open air of a secluded country-side, where we shall find again the calm night world of Nature.

2

Nature, the Earth, Unconsciousness and Death. We are drawn back and down towards them in the Night.

3

Nocturnal Music. Meditations in dark gardens. Gradually forming thoughts pursued in gardens by such solitary strollers as may now find themselves outdoors, taking a turn or two before retiring; taking a breath or two of fresher air.

4

Walking there without a predetermined object; in the starlight; at a slow pace, uncertainly. Standing still from time to time as though to listen, yet not attending to any clearly determined sound.

5

The Night Music drifts away into remote serenity, leaving the hearer standing still to listen to the stillness of the garden, waiting to hear what may be born out of the stillness.

6

He stands still and seems to listen to some unknown distant thing; something that may be reaching him from . . . from where? What echo from beyond what last horizon?

7

There is nothing to be heard. The garden is quite still. There is only silence in the darkness.

8

Yet there is seldom experienced anywhere on the inhabited earth, for more than a moment or two at a time, such a thing as silence. For Silence is something we imagine only, an idea that we have of what a complete absence of sound would be like. Real Silence is the message spoken to us that we fear most of all to hear. What is usually called silence is most often no more really than a confused medley of diminutive sounds to which it would be too tiring to pay conscious attention.

9

Everywhere about us, day and night, goes on the eddying stream of murmur: little drifting sighs and rumblings, whispers, coughing, whistles, moans. Goes on rising from the earth, the home of life, birthplace of restlessness, where all the rhythms meet, and cross, and intertwine uninterruptedly.

10

Night music of mysterious hazard. Dream-fugues; variations on fortuitous themes; intricate tracery unwinding like designs drawn in a trance across the taut sky of the universal Ear.

11

Decrepid gust-blown tinkling of a crumbling pagoda's bells.

12

Intensely complex tightscrewed-up tattoo of tiny drums.

14

Velvet-padded hammering of the life-blood's changing pulse.

15

The pulse of changing life is the deep underlying constant. And the Unchanging also is a pulse, flowing through all that lives; a single pulse.

16

The changes and the pauses and occasional recurrence of abrupt irregularity make sound-patterns we overhear but never really hear. Our hearing intercepts no more than one bar at a time. These patterns are upon a scale not measurable in hours. Attention wanders; thinking intervenes.

17

The boundaries of the senses are not often clearly realised. The Infra and the Ultra are fields easily forgotten. Out of hearing stays unthought-of; out of sight is out of mind. And yet, how haunted we all are.

18

The night-walker, on a terrace in the garden, unaccompanied, hardly aware of it, half hopes to overhear – that haunting. Something that hovers, hovers maybe only just beyond the rim. A thing no-one has thought of yet, that he has never heard.

19

The weir, the misty, distant falling waters of the weir among the meadows make a whispering that swells and faints but never quite subsides.

20

The City blazing with electricity just over the horizon flings its glare-reflection like a continual exclamation of astonishment into the sky, emitting intermittently a high-pitched filtered rumour of its roar.

21

The whisper drifts, the faint roar flutters in the upper air. Both rise and fall. And presently a sudden fine and quite unearthly whistling sound comes sliding down from emptiness, lasting no longer than it takes a shot star's dust to drift and disappear.

22

And then a brisk salt *wind blows from the other side of the black sleeping downs, and for a while the sea in its perpetual passion of frustration at the shore is to be heard vociferating.*

23

A salt breeze seems at least to bring some echo of that sound.

24

The sound of the sea's ebb and everlasting obstinate resurgence, from afar.

25

On a terrace in the garden, the solitary stroller has at last come to a standstill. He leans over a parapet and gazes out ahead into the starlit tranquil dark. He thinks of nothing. He lifts his head and gazes and is blind. His heart beating strikes midnight. He breathes in the night's ancientness and freshness, slowly absorbing strength and courage for a coming time when he will have to be reborn.

26

He thinks: '*I stand here staring into darkness and see nothing. Yet it is not nothing that stretches away there before me for ever in whatever direction I turn my eyes. It is the Universe. It is I myself that am nothing. Through my eyes, Nothing gazes at Reality, that utterly unqualifiable Something. And slowly the question rises out of nothing's depths, Can I be real if I remain unseen? If I speak out of my own inmost reality, shall I not be heard? Why should it be more extraordinary that I who am nothing may be none the less perceived, or that my speaking may be heard, than that nothingness should wonder, gaze and listen?*'

27

He speaks: '*I stand here speaking of my nothingness; and yet I am a man. It is my heart that speaks, abasing itself in dread before that colossal inscrutability; overwhelmed by the total evidence that what is there must be. I cannot ever understand how I am able to address what faces me; and yet I know I must somehow respond. From out of that profound star-strewn abyss of night-blue vacancy comes the command: "Lift up your heart"* . . . *I raise my spellbound head and face to face with what I cannot name I worship and adore. I lift my heart up and it speaks my prayer.*'

28

He asks: '*O Being, be! O be what faces me, to whom my heart may speak.*

'*Almightiness, O be the Face bent over me, O be aware and hear.*

'*Acknowledge me, accept me, and may my response responded to help me to know how we are thus akin.*

'*O be the One, that I may be no more alone in knowing that I am. Let my lost loneliness be illusory. Allow to me a part in Being, that I may thus be part of One and All.*'

29

He reflects: *'I am a man of a benighted century, famished for light and praying out of darkness in the dark. I do not really any longer know what praying means. To pray by rote, repeating time-deconsecrated words, seems vanity to me. I cannot bear to hear myself repeating words of prayer that might be mumbled and not meant. Men of this time seem not to know that there is meaning, nor to know what Being is. All of us talk and talk of all and everything, and shut ourselves up in ourselves, and with the curtain of our words shut out the fact that we are blind and dumb. We are afraid of silence, and afraid to look each other in the eye. Talking, we do not speak to one another; and one who speaks of many others seldom fails to disparage them all indiscriminately. Many speeches are made to urge men on to secure peace through understanding; but I will speak no more of speaking:*

Man has become above all the most indefatigable mimic of all the ways of being man that have ever been thought striking. Men imitate, and I am imitating them. I say 'Man' and 'men,' and thus invest abstractions with my own deficiencies, and think I somehow thus may be absolved of the whole failure to be truly man. I am a man. I cry out of my darkness. I could not cry if I were in complete despair.'

30

In the gardens of the Night, breathed on by newly freshened air, wrapped in the sheltering arms of shadows cast by slowly growing things, the consolation of profound serenity is to be found. Here, in forgetting by degrees the crude immediacies of day, talk's trivialities, the well-worn props and tokens of habitual routine, it is possible to recall to mind and to draw near again to something vastly fundamental, self-effacingly withdrawn, that has been lying there and is there all the time. It is an ever-new discovery to find it still awaiting our return, unsmiling, taciturn, yet limitlessly tolerant and all-comprehending, ready to take us back into obscurity, to share with us its poverty, to close and soothe our eyes.

31

Nature, the Earth, Unconsciousness and Death. We are drawn down and back towards them in the Night. But there is Vigil where the walker in the gardens stands and wonders in the dark.

32

Now the man who spoke aloud out of his dark into the darkness: to no-one, to someone? the mystery is not mine to solve that each must face alone – the man who said: 'I could not cry if I were in despair,' turns presently towards the lighted windows he had left behind him earlier, and slowly makes his way back through the sleeping garden's scented plants and dangling leaves to where await him wife and home and books and bed.

33

He begins to realise, as he goes, something has changed in him. The open air, the space about him had first stirred his heart, he lifted up his heart and it had opened, and the wind that blows when it will and comes from nowhere that we know and passes on as unaccountably, had inspired it with its own more vital, lighter, unrestricted and revivifying breath. Silence had delivered its essential message to him, and he had responded. Now he feels that he no longer has the need to reassure himself with words.

34

He goes back to the house, he returns to his wife and children. The children upstairs have long been asleep in the night-nursery. His wife is sitting where he left her, under the reading-lamp. She closes her book as he enters; looks up at her husband and smiles slowly at him, sleepily. He kisses her.

35

They are together. The primary division of the human family at night is that which sets those who are alone apart from those who are together. And yet, all are alone, as the man realised in the garden earlier; and all those who are isolated in their solitude are really alone only because they fail actually to realise the presence of other beings like themselves in the world.

36

Greetings to the solitary. Friends, fellow beings, you are not total strangers to us. We are closer to one another than we ever realise. Let us remember one another at night, even though we do not know each other's names.

p. 1956

SENTIMENTAL COLLOQUY

Daphne: The evening in the towns when Summer's over
Has always this infectious sadness, Conrad;
And when we walk together after rain
As darkness gathers in the public gardens,
There is such hopelessness about the leaves
That now lie strewn in heaps along each side
Of the wet asphalt paths, that as we turn
Back to the gardens' closing gates, we two,
Though in our early twenties still, seem elderly,
Both of us, Conrad, quietly quite resigned
And humbled into silence by the Fall . . .

Conrad: My dear, even your Mother is not elderly!
A woman is a girl or an old maid.
Yet I too do feel muted by this twilight;
For as it ever is the tendency
Of dusk to fall, and of past Summer's leaves,
At this time not of day but of the year,
To drop from trees, so surely must we fall
Silent if we take lovers' strolls in Autumn
Hoping we'll not fall out before the Spring.

Daphne: I hate you, Conrad, if that's what you're hoping!
I don't believe you think I'm a 'young girl'.
There is already in the air that hint of death
That when we breathe it makes us winter-wise.

Conrad: I do not think we to ourselves appear
A pair of fledglings. Let the middle-aged
Be sentimentally aware of their maturity
But let us not seem to invite their envy.
We shall be like them sooner than we think.

Daphne: There go a couple really bent with care:
Oh, look! how they both love each other, though,
In spite of –

Conrad: Why, you only speak your wish,
Daphne, you've not looked close enough!
A pair of ancient fish, my love, out of the deep:

            Mute and expressionless they loom and pass
            On their dim way across the ocean floor
            Of roaring London.

Daphne: Conrad, how long ago
            Did we sink drowned in it? Little you care
            For two such poor old phantoms. Sink or swim,
            We have no choice, since gravity descends
            And we although our love's still young
            And though true love's immortal, are as old
            And sink as fast as hearts of stone, if we pretend
            We care for no one but ourselves,
            Failing to recognize that that's who they are.

Conrad: You will become a Sybil, sweetheart, soon.

p. 1954

ELEGIAC IMPROVISATION ON THE DEATH OF PAUL ELUARD

A tender mouth a sceptical shy mouth
A firm fastidious slender mouth
A Gallic mouth an asymmetrical mouth

He opened his mouth he spoke without hesitation
He sat down and wrote as he spoke without changing a word
And the words that he wrote still continue to speak with his
    mouth:

Warmly and urgently
Simply, convincingly
Gently and movingly
Softly, sincerely
Clearly, caressingly
Bitterly, painfully
Pensively, stumblingly
Brokenly, heartbreakingly
Uninterruptedly
In clandestinity
In anguish, in arms and in anger,

In passion, in Paris, in person
In partisanship, as the poet
Of France's Resistance, the spokesman
Of unconquerable free fraternity.

And now his printed words all add up to a sum total
And it can be stated he wrote just so many poems
And the commentators like undertakers take over
The task of annotating his complete collected works.
Yet the discursivity of the void
Diverts and regales the whole void then re-enters the void
While every printed page is a swinging door
Through which one can pass in either of two directions
On one's way towards oblivion
And from the blackness looming through the doorway
The burning bush of hyperconsciousness
Can fill the vacuum abhorred by human nature
And magic images flower from the poet's speech
He said, 'There is nothing that I regret,
I still advance,' and he advances
He passes us Hyperion passes on
Prismatic presence
A light broken up into colours whose rays pass from him
To friends in solitude, leaves of as many branches
As a single and solid solitary trunk has roots
Just as so many sensitive lines cross each separate leaf
On each of the far-reaching branches of sympathy's tree
Now the light of the prism has flashed like a bird down the dark-blue
    grove
At the end of which mountains of shadow pile up beyond sight
Oh radiant prism
A wing has been torn and its feathers drift scattered by flight.

Yet still from the dark through the door shines the poet's mouth
    speaking.
In rain as in fine weather
The climate of his speaking
Is silence, calm and sunshine,
Sublime cloudburst and downpour,
The changing wind that breaks out blows away
All words – wind that is mystery
Wind of the secret spirit

That breaks up words' blind weather
With radiant breath of Logos
When silence is a falsehood
And all things no more named
Like stones flung into emptiness
Fall down through bad eternity
All things fall out and drop down, fall away
If no sincere mouth speaks
To recreate the world
Alone in the world it may be
The only candid mouth
Truth's sole remaining witness
Disinterested, distinct, undespairing mouth
'Inspiring mouth still more than a mouth inspired'
Speaking still in all weathers
Speaking to all those present
As he speaks to us here at present
Speaks to the man at the bar and the girl on the staircase
The flowerseller, the newspaper woman, the student
The foreign lady wearing a shawl in the faubourg garden
The boy with a bucket cleaning the office windows
The friendly fellow in charge of the petrol station
The sensitive cynical officer thwarting description
Like the well-informed middle-class man who prefers to remain
    undescribed
And the unhappy middle-aged woman who still hopes and cannot
    be labelled
The youth who's rejected all words that could ever be spoken
To conceal and corrupt where they ought to reveal what they
    name.

The truth that lives eternally is told in time
The laughing beasts the landscape of delight
The sensuality of noon the tranquil midnight
The vital fountains the heroic statues
The barque of youth departing for Cythera
The ruined temples and the blood of sunset
The banks of amaranth the bower of ivy
The storms of spring and autumn's calm are Now
Absence is only of all that is not Now
And all that is true is and is here Now
The flowers the fruit the green fields and the snow's field

The serpent dance of the silver ripples of dawn
The shimmering breasts the tender hands are present
The open window looks out on the realm of Now
Whose vistas glisten with leaves and immaculate clouds
And Now all beings are seen to become more wonderful
More radiant more intense and are now more naked
And more awake and in love and in need of love
Life dreamed is now life lived, unlived life realized
The lucid moment, the lifetime's understanding
Become reconciled and at last surpassed by Now
Words spoken by one man awake in a sleeping crowd
Remain with their unique vibration's still breathing enigma
When the crowd has dispersed and the poet who spoke has gone home.

PAUL ELUARD has come back to his home the world.

w. 1952, p. 1954

NIGHT THOUGHTS
Radiophonic Poem

(1956)

> Aber weh! es wandelt in Nacht, es wohnt, wie in Orcus Ohne
> Goettliches unser Geschlecht . . .
>
> HÖLDERLIN

But alas! our generation walks in night, dwells as in Hades, without the Divine . . .

1 THE NIGHTWATCHERS

[Voice A]
Let those who hear this voice become aware
The sun has set. O night-time listeners,
You sit in lighted rooms marooned by darkness,
And through dark ether comes a voice to bid you
All be reminded that the night surrounds you.

[Voice B]
Around us, as within us, battle rages.
Enveloped in obscurity, our enemy,
An emissary from the world of shadows,
Assails us from an unknown vantage-point,
Observes us unawares, usurps initiative
And uses it to inspire such distrust in us
That we must now suspect him everywhere.

[Voice C]
Let those who hear my voice become aware
That Night has fallen. We are in the dark.
I do not see you, but in my mind's eye
You sit in lighted rooms marooned by darkness.
My message is sent out upon the waves
Of a black boundless sea to where you drift,
Each in a separate lit room, as though on rafts,
Survivors of the great lost ship, *The Day*.

[Voice A]
Let those who hear our voices be aware
That Night now reigns on earth. Nocturnal listeners,
The time you hear me in is one of darkness,
And round us, as within us, battle rages.

[Voice B]
A war goes on within against the shadows.

[Voice D]
Who speaks tonight of war and battle? Go to bed!

[Voice E]
The war? What war? We've had too many wars.
The last War's over.

[Voice F]
                        Go to sleep. Put out
That light. The War is over now. It's late.
Why don't those people go to bed?

[Voice G]
                         Why must we hear
Night-voices always arguing about the state
The world's in? Why can't they forget about it?

[Voice E]
                            War?
Why must we always worry about that? Make them put out
Those lights.

[Voice F]
I'm O so sleepy . . . Now let's talk no more.

[Voice B]
The plane-trees in the court outside my window
Suspend their leaves between me and the street-lamp
That burns all night beside the entrance-arch;
And when the night-wind sets their branches waving
The shadows drift in tattered velvet bunches,
Thick-tangled rags of shadow are set swaying,
That dance like the black flames of a cold bonfire,
Leap up and are cast writhing on my bed.

[Voice C]
Anxiety and dream assail the watchman
Who waits in solitude for night to pass,
And shadowy multitudes with muffled tread
March menacingly round about the vigilant.

[Voice A]'
'Anxiety and dream,' the watchman said,
'A shadowy tumult that I cannot quell,
Stir round me like a wind through sleeping grass.'

[Voice B]
I cannot sleep. These nights are terrible. Yet there is now
Nothing more terrible to be afraid of: We have won
The worst; now we need fear no more, nor hide
Our disbelief in anyone.

[Voice D]
Can you believe,
O foreigner I'm thinking of, woman unknown to me,
Lying awake somewhere in Europe, can you now
Believe that you have friends lying alone,
In darkness, overseas, who can imagine how you feel
And wish, and wish – ah, what? What can be done
For anyone, what can we do alone, alas, how can
The lonely people without power, who hardly know
How best to help neighbours they know, help those
Who surely would be neighbours like themselves, if they but knew
How to break through the silence and the noise and the great night
Of all that is unknown to us, that weighs down in between
One lonely human being and another? Who can hear
My thoughts, or know how my heart grieves, or feel
That I just like themselves long to believe
That lonely human beings love each other?

[Voice E]
                                                                 I believe

There's bound to be another war one day.

[Voice F]
                                                              You can't believe

Everything that the papers say.

[Voice C]
                                                        Russia, the U.S.A.,

Atomic Power, Foreign Powers . . .

[Voice F]
Go to sleep. Put out
That light! The War is over now. It's late.
Why don't those people go to bed?

[Voice E]
                                              They're all alike
Those foreigners, you can't trust them, can you?

(Confused Grumbling Voices Fade Out)

[Narration One]
The Tyrant Negativity has usurped power and thrown
Men's captive souls into the silent pit
Of self-confounded Subjectivity.
Immortal souls that know themselves to be
Immortal souls have wings.
But in that pit
All doubt-blindfolded souls must fall like stones –
Fall down without the power to cry out
Unless inspired by Anguish.

[Narration Two]
A stone that falls feels nothing, has no fear
And knows no need, and cannot cry.
A falling stone is not a fallen soul.

[First Mortal Soul]
Now Man benighted huddles in his cave,
In mighty ignorance of what he is and what he's not:
Cave-night which every night
His all-aloneness drives him back into:
This is the dark, familiar, fearful place
Where once again flung down I fallen lie!
Oh! could I but release from far within
My own benighted selfish inmost dark, from deep within
The ever unknown part of me, could I release
One long, long harsh heartbreaking broken cry
That would for once express all that the night
Awakens in me, all that words betray,
Being too flimsy and approximate and too
Precise: could I unsay

All I have clumsily but half-expressed, O could I howl
Instead the protestation of my impotence against
The dull omnipotence of stifling soundlessness,
Dull swelling vacancy, that from all sides
Drives with the pressure of incessant passing time
Inwards on me, thrusting back into the lapsed
Being become non-being where annihilation waits
To swallow all that I have ever been,
Then might I sleep like one whom his own soul no longer hates.

[Narration Two]
The cry of mortal anguish from the soul's dark night
Reaches you now, if you will hear it. I will ask
Myself whether you hearing it, if you were God
Would pay no heed but turn away your ear.
You have heard one, but there are countless cries.

[Second Mortal Soul]
Shut up, shut off that hateful voice.
Shut up, shut out the Night.
I do not want
To sense the world's obscure plain spread
Out under empty heaven, or to know
That we lost in obscurity are stranded on a sphere
Of earth that spins amidst infinity
Among unnumbered galaxies of spinning spheres
Dispersed in distances so vast that human sight
Swerves backward sickened by the senselessness
Of so much space without a single sign
That consciousness, pinprick adrift in it,
Can seize on to decipher.
Let me be stupefied.

[Narration One]
We are always free
To turn away. Our hearts can always harden to refuse
To suffer mortal anguish. There are many anodynes.

[Third Mortal Soul]
Drink strength and comfort now out of the well
Of Night, that can so quickly quench our thirst
And as it slowly slakes its own, consumes us all.

The sun sank out of sight and darkness covered us.
I will sit down and close my eyes and wait; sit still and wait,
Though I still somehow cannot yet relax, I feel a weight
Of heaviness that will not let me rest, a load that stirs
And slackens in me, weighing down, wearing away,
With weary will to stay awake when I lie down,
My wish to give up vigil for repose.

[Nightwatcher's Voice]
At Night, I often sit an hour out thus,
Attentive to a dull insistent roar –
Or not a roar, rather a kind of cry, and yet
No cry, for that would be a sound too clear,
And what I hear might come from underground,
It is so thick and muffled, and yet hollow-sounding too,
Although not resonant at all, but harsh and dead,
If dead is not too definite a word:
And whatsoever this dull urgent rumour be,
It holds me spellbound by the hour and more,
While I, with a great longing to be free
From doubt about what it can signify,
Gaze up through a small skylight's panes and see
Nothing at all of my star's watch-fire
That may be burning in the black neglected sky;
Do not see even that blank square the window frames –
As though all sight lay blinded in my ears.
And then, returning suddenly again
To consciousness of my immediate self,
I've had a moment's glimpse into the depths
Of solitary absence through which stray
Our tired and restless bodies among all the dead things found
Strewn round them on all sides in an unanimated dream:
Dread has distracted us away from what is here
And what we really are when faithful to the truth;
So we must suffer hopelessly the sullen apathy
That reigns on a deserted theatre's stage
Where all night long we play out our null roles,
In a Morality that could be called *'No Man'*.

[Second Nightwatcher's Voice]
I hear a voice that speaks from No-Man's Land
And when just now he said he'd heard a cry

Or some strange sort of sound I thought I recognized
That what I listened to him speaking of I too had heard:
For listen, listen, it begins again! It's the same sound, I'm sure!
On many other nights before I have heard this,
Like sound of distant rioting, that angry voices' sound,
Popular uproar from afar, as though crowds underground
Were pushing upwards boiling to invade the city streets
With hell-hordes hoarsely clammering for blood!
For Blood! For Justice! Bloodshed and Revenge! What cry
Is that I only hear an echo of? Why after all should I
Feel threatened by a thing so far away? Does no one else
Hear what I hear at night?

[Third Nightwatcher's Voice]   Yes, neighbour, I can hear.
I too have heard those ominous night voices. I hear yours,
You are my neighbour, not a crowd, I'm not afraid of you,
Although I cannot see your face. Then let us not
Mistrust each other, nor be too much disturbed by them.
And do not be afraid of it. If you can hear
The echoes of your own anxiety, if you can bear
To listen to that rumour, then you know at least that dread
Of hearing what you fear has not yet deafened you.

[Anonymous Mass Voice]
Fear, fear: you speak of fear.
What is this fear? Is it the fear we dare not fear,
That fear of fear itself, or fear of other's fear,
Such fear as ends
In passionate untruth, self-justifying falsehood without end?
Demonic fear
Of individual guilt, of being caught, of doing wrong,
And fear of failure or of being found a fool,
And fear of anything that might contrast with me
And thus reveal my insufficiency,
My lack, my weakness, my inferiority,
In showing up my difference from itself;
Fear of uncertainty and loss, fear of all change,
Fear of all strangeness and all strangers; and above all else the fear
Of Love, of being loved, of being asked for love,
Of being loved yet knowing one has no love to return;
Fear of forgiveness –

Fear of that love which is so great it can forgive
And the exhausting fear of Death and Mystery,
The Mystery of Death, of Life and Death,
The huge appalling Mystery of everything;
Arid fear of Nothing,
Yes, after all the fear of Nothing really,
Fear of Nothing, Nothing

Fear of Nothing, Nothing, absolutely Nothing.

[Voice C]
Dread of life, and fear of Nothing,
Anxiety and dream assail the vigilant
Watchman who waits in solitude for the Night to pass.

[Voice A]
A blind wind whispers in the sleeping grass.

2   MEGALOMETROPOLITAN CARNIVAL

[Voice A]
When Night has been announced as theme, will it not cause surprise
If there is nothing said about the stars? Also it has
Been immemorially the custom to apostrophize the Moon –
In courtly terms, calling her Queen of Night, and to refer
To Cynthia's argent chariot, or some such-like stage-property,
Or improvise some image like that Gallic wit's who saw
The Moon above a steeple like the dot above an I.
Planets and constellations tend to lend themselves to rhapsody,
Having like hosts of lesser stars most ornamental names:
Orion, Mars and Venus, Betelgeuse and all the rest,
That are godsends to poets, shedding lustre on their lines.

[Voice B]
But if I stand tonight,
Not in a poem but in actual fact in, say, Trafalgar Square,
And stare up at the heavens there, what can they mean to me,
The glories of the Zodiac, the lovely names of stars?
Do I see splinters of old myths stuck in the sky above my head?
If stars are visible at all, they're but a sprinkling of pinpricks
Blurred into insignificance by the brilliance on the ground,

Where the City round me celebrates the triumph of the brain
Of man over his darkness, in the effervescent blaze
Of a commerce-sponsored carnival of multicoloured bulbs.
The soot-suffused sky-canopy, shot through with bluish red,
Shuts off from me as surely as do too-familiar names
The mystery of Space.

[Voice C]
At night I've often walked on the Embankment of the Thames
And seen the Power Station's brick cliffs dominate the scene
Over on the South Bank, and its twin pairs of giant stacks
Outpouring over London their perpetual offering
Of smoke in heavy swags fit for a sacrificial rite
Propitiating some brute Carthaginian deity;
And thought they stood like symbols for the worship of our age:
The pillars of a temple raised to man-made Power and Light.

[Voice A]
And I have sometimes gone out towards midnight
Through streets of dwelling-houses and apartment–blocks
Behind the rows of window-squares of which
Innumerable tired executives prepared for bed,
While past street-corner lamps dogs' pensive escorts
Tugged them on leads along their late patrol;
Through districts full of narrow shady gardens
With strips of black lawn stretching from french windows
To sooty shrubberies, a seedy tree or two,
Laburnum to o'erhang the pavement pilgrim
When summer has transformed these dormitories
By splashing blossom-sprays across their drabness
For a few weeks each year. And have walked on
Until I came out on an open hillside,
A public park space from which one looks down
Upon the mighty Nocturne of the Capital
Whose twinkling panorama's spread below:
Arena sprawling dazed in concrete gloom,
Freckled with sparks and smeared with arc-lights' gleams,
With crawling glares and melancholy glazes,
Slow-sinking monuments and stoic lighthouses:
Mile after mile of tenements and terraces,
League after league of palaces and parks.
Here hover hazes of green sick-ward light,

And there red neon blurs flick on and off,
In fixed directions avenues stretch sleekly
To disappear in ultimate uncertainty
In regions where the bottom of the sky
Mingles with fumes that rise from the abyss . . .
Fearful and wonderful, that sleepless monster,
Sphinx among cities, Megalometropolis,
Stuns with her grave immensity all eyes beholding her:
One's wonder gapes and quickly palls and falls into dismay,
Knowing the roaring labyrinth deepsunk in Night below
Teems with noctambulists too multitudinous
For any now to fear the Minotaur.

[Voice D]
Effulgent filaments in bulging bulbs
Persist in stinging blackness till they've tinged with pallid stain
All wilting areas of opaque obscurity;
Innumerable bulbs that like frost-glazed unpupilled eyes
Pour out incessant bleared lacklustre glare
Upon all public places all night long.

[Voice E]
No trace remains in any place of daytime's busy throng.

[Voice F]
Behold how every building-block, each bank,
Walls behind which wait bales of ware in yards,
Forums, exchanges, business-houses, stores,
Stand back drawn up behind a film of blankness,
A foreign aspect hazing all façades.

[Voice E]
The absent inmates have locked all their doors.

[Voice D]
Scarcely a soul is to be seen on any sidewalk at this hour.
Scarcely the word is soul perhaps for such as might be seen.

[Voice F]
Their desultory feet move slow and furtively,
Few footsteps far between.

[Voice E]
Seeing it now, you'd hardly know the city scene.

[Voice D]
Street-crossing islands stand becalmed; round them no traffic roars.

[Voice E]
All waking feelings now are dimmed, the day-time's passions curbed.

[Voice F]
The decent sleep in duty bound. They may emit some snores;
Otherwise they are mute and must by no means be disturbed.
They've made their beds; now they must lie in them.

[Voice D]
They have retired in consequence to do so and are prone.

[Voice F]
Between the sheets, beneath the blankets, parked in cots and bunks,
Stretched out in alcoves, side by side or all alone,
In double-beds or on divans, with lamps out, curtains drawn,
Immobile many millions lie, all interchangeable,
All horizontal humans out of use until next morn.

[Voice E]
No household has been able any longer to refuse
Sleep's standing invitation to its old home castle-keep
There to recline like lords at ease unconscious till next day.

[Voice D]
Everything now has been closed down, shut up and locked away.
The population's breathing is slow regular and deep.

[Voice F]
Although Megalometropolis is unsleeping, night and day,
At times even the city seems to doze off for a spell.
Whether or not it sleeps is hard to tell. I couldn't say.
Brought to a standstill it stands waiting. Empty.

[Narration One]
Enter the Dreams.

[Narration Two]
The Dreams enter the City.
Drifting in swiftly twisting clouds above the roofs,
Their whirling fever-coloured smoke crosses the moon;
As they race past, its contours blur and tremble.
A moment after, real clouds blot its face.

[Narration One]
Enter the Dream.

[Narration Two]
Enter the Dream's great glimmering park.
Only at first is it still dead of night.
Slide softly, stepping rapidly, at first.
Here there still lingers a strange stealth and stillness.
The beams that fill the early dreams are soft as twilight
In the first place. In this faint light you must move swift as swimmers,
Move with short strokes beneath the lowslung boughs,
The grey, long-bearded, overhanging branches
Of ancient trees still lining all these avenues.
You'll have to hurry down these thoroughfares,
Though splendid shops and gardens catch your eye.
All signposts point in only one direction.

[Narration One]
Follow the fingers, you can't lose your way,
It won't take long to reach the central space,
That is the special place you have to find.
Just one street further. Here at last you are.

[Narration Two]
Here is the Circus in the Square that represents
The very heart of the primeval City. Now's the time
To recollect that you've received a secret summons
To a rendezvous with the Unknown, at the foot of the Fountain
That leaps without spray, a thin glimmering quicksilver pillar,
Above the memorial marking the first fatal spot,
The meeting place of the First Person with Persons Unnamed
At the heart of the Forest that grew where the City now stands.

[Narration Three]
The quicksilver Fountain that's hovering there like a column allures
All who enter the lair of the Labyrinth-Omphalos Boss,
Whose domain lies beneath, in the earth. Yet if anyone nears
The Basin too closely, at once it will sink underground.
By the time you've got right to the axis round which the square circles,
You will find that it's no longer there.

[Narration One]
Just stand still for a moment. No need to be scared.
Pay no heed to the thunder of traffic, the dazzle of lights
On the walls flashing messages round you on every side.
Soon, just where the Fountain has vanished, the earth at your feet,
At the heart of empirical hubbub, will yawn open wide
And the cavernous Subway's mouth show you the way down inside.

[Narration Two]
Now you follow the steps and descend to the City's true heart,
And are soon in a Plaza illumined more brightly than day
Where more people are hurrying in all directions than up there
 above.
Close at hand is the brisk business district, just under you lie
The platforms from which the incessant electric expresses
Go rushing from City to faraway Suburbs, and back from the
 Suburbs again.

[Narration Three]
Here are underground Boulevards bright with Bazaars, here you'll
 find
Vast fields for the shop-window gazer to graze in. Arcades
Branch off on each side, endless Galleries lined with glasscases
 invite
To inspection of carloads of diamondmine loot, of forests of
 flowers,
Tropic fruits piled in tiers, Pin-up waxwork girls posed in parades
To show off new nylons, new sequins, new rhinestones, new lace-
 trimmed furcoats.

[Narration One]
But don't linger too long for a rush-hour approaches and here it's
 unwise

To risk getting caught by the tide of the throng that flows through
   at its height.
Better make your way now to the flights of steps all leading down
To the slow-moving staircases, up to the fast escalators
Descending past columns of spiralling stairs to the level where
   tubes
Have been bored for the feet to press through from the foot of one
   flight

[Narration Two]
Of stepping stones, on to the passages in, then the passages out,
To the thoroughfares out of which more escalators are moving,
   some more
Slowly, the others more quickly, first up and then down, on and on,
On and off, up and up, down down down, go on down, till at last
The wonderful system will crown the true will to success with
   success
As the peace known at zero-hour's peak on the heart of the rusher
   descends.

[Sleeping Citydweller]
    Oh! Let me stop, I must sit down!
    I've been deceived, I am confused!
    I must wake from this nightmare soon.
    Among these crowds I've got quite lost –
    Words in the tunnels' roaring drown!

[Train-Wheels Chorus]
Hurry up and get on Hurry up and get on Hurry up and get on Hurry
I couldn't care less I couldn't care less I couldn't care less I couldn't
The Main Chance The Main Chance The Main Chance The Main
Get on Care less Get on Care less Get on Care less Get on Care less
Teach a lesson teach a lesson teach a lesson teach a lesson teach a
The Damned are the Damned are the Damned are the Damned are the
The Day of Wrath the Atom Plan the Wrath to Come the Atom
Bomb the Coming Day the Greatest Bang the Biggest Bomb the
Wrath of God the World of Man the Day to Come the Bang the
   Bomb . . . (ad inf.)

[Guide Voice]
As you move at a pace that gets constantly faster, your eyes
Are increasingly caught and held fast at each step by one after

Another phrase, slogan and image set up to solicit as much
Of the crowd-individual's attention as each in his hurry can spare.

[Narration One]
You may look where you like for the public's fastidious and only permits
Its favourite posters to brighten the walls of such sanctums as these:
Now the principal stations afford a great treat with the constant variety
Of the attractions inviting the traveller's mind's eye to rove towards
All sorts of model resorts; at his journey's end wait to stare down on him
On his arrival more posters depicting the places abroad he must
Hasten to visit as soon as he can to discover:

[Narration Two]
NEW VISTAS NEW THRESHOLDS NEW PLEASURES NEW BEAUTIES NEW BEACHES NEW LIGHT
ON OLD-WORLD INNS NEW WORLDS IN DISGUISE OLD CATHEDRALS SPOTLIGHTED
NEW CRUISES TO BEAUTYSPOTS SEA-COASTS BEST SUITED TO NUDES

[Narration Three]
Look! Here posters plaster the best people's eye with huge glimpses
Of Scenes from the Very Best Shows of the Year by the Star-Chamber
Critics' Assembly Selected: The Most Highly Praised, the Best Advertised, then
The most Noted for Highlypaid Acting, the Most Controversial,
The Brightest, the Loudest, Most Daringly Brutal, and Quite the Most Crude.

[Narration One]
The Crowd's hardheaded leaders alone have the leisure to cast a glance over them
As they press past down the passage from exit to box-office queue but they turn
To present to the next passerby their opinion for what it is worth and
He'll then in his turn send it on to be sent on till common consent
Has agreed that it's fit to be fully divulged to the public at large.

[Narration Two]
Now here you must follow the people in front of you down some
    more stairs
Where as you descend you will find on each side are arranged on the
    walls
More advertisements eager to snatch at your glance as you pass:
If you miss one or two it won't matter, you'll find them again
    further on.

[Publicity Chorus]
STRAPLESS BREASTAPPEAL BRA MAKES YOU HARDER TO GET
NEW LYNX LIMOUSINE WITH LOW FAMILY EYELINE
DON'T LET THEM DESCRIBE YOU AS DIRTY! GET 'WET'
HOW'S YOUR COLON LOOK? TREAT IT TO LIQUORICE SOAP
WATCH APPROACH OF PHENOMENAL NEW STAR ON SKYLINE
VAN WORMWOOD EXCLUSIVELY FEATURED IN 'DOPE'
'THIS SOULTWISTER BLISTERS THE PAINT OFF THE SET!'
DRINK MORE DRINK! WEAR MORE CLOTHES! DON'T LOSE HOPE!
    DON'T FORGET!
WEAR MORE SMILES PLEASE! LAUGH LOUDER! LOOK AFTER YOURSELF!
USE CHARM AND DISCRETION! BE TOUGH! DON'T GET LAID ON THE
    SHELF!

[Train-Wheels Chorus]
I couldn't care less I couldn't care less I couldn't care less I couldn't
A chance you can't afford to lose a chance you can't afford to lose a
Smooth as glass and tough as hell as smooth as glass and tough as hell
The damned are the damned are the damned are the damned are the
The World to come the Atom Plan the World of Man the Atom Bomb the
Coming Day the Biggest Bang the Wrath of God the Atom Age the Day
    of Wrath . . . (ad inf.)

[Narration One]
The Sleeper came here on a Quest, to find that he is lost,
Deepsunk in the confusions of a City underground,
And now looks round him, lonely and bewildered, in the midst
Of anonymous masked multitudes, surrounded by the sounds
Of Latter Pandemonium, Hell's ideal up-to-date
Metropolis of Commerce-cum-Cacophomonium,
The Capital of Every Pseudo Super-City State.

[Commentator]
Tonight is Carnival Time in this great underworld city of platforms and staircases and here I am on the spot to give you a ringside description of the scene in the Pluto Plaza, where a vast number of masked revellers are already waiting on the great black ice ballroom floor for the New Season to be officially declared open by – why yes, here he is, it's a top secret but I think I can let you in on it, it's a very important V.I.P. indeed, now I can see his flaming whiskers and gaily pointed tail as he goes past on his way to the rostrum. Everyone's tense with excitement, the ice of the ballroom floor's going to melt in a moment, I think he's going to address them, yes, now here it comes, this is the moment everyone's been waiting for, you're actually going to hear the Old Man himself speaking.

[V.I.P.]
I have every hope that those of you who hear me speak tonight will be as deeply stirred as I have been to learn that it is to be my special privilege to have the honour of presenting to Charity for auction on your behalf this most artfully designed and purposeful-looking Pair of Silver Ceremonial Scissors, having first severed with them in a single snip – the mile-long cordon-bleu communication-ribbon which has been arranged so as to run round these entire fully licensed premises.

(He cuts the cordon)

I hereby declare endless Carnival to be left open to the Four Winds of Publicity, Gossip, Idletalk, and Rumour, and have much sly pleasure in handing over all responsibility for the conduct of further proceedings to the Master of Spring Opening Ceremonies, who is already seizing the Microphone to Address you.

(Applause)

[Master of Spring Opening Ceremonies]
Applause comes first! That's what I like to hear! Just one more burst! Now when
I give the sign, let there be music. Bandsmen may burst their drums but have no fear,
Dear Dressdesignstars and neat Grooms. Dance, dance until you faint.
Abandon everything. No one would think that *your* death might be near.

Have no anxiety at all. You'd look a million dollars at your worst.
Never let laughter falter lest its note sound forced, nor let your feet
Trip the less lightly over foolish fear; no one looks quaint
By being opulently over-lightly clad. Dance in the street!
Let the rare joy of true extravagance in dress carry you on
From whirl to whirl, and through hall after hall
Of topflight fashion, as from square to square dance floor!
May I remind you that there are none so mad
Among these streetwalkers that the red carpets spread
For your fleet crystal-slippered toes alone to tread
Will not inspire in them a rapt respect while you are revelling; not one
Who following your least step close as facsimile permit
Will not wish that she might be at once flash-photo'd dead
Were she but gowned with the unerring taste shown in your very shroud!
So fling yourselves headlong into our Carnival, and let your joy in it
Be long as night, and very, very loud!

[Chorus of Masks] (confusedly)
Out of this world. Marvellous! Of course, this is sheer Heaven!
  Out out of this World World. Exquisite.
Divine! Out of this World. Heaven!
  Out of this World. Darling! Such heaven!
I simply worship him. Ah, what Heaven! Worship her worship it
            Simply Divine! I do adore to dance!
  Divine! Out of this World! Sheer heaven, my dear, but too divine!
  This world is heaven! Divine! I adore it, Darling!
You do look heavenly! Adorable! I think your make-up's too divine!

[Narration One]
Although the style's incongruous, one may quote here, I hope,
These apposite Augustan lines from Alexander Pope:
    'Hell rises, Heaven descends, and dance on earth:
    Gods, imps, and monsters, music, rage and mirth,
    A fire, a jig, a battle, and a ball;
    Till one wide conflagration swallows all.'

[Voice of a Mask]
Smoothburnt by artificial sunrays, cold with sweat
Under our swathed robes' sheaths since zero lies within,
Perplexed apparently by our perdition, inwardly

Rehearsing rigmaroles of self-defensive calumny, we go
The tortuous easy way towards uncertainty out of
The pit of ages past. Ours is harsh music. Masks
Like snailshells are become, the glossy whorled
Concealment we excrete to screen our softness from ourselves.
Should silence fall, we'd shake like withered leaves and surely tell
How easy paralytic souls a prey to terror fall
Stonedeafened by midwinter's blasts at last! So endless noise
We need to stuff our burning ears with, huge uproars
Must keep on breaking out lest we should judge
Unwillingly how far and near are all one to the void
Whose dungeon swallows up the instant after our least sound.
When buffeted by pangs of dread of failure, we at once
Wrap blankets of cacophony about us, plucking strings
Of strident resonance to death with frantic fingers, while alas,
The only ground-note to all songs is like the throbbing sob
Of childhood by our cold sophistication throttled, choked
Back in our lying throats, to underlie, pent in our breasts,
Each cry during the long spell of our carnival expelled
To swell the roar that rises with each climax repostponed.

(The Music, in which the Dies Irae *has been distinguishable, played simultaneously with* Boys and Girls Come out to Play, *here reaches the summit of its crescendo with a high, piercing trumpet note.)*

[Narration One]
Sleepers, Awake! Awake from Sleep! Back from the world of
   Shades!
The trumpet sounds, the curtain falls, the fabric strange dissolves
And the familiar scene shows through: the darkened stage
Which is the sleeper's bedroom; the familiar properties
Of daily use arranged around the bed. The ordinary street
Outside the window and its streetlamps in the ordinary night.
You awaken from the Pandemonium of your dream, the midnight
   carnival,
And find yourself in the Dark City of the present day again.

[Narration Two]
We think at night. We break the spell of every-day if thought can
   wake
From the deep twilight sleep of thinking darkness light.

[Narration Three]
It has been said that in the Marketplace, man sleeps his deepest sleep.

[Narration Two]
Purely material reality, if reality it were, would be lived in by no more
Than animated corpses, dead-alive, with ghosts of thoughts
Haunting their brainpans' coils of cells in an irrational way,
However rational their words and meanings were.

[Narration One]
Tonight you in the dark attentive to the Night
Thoughts we have here assembled, may be more
Than merely thinking that you wake. When the new day
Emerges from the everlasting East perhaps you may.

3 ENCOUNTER WITH SILENCE

[Narration One]
Night Thoughts. Night Music. Now from buried labyrinths and caves of the town-dweller's anxious dream, from claustrophobic corridors of nocturnal soliloquy, we move away until we can emerge into the open air in a secluded countryside.

[Narration Two]
There we shall find again the calm night world of Nature.

[Narration One]
Nature, the Earth, Unconsciousness and Death. We are drawn down and back towards them in the Night.

[Narration Three]
Nocturnal Music. Meditations in dark gardens. Gradually forming thoughts pursued in gardens by such solitary strollers as may now find themselves outdoors, taking a turn or two before retiring, taking a breath or two of fresher air.

[Narration One]
Walking there without a predetermined object; in the starlight; at a slow pace, uncertainly. Standing still from time to time as though to listen, yet not listening to any clearly determined sound.

[Narration Two]
The Night music has drifted off into remote serenity, leaving the hearer standing still to listen to the stillness of the garden, waiting to hear what may be born out of the stillness.

[Narration Three]
He stands still and seems to listen to some unknown distant thing; something that might be coming from . . . from where? What echo from beyond what last horizon?

[Narration One]
There is nothing to be heard. The garden is quite still. There is only silence in the darkness.

[Narration Two]
There is seldom experienced anywhere on the inhabited earth, for more than a moment or two at a time, such a thing as silence. For it is something we imagine only, Silence, an idea we have of what a complete absence of sound would be like. Real Silence is the message spoken to us that we fear most of all to hear. What we usually call silence is most often no more really than a confused medley of diminutive sounds to which it would be too tiring to pay conscious attention.

[Narration Three]
Everywhere about us, day and night, goes on the eddying stream of murmur: little drifting sighs and rumblings, whispers, coughing, whistles, moans. Goes on rising from the earth, the home of life, birthplace of restlessness, where all the rhythms meet, and cross, and intertwine uninterruptedly.

Chorus 1:   A window rattling in the wind
Chorus 2:   That everlasting rear-exhausting, gear-exhausted car
Chorus 3:   Bark of a mongrel
Chorus 1:   Tap of an old benighted blind-man's cane
Chorus 2:   Another mongrel's barking
Chorus 1:   An infinitesimal insect's lovesong, scarcely a second long
Chorus 2:   That wretched child . . .
Chorus 3:   An ancient iron engine shunts and shunts
Chorus 1:   O the wind and the rain in the rain and the wind in the rain in the wind
Chorus 2:   O love return, return, O darling come . . .
Chorus 3:   A mammoth feather's smothered fluttering

Chorus 1:	And screams like hell and shunts and shunts and shunts
Chorus 2:	Bark of another mongrel
Chorus 3:	The same everlasting car
Chorus 1:	Old oak's slow taut-slack creak, clock's low quick-slow-quick tick
Chorus 2:	Sand trickling underneath the door, dust blown across the floor
Chorus 3:	The sleeper's snore soon swells the stream which never dies away
	But flows on till with dawn it joins the streaming sounds of day.

[Narration One]
Night music of mysterious hazard. Dream-fugues: variations on fortuitous themes; intricate tracery unwinding like designs drawn in a trance across the taut sky of the universal Ear.

[Narration Two]
Decrepid gust-blown tinkling of a crumbling pagoda's bells . . .

[Narration Three]
Intensely complex tight-screwedup tattoo of tiny drums . . .

[Narration One]
The velvet-padded hammering of life-blood's changing pulse.

[Narration Three]
The pulse of changing life is the deep underlying constant. And the Unchanging also is a pulse, flowing through all that lives, a single pulse.

[Narration Two]
The changes and the pauses and occasional recurrence of abrupt irregularity make sound-patterns we overhear but never really hear. Our hearing intercepts no more than one bar at a time. These patterns are upon a scale not measurable in hours. Attention wanders; thinking intervenes.

[Narration One]
The boundaries of the senses are not often clearly realized. The Infra and the Ultra are fields easily forgotten. Out of hearing stays unthought-of; our of sight is out of mind. And yet, how haunted we all are.

[Narration Two]
The nightwalker, on a terrace in the garden, unaccompanied, hardly aware of it, half hopes to overhear – that haunting thing. Something that hovers, maybe hovers only just beyond the rim. A thing he has not thought of yet, that no one ever heard.

[Chorus 1]
The weir, the misty distant falling waters of the weir among the meadows, make a whispering that swells and faints but never quite subsides.

[Chorus 2]
The City blazing with electricity just over the horizon flings its glare-reflection like a continual exclamation of astonishment into the sky, emitting intermittently a high-pitched filtered rumour of its roar.

[Chorus 3]
The whisper drifts, the faint roar flutters in the upper air. Both rise and fall. And presently a sudden fine and quite unearthly whistling sound comes sliding down from emptiness, lasting no longer than it takes a shot star's dust to drift and disappear.

[Chorus 1]
And then a brisk salt wind blows from the other side of the black downs, and for a while the sea in its perpetual passion of frustration at the shore is to be heard vociferating.

[Chorus 2]
A salt breeze seems at last to bring some echo of that sound.

[Chorus 3]
Of ocean's ebb and everlasting obstinate resurgence, from afar.

[Narration One]
On the terrace in the garden, the solitary stroller has at last come to a standstill. He leans over a parapet and gazes out ahead into the starlit tranquil dark. He thinks of nothing. He lifts his head and gazes and is blind. His heart beating strikes midnight. He breathes in the night's ancientness and freshness, slowly absorbing strength and courage for a coming time when he will have to be reborn.

[Voice of the Solitary]
I stand here staring into darkness and see nothing. Yet it is not nothing that stretches before me away there for ever in whatever direction I turn my eyes. It is the Universe. It is I myself that am nothing. Through my eyes, nothing gazes at Reality, that utterly unqualifiable Something. And slowly the question rises out of nothing's depths, Can I be real if I remain unseen? If I speak out of my innermost reality, shall I not be heard? Why should it be more extraordinary that I who am nothing may be none the less perceived, or that my speaking may be heard, than that nothingness should wonder, gaze and listen?

I stand here speaking of my nothingness; and yet I am a man. It is my heart that speaks, abasing itself in dread before that colossal inscrutability; overwhelmed by the total evidence that what is there must be. I cannot understand however I am able to address what faces me, and yet I know I somehow must respond. From out of that profound night-blue abyss of starry vacancy comes the command: 'Lift up your heart! . . .' I raise my spellbound head and face to face with what I cannot name I worship and adore. I lift my heart up and it speaks my prayer.

O Being, be! O be what faces me, to whom my heart may speak.

Almightiness, O be the Face that bent over me, O be aware and hear.

Acknowledge me, accept me, and may my response responded to help me slowly to realize how we are thus akin.

O be the One, that I may never be alone in knowing that I am. Let my lost loneliness be illusory. Allow to me a part in Being, that I may thus be part of One and All.

I am a man of a benighted century, famished for light and praying out of darkness in the dark. I do not really any longer know what praying means. To pray by rote, repeating time-deconsecrated words, seems vanity to me. I cannot bear to hear myself repeating words of prayer that might be mumbled and not meant. Men of this time seem not to know that there is meaning, or that Being is. All of us talk and talk of all and everything, and shut ourselves up in ourselves and with the curtain of our words shut out the fact that we are blind and dumb. We are afraid of silence, and afraid to look each other in the eye. Talking, we do not speak to one another; one who speaks of many others, seldom fails to disparage them all indiscriminately. Many speeches are made to urge us on to secure peace through understanding; but I will speak no more of speaking: Man has become above all the most indefatigable mimic of all the ways of being man that have ever been thought striking. Men imitate, and I am imitating them. I say 'Man' and 'men' and thus invest abstractions with all my own deficiencies and think I somehow thus may be absolved of the whole failure to be truly man. I am a man. I cry out of my darkness. I could not cry if I were in complete despair.

[First Voice]
In the gardens of the Night, breathed on by newly freshened air, wrapped in the sheltering arms of shadows cast by slowly growing things, the consolation of profound Serenity is to be found. Here, in forgetting by degrees the crude immediacies of day, talk's trivialities, the well-worn props and tokens of habitual routine, it is possible to recall to mind and to draw near again to something vastly fundamental, self-effacingly withdrawn, that has been lying there and is there all the time. It is an ever-new discovery to find it still awaiting our return, unsmiling, taciturn, yet limitlessly tolerant and all comprehending, ready to take us back into obscurity, to share with us its poverty, to close and soothe our eyes.

[Second Voice]
The Earth, Nature, Unconsciousness and Death. We are drawn down and back towards them in the Night. But there is Vigil where the walker in the gardens stands and wonders in the dark.

[First Voice]
Now the man who spoke aloud just now out of his dark into the darkness: (to no one? to someone? the mystery is not mine to solve that each must face alone) the man who had said: 'I could not cry if I were in despair', turns presently towards the lighted windows he had left behind him earlier, and slowly makes his way back through the scented plants and dangling leaves of the dumbly sleeping garden to his wife and home, his books and bed.

[Second Voice]
And as he goes, begins to realize that something has changed in him. The open air, the space about him had first stirred his heart, he lifted up his heart and it had opened, and the wind that blows when it will and comes from nowhere that we know and passes on as unaccountably, had inspired it with its own more vital, lighter, unrestricted and revivifying breath. Silence had delivered its essential message to him, and he had responded. Now he feels that he no longer has the need to reassure himself with words.

[Third Voice]
He goes back to his house, he returns to his wife and children. The children have long been asleep upstairs. His wife is sitting where he left her, under the reading-lamp. She closes her book as he enters, looks up at her husband and smiles slowly at him, sleepily. He kisses her.

[First Voice]
They are together. The primary division of the human family at night is that which sets those who are alone apart from those who are together. And yet all are alone, as the man realized earlier in the garden; and all those who are isolated in their solitude are really alone only because they do not actually realize the presence of other beings like themselves in the world.

[Second Voice]
Greetings to the solitary. Friends, fellow beings, you are not strangers to us. We are closer to one another than we realize. Let us remember one another at night, even though we do not know each other's names.

LATER POEMS

1956–1995

THE GRASS IN THE WASTE PLACES

To Danilo Dolci

What does the grass say?
The Buddha's smile will never tell us quite.

No propaganda, no 'ideas'.

Grass, grasses, fields, the field, 'la terre', our home.
All flesh,
    'cut down, dried up, withereth . . .'

Teeming, brave, swayed by the wind,
Sweet in the shine and shade.

Grass and flowers. Weeds and tares.

Anarchy the law of nature.

A blade of grass glistens with dew
That the Franciscan sun devours.

w. 1956

HALF-AN-HOUR

To Meraud Guevara

. . . and grass grows round the door. The ground,
Without, is grained with root and stone
And yellow-stained where sunlight pours on sand
Through listlessly stirred chestnut-leaves.
This is the long-sought still retreat,
This is the house, the quiet land,
My spirit craves.

   A burning sound,
Uninterrupted as the flow of high-noon's light

    Down on the trees from whence it emanates,
    The song of the cigales, slowly dissolves
    All other thought than that of absolute
    Consent, even to anxious transience.

w. Aix-en-Provence 1960–61, p. 1974

ON REREADING JACOB BOEHME'S 'AURORA'

    Now no one can deny
  That what the blessèd shoemaker foretold
Is come about indeed. Babel stands builded high
    About us. Nothing avails to save
The old world like a brand from burning. We must die
  Before our eyes can see. The dead must live
  Before lament and mourning cease to be
  The only song heard rise from earth's vast grave.

    All shall at last affirm
  The Being Boehme faithfully recalled
To have become again real at the final term
    Of chaos. Out of the triple void
Of no religion, no communion, no hope, Boehme
  Foresaw the sun at midnight would be seen
  To rise with rays like healing wings and shine
  On the whole world man's fears had else destroyed.

w. 1953 (retitled, modified 1969), p. 1975

THREE VERBAL SONATINAS

1 HISPANIC

To Rafael Nadal

This is for reading
One wild long winter night
Before the long and dreary
Wild winds have come to fright
Us all with their emotion-
al and spicy Winter's tales,
Have come and gone and broken
With the force of heavy gales,
Leaving spume upon the mantel
And ice upon the floor –
Where are we now? Good gracious,
It's only half-past four!

If you want to eat them,
These words will always do,
For that's the way to treat them,
And wild Cassandra's too!
There is no time to sweep up
The tears upon the floor,
So crystalline and icy,
Since 'that was half-past four!'

For since that long-past cry went
Up into empty space
The birds have come, and by went
The thrilling parrot race!
O human, all too human,
Are those they left behind,
Baboons are we, to some of us,
And bloody pansies, mind!
But Christmas comes but once a year,
Can Spring be far behind?
I've lost my rhyme, and metre too,
Whatever shall I do?
The time has come to wipe us up
Again, thou Winter Wind!

O thrilling Sound, the Winter round
'We have had Spanish Flu!'
And when the wind-up wind does sound
T'will come again for you!
The pen, the pen, the bright blue pen,
It has turned up again!
So now we'll write till candle-light
Has drenched the world, the Main
(The Spanish One), and all
Oh, all the World's in sight!

2 NEO-CLASSICAL

To Terry Clare

This is a strict
And very clean song,
Not without words but,
Not to be *too* long,
Without a tune,
Unless you like to
Make up your own
('Ere the clock strikes two!)

It's very brief,
(A Sonatina
Has to be!) and rolled-
Up like a concertina,
The basic row,
The saying goes
That life is grief
Without a song, so
Anything goes!

A Spanish song's
No more in order
Since 'Half-past four!'
Came in and roared a
Great rallying cry,
The other evening,
Another time, another . . .
(What rhymes with 'evening?')

This, as I said,
Is meant to be
A poem read,
No symphony!
Don't try to sing
But only listen
A bit to that,
And then to this'n

We'll soon be through!
I think so, don't you?
Be through 'ere two,
Eh? Will you, won't you?
Well, we shall see
As soon as sight comes
To light the burden,
And some light hums

May see us through, till
This opus ends, as
It opened, with a
Nice strict (has
It been that?) tune
In words, so
That we will soon
Reach the last stanza.

(What rhymes with that? Oh,
It doesn't matter!) Then
If not too flat, Oh,
We will have done well,
And eight lines each
A stanza helped
Us to at last reach

This final one!
It's been brisk going.
But we've had fun!
Such Ah- and oh-ing,
Have done at last,
And well before two!
Just not too fast!
Now we are right through!

3 SERIAL

To Humphrey Searle

This starts with ATO
And then goes on to be
A set
Of variations. Of variations
On ATO. These three
Letters comprise
The basic row,
Like ABC. Instead of Twelve
Notes, we have three basic
Letters. Compare
These three
With their associations,
As, for instance, Ash,
And Tin and Oranges. And then
Shh. Wait for the next,
The next world coming on,
This earth to change: W.R. & B.
Nice to be good
Nice to be rich
Nice to be full
And beach

As I was saying,
Before I was
Politely interrupted, take
Verbal associations, such as
This time,
Ants, Offal, Tunes.
On some such tunes as these
All variations are composed.

Next Variation: Take
Three Basic Rows, such as
We have above. Then choose
Some completely new associations
This time. Take Orange,
Antiques and Turpentine.
These form an as it were
Complete

Contrast with the previous
Variation. (At least I hope
So.) Then,
After such an ATO,
Atonal kind
Of variation, we pass on
To the next variation which
Is this time once again
On OTA,
So that we have
By this time come
Back to the basic
Triad: O for Oxford,
T for Times, A
For Alphabet.

But what comes next?
Let's see.
The ABC. I see.
C is the Basic Note,
C major, that is,
For all atonalists
Who know their Latin. Let's
Conceive that A is B, and B
Is C. Where does
That get us?
Cannibals, Beach-girls.

And Anannapolis.
This will be Greek to those
Who think that Prose
Is Simple Gospel. Now I think
That Variation's
Done with. What comes next?
Next comes a further,
A yet further variation,
This time on OAT
(I do not mean the cereal)
Now, oats are sown,
But that's not Serial.
And so we're back
To Purely Verbal

Associations, this time: Octaves,
Apples and Tintype.
That should be plain,
Quite plain and simple
As quite befits
This plain and simple set
Of Variations.

So to complete
This complex set
Of simple variations, let
Your mind next dwell
On OAL, just to make one
Small unexpected and
Discordant letter creep
Into the Game. With L
Let us associate a single thing,
Say Lint, or Lemon, Light
Or Loganberry. This
With O and A makes up
A sort of supersidiary
Penultimate
And temporary variation,
LOA, loa, as in Loaves,
Though, unfortunately, we
Can't work in Fishes
So let's get back
And let us see,
Once more, just how
To bring this Sonatina (Verbal)
To a conclusion fit
For such a thing. Suppose
We now again evoke
The Basic Three. No?
That would be rather dull? Well
Let's try a free
And definitely final this time
Association. Say O for Oak,
and T for Tank, and A
For Arcady. OK. Let's go.

Well, that went quick! Now let's
Go slow, a little. Then
Will come the turn
For ATO to grow
Once more familiar, like a rare
And convoluted tune;
And soon
Will come the Twin
For Ashes, Oats and Trees
To come at last
To their last Resting Place.
An English man here says
That English men are
Liars: Is he reliable?
That is the final, unexpected
Intermitted question that makes this
Still a surprising variation.
If only LIA
Had crept in earlier, we could
Account for it. But no,
Mere wordplay cannot lie.
So let us say goodbye
To ATO and ABC, and
LOA and all
Their variants, and end
Not with a dying Fall, but with
The Final, First and Tonic C,
True 'Art of Harmony'!

w. 1969

SPEECHLESSNESS

A soldier at Mountbatten's funeral
To the interviewer from the BBC:
'I don't care what the poets will say,
Our fine old mottos's good enough for me . . .'
I think he's right, of course he is.
'We loved him,' said the Romsey paper's editor,
'But what does a word like love mean nowadays?'
'Words, words, words': Impatience or despair?
Mere wornout husks, devalued coinage, 'strain,
Crack and sometimes break . . . '
'Decay with imprecision.'
'What can one say?' asks everyone.
Some withering wreaths: Imperishable memories?
Such is our ever-increasing impotence
In this our more and more blood-reeking world.
Is silence therefore really best?
Even a poet can no longer say.

w. 1979

WHALES AND DOLPHINS

A Poem for the Greenpeace Foundation

We're told that we must never anthropomorphize
When we are writing about animals, or 'creatures'
as we'd prefer to say; nor are we now allowed,
of course, to speak of 'all God's creatures' either,
since there are few today who can believe
that He exists and once created them and us.
To write a poem about whales or dolphins, then,
presents a challenge to all those who see
in the great whale the dread Leviathan
which Scripture teaches man should look upon
as the huge proof of the Creator's mightiness,
the ruler of the deeps, and in the guise
of the White Whale of Melville's 'Moby Dick'
a mighty symbol of both Death and Mystery;

or who, as I do, see in the dolphin's face
the look both of the cherubim and of the unborn child
safe in its mother's womb, with the angelic, innocent
smile worn by all the creatures of God's Paradise.
Many the myths about the dolphin. *Dauphin* means,
or used to, dolphin and also 'first-born'; and
a boy upon a dolphin's back is such an old
image, it surely tells us men have always sensed
some sort of kinship that the reason can't explain
between the amphibious being and our own.
Then there's the recent question or new myth
about the dolphin's sort of speech: a mystery
indeed! Poets and thinkers are increasingly
concerned with the great problems language sets.
A poem should avoid abstraction and all forms
of private declaration of belief; yet I must state
that I'm convinced by what is called the Fall of Man.
We've been turned out of Paradise; we've made the world
into a shambles and a slaughter-house; we've lost
the primal *Urspräch* which may once have been
also an aid in our communion with the beasts
we now exploit and prey upon. Polluted earth,
polluted souls: Now finally, perhaps too late,
we try to care, if not to pray, for some Salvation.
A poet friend of mine[1] wrote lately that: 'We live
in the mind of God, here, now and always, for there is
no other place.' And R. Buckminster Fuller wrote
in Nineteen Sixty-three: 'Stop "calling names"
names that are meaningless; you can't suppress God
by killing off people which are, physically,
only trans-ceiver mechanisms through which God
is broadcasting.' And too: 'The more man becomes man,
the more it will be needful for him to,
and to know how to, worship: thus the Père
Teilhard de Chardin. I do not digress.
If you have faith you may not have it every day
but somehow you believe that we shall not destroy
ourselves and God's creation; though we can
'kill off people' and, be it added, species like
the direly menaced whales and dwindling dolphins.
Now 'the light of the public darkens everything.'[2]
But still the animal kingdom and the world of nature can

remind us of our long-lost innocence. All things shall be
made new. Let chaos come. The mortal must first die.
Yet even an atheist poet[3] could write: 'The rose
tells that the aptitude to be regenerated has
no limit': and, 'what selectivity there can occur,
only just in time, and succeed in imposing its law
in spite of everything. Man sees this pinion tremble
which in every language is the first great letter of
the word Resurrection.' Redemption. Paradise Regained.
God's Kingdom here on earth. Absurd, discarded dreams?
Not only fools can still believe and fight for faith
and meaning: to preserve our innate, obstinate capacity
for love, for wonder at the miracle of life:
to speak out even if the words one's forced to use
seem worn nearly to death, and say: Yes, we can still
do what we can to preserve not only such rare things
as whales and dolphins, but the eternal Mystery of which
they are both emblem and incarnate form.

[1] Kathleen Raine
[2] Martin Heidegger
[3] André Breton

p. 1980

PRELUDE TO A NEW FIN-DE-SIÈCLE

Incessant urging, curt, peremptory:
Write what you will, in verse, or otherwise,
Intelligible, using simple metaphors.
Address a reader not just hypothetical
But flesh and blood in no need of harangues.
The time has come. We're on the very brink
Of what? Can any prophet, true or false,
Make himself heard above the mad uproar
Of all the mingling and ambiguous,
Self-righteous or dismayed denunciations,
Warnings and dire predictions that assail us from
All 'informed sources', media-debased and bent?

– If this is a poem, where are the images?
– What images suffice? Corpses and carrion,
Ubiquitous bloodshed, bigger, more beastly bombs,
Stockpiled atomic warheads, stanchless wounds,
Ruins and rubble, manic messiahs and mobs.
– But poets make beauty out of ghastliness
– You think I want to? Think truth beautiful?
– 'A terrible beauty is born . . .' – It is indeed.

In youth I did in spite of everything
Believe with Keats and Shelley such things as
That poets can 'legislate' and prophesy;
Or like Stravinsky when he wrote 'The Rite'
Become transmitting vessels for new sounds
From an inspiring, unknown world within.
I'm over sixty now, my dubious gift has gone,
I can but grope for unexpected similes.
But now as in the 'Thirties I can once again
Feel passion and frustration and that sense
Of expectation, imminence and pressing need
To express something that just must be said.
Mature awareness knows that poetry
Today demands the essence and the minimum;
That only Silence such as God's could say the Whole.
One stark vocabulary at least remains.
The litany of lurid headline-names
Merely to mention which can nag the nerves:
Vietnam, Angola, Thailand and Pakistan,
Chile, Cambodia, Iran, Afghanistan,
Derry's Bogside, Belfast and Crossmaglen;
Up in Strathclyde or down on Porton Down,
On Three Mile Island or in Seveso Italy
Then there are Manson, Pol Pot and Amin,
To name at random just three myth-monsters,
Too many more to mention, all mass-murderers:–
None of them need an adjective and though we're sick
Of being sickened by them they will stay engraved
Or branded on even callous consciences.

And yet I yearn to end by trying to evoke
A summer dawn I saw when I was not yet eight,
And having risen early watched for an hour or more

A transcendental transformation of auroral clouds,
Like a prophetic vision granted from on high.
I cannot see much now. The dawn is always new
As nature is, however much we blind ourselves and try
To poison the Earth-Mother. But an ancient text
Tells of what I believe may happen soon today:
The raven disappears as night draws to its close,
Then as the day approaches the bird flies without wings;
It vomits forth the rainbow and its body becomes red,
And on its back a condensation of pure water forms.
For that which is above is still as that which is below
For the perfecting of the One Thing, which is now
As it shall ever be, World without End, D. V.

w. 1980, p. 1980

VARIATIONS ON A PHRASE

'le lièvre fit sa prière à l'arc-en-ciel à travers la toile de l'araignée . . .'

RIMBAUD

The hare sent up his prayer to the rainbow
Through the spider's fine-spun filmy web,
Despite the huntsmen tracking it below.

The hunters set their snares, the Norns weave threads;
Hephaestus' net awaits all peccant pairs.
A filament of light through heaven spreads.

A shaft of sunshine transpierces the dust
That rises as the shell's target explodes,
And glorifies it. Deep in mud we must

Unseal our eyes through choking smoke to see
How slaughter and compassion can combine
To trace a liberating filigree.

A hostage prisoned in a stinking cell
For just an instant saw a glinting fly
Above him as a sign from heaven not hell.

In chthonic labyrinth where we now stray
Do Thou in us make peace, O lightbringer.
Submerged in darkness glows the serene day.

While raw-scabbed refugees without end file
Past numbed spectators, an aeon elsewhere
Some insane sanity sustains its smile.

Yet jackals howl across the wastes of thyme.
The drunken boat speeds on. The skilled music
Still needed by desire runs out of time.

The Charleville boy ended up peddling guns
In Ethiopia, amnesic of dream.
We can end roasted by our man-made suns.

p. 1982

RARE OCCASIONAL POEM

May 13th 1982

The 'Thought for Today' that was broadcast this morning
Told us that Crisis means Judgement. But who is the Judge?
You may or you may not believe that one exists.
Judgement can signify verdict, decision or
Fate, among other things. Yesterday, Fatima:
Priest tried to stab Pope. There was one more announcement
That a new Incarnation of Christ will appear
On TV before June has ended; by which time
Perhaps the dense fog which just now envelops us
May have somewhat dispersed, thus revealing at least
Whether fervour for fatherland, freedom or force
Have prevailed in the South Atlantic . . . or foresight.

p. 1982

DODECATRIBUTE TO MIRON GRINDEA AT 75

Many years, many memories, my dear Miron . . .
I met you early, an ignescent incomer,
Raw yet ready to recognize your rare repute
Of openness to all original output.
Now none can ignore your initiative nous.

Great is our gratitude for your genial gift:
Rampart of rance amidst Ragnarok's rioting,
Indispensable international index,
Nonesuch never needless of normative notions,
Doyen of discerningly diglot dossiers,
Exemplarily edited for an era –
ADAM, acme of annals of authentic art.

p. 1983

ARBRES, BÊTES, COURANTS D'EAU: IMPROVISATION

pour Salah Stétié

« With the situation as it is in
Beirut at present, anywhere is home. »
BBC TV News commentator: 6.XII.83

Dans ma première enfance en pèlerinage
avec ma mère vers le littoral prochain
certain midi nous nous assîmes
sous l'ombre d'un gros pin quand soudain,
étonnement inoubliable, notre siège gréseux
se révéla fourmilière remuante rouge au soleil.

Garçonnet je chantais sous la flèche
la plus haute de mon pays
qu'entoure un vaste tapis d'herbe
de pâquerettes et de thym parsemé
duquel un cèdre se dresse
bibliquement vénérable.

En vacances j'adorais
surtout le riverain sableux
d'un ruisselet roulant ignoré
derrière notre logis: et grimper
en chaman apprenti le jeune peuplier
montant droit comme l'index

auprès de mon antre buissonnier
tandis qu'à l'alentour
s'étalait une prairie soucieuse d'eau
hantée par mes amis mystérieux
le héron et le martin-pêcheur:
un cygne passait parfois par là.

Dans la contrée de lacs des poètes
longtemps plus tard j'ai entrevu
par hasard un cheval blanc bien vieux
sur la verdeur d'un versant néanmoins gambadant,
pégase nordique perpétuel partenaire
que je n'oublie jamais.

Dans l'île où j'habite
que le fleuve Medina en raccourci pénètre
un jour j'apercevais, blanchâtre grisaille,
une truie que je n'oublierai jamais
dans la boue de son enclos ruminant son deuil:
Niobé stoïquement endurante.

Mon compagnon c'est à présent ce Medina
comme l'était jadis le ruisselet secret
tributaire d'un Avon; et autrefois la Tamise
a porté mon reflet rêveur, comme la Seine
emportait les jours de ma jeunesse sous ses ponts,
tandis qu'estivant je me trempais dans l'Arc.

★   ★   ★   ★

Mirage là-bas, obsédante actualité:
fresque foudroyée, façades grêlées de mitraille,
dans les moellons le marasme des massacres
que dominent des orbites de crânes bourrées d'affres,
hérissement de barbelés et de brandons brandis:
dans l'arrière-pays cependant toujours les monts de cèdres.

Reste à jamais l'oasis par le mirage caché
où coule la source qui seule peut adoucir
le venin de la nostalgie innée, abreuvante
et le cheval et la truie ainsi que toute bête.
reverdissante toujours peuplier, pin et cèdre:
oasis outre-lieu de tous nos lieux terrestres.

« La jeunesse se plaint de la vie; la mort la guérit.
La terre est ma chambre à coucher, la vôtre aussi;
personne jusqu'à présent n'a quitté sa dernière demeure.»*
Quoique l'on chasse jeunes familles et vieilles
chaque jour harcelées de leurs logis,
une terre paisible nous attend tous.

p. 1984

HAGUE HAIKU (for [Salah] Stétié)

In the garden of Salah
The silence is soothed
By the whispered lisp of leaves.

w. 1984, p. 1995

*Abu Al-Ala Al-Ma'arri (903-1057)

THALASSA: THE UNSPEAKABLE SEA

For Mimmo Morina

Sitting on a beach facing the foaming collapse of the waves of a vast expanse of acrid water stretching away as far as the distant line that indicates the curvature of the globe

Sitting in a deckchair with ballpoint and notepad facing the theme of Thalassa

Vociferations uninterrupted since the first emergence of all animal life. Thunders – murmurs: furies – calms. Ultimate challenge to language. Total proscription of words

Primal matrix: insatiable grave. Unalterably other. Unlikeness extending out of sight

We are a minority inhabiting an environment unaware of having given us birth

Swimming, sailing and fishing: ephemeral superfluities

How long before the final drowning of that book wherein it is written that our finest order is no more than a heap of garbage dumped at random on the verge of the purest and most polluted of waters, undrinkable and deadly to all but the Kraken and its countless amphibious hordes?

Triumphant rise, fall and crash of a last billow against the definitive deserted shore: all too human imagining that no incarnate consciousness can ever realize.

p. 1985

ENTRANCE TO A LANE

on a painting by Graham Sutherland

To Elizabeth Jennings

Memento rectangled to lead the gaze
From outer levels to a hub of white,
An elsewhere that recedes from coiling planes

Sequestered rural scene reputed Welsh,
Season's regalia reduced to tones
Of veld and verdure, leaves to sprays of blotch

A static vortex wherein ochre glows
Softly in strata linked by streaks and zones
Of compact shade and layers of virid light

The felt-floored lane leads to a blank where hues
And perceptions vanish as fast as time
Into the *non-lieu* beyond mortal reach

Where red is not an opposite of rot
Or devastation the reverse of peace
And all those things that were the case resume.

w. 1985, p. 1986

A FURTHER FRONTIER

Viewed from Corfu

To Lawrence Durrell

Seen across leagues of amethystine calm,
Two facing foreheads, one afforested,
The other sparsely greened as with Greek-hay,
An isthmus vista in between them hazed
By distant fluorescent shimmering
Of drowsy blended colours in which soot
Suffuses violet, peach and ivory.
Far to the East, a tranquil smoulder veils

Some remote city old as Trebizond,
Sated with myth and stunned by history,
Where linger shades of despots, peasants, saints,
Lost in oblivion's drifting dust. The end
Of afternoon approaches, the tenth month
Is almost here, further to obumbrate
A land once white with dawn, the nearby shore
Of North Helladic rock, whose dwellers owe
Fealty alike to thoughts of men long dead.
Night hovers like the question haunting all
As to whether *eschatos* has not come:
Unseen above hangs Saturn's fractured scythe.

w. 1985

A SARUM SESTINA

To Satish Kumar

Schooldays were centred round the tallest spire
In England, whose chime-pealing ruled our lives,
Spent in the confines of a leafy Close:
Chimes that controlled the hours we spent in singing,
Entered the classrooms to restrict our lessons
And punctuated the half-times of games.

The gravel courtyard where we played rough games
During the early break or after singing
In the Cathedral circled by the Close
And dominated by its soaring spire
Saw many minor dramas of our lives.
Such playgrounds predetermine later lessons.

Daily dividing services, meals, lessons,
Musical time resounded through the Close,
Metered existence like the rules of games.
What single cord connects most schoolboys' lives?
Not many consist first of stints of singing.
Our choral rearing paralleled a spire.

Reaching fourteen within sight of that spire
Unconsciously defined our growing lives,
As music's discipline informed our lessons.
We grew aware of how all round the Close
Households were run on lines that like our singing
Were regulated as communal games.

We sensed the serious need for fun and games,
What funny folk can populate a Close.
We relished festive meals as we did singing.
Beauty of buildings balanced boring lessons.
We looked relieved at times up at the spire
Balanced serene above parochial lives.

Grubby and trivial though our schoolboy lives
Were as all are, we found in singing
That liberation and delight result from lessons.
Under the ageless aegis of the spire
Seasonal feasts were ever-renewed games.
Box-hedges, limes and lawns line Sarum Close.

Choristers in that Close lead lucky lives.
They are taught by a spire and learn through singing
That hard lessons can be enjoyed like games.

w. 1984, p. 1986

NOVEMBER IN DEVON

Leaving Plymouth last seen after first smashed by bombs,
   Driving North all the morning after rain
      Towards Hartland's hospitable hearth
   Through landscapes clad in disruptive pattern
Material edged by hedge or walls of dry-stone:

Under a cover of commingling cloud and clear,
   Drifts of drab haze transpierced by wet blue slate,
      Between lofty moor and deep glen
   Past lanes twisting off into the arcane
We spin towards midday's strengthening sun.

After Launceston eleven o'clock approaches
   At a thousand revs per minute four times
      Beneath us: the car radio
   Picks up brass playing *Nimrod* in Whitehall,
Rearousing a reticent love for this land.

While memory brings back like a sepia still
   Holding my mother's hand in a Bournemouth
      Doorway during the first of all
   Remembrance Days' two minutes of silence,
Today I anticipate the advent of death.

A parade of folk sporting mass-produced poppies
   In the next village briefly delays us
      At a border-point round which spread
   Areas of age-old non-violence.
In ivy-dark gardens hang white rags of late rose.

An abrupt paranoia wonders just how sure
   One can be now that no secret convoy
      Was out during last night on roads
   Linking Hinckley Point and Bull Head, that near-
by tin-mines or tumuli hide no lethal hoards.

At half my age this might have worried me more.
   The South country kept my childhood secure.
      Now I know that to Whinny-moor
   Before long I shall come, as one more year
Declines towards departure in deceptive calm.

w. 1986

THREE REMANENCES

SCOTLAND 1919

In Kinghorn on Forth
held up to the sill
I saw dim shapes cross
the Firth's distant mouth –
the Kaiser's whole fleet
on its way to be sunk
in remote Scapa Flow
Nineteen years had to pass
before one could guess
what revenant would rise
from reprisal's sea depths

SPUTNIK OVER AIX

Every day for a week
like a steel astral tine
from the apricot West
slicing evening's swart skin
slowly but quick
on its way towards Cannes
slid fugacious sputnik

PROVENCE MARITIME

Half way between
L'Estaque and Aigues-Mortes
he she and I
after sardines and wine
lay spread on a bed of
couch grass and grey sand
like a twelve-limb-rayed star
beneath a taut awning
of cyan velour
sprayed with Milky Way sperm

Waking soon before dawn
I had to decide
between grasping her wrist
or caressing his nape

By the time light arrived
I still hadn't stirred
to wake them from sleep

w. 1992, p. 1994

IVY

The ivy invading my window-sill
Needs perennial cutting-back.
An ivy-leaf fluttering in the wind
reminds me of inhuman nature's
                            obstinate beauty.
A patch of pale blue behind it
portrays a persistent faint yearning
while the cloud crossing it
                            grey as boredom
is yet tinged with a flush
                            of residual hope.

w. Isle of Wight, 24 August 1994, p. 1995

APPENDIX A

UNPUBLISHED POEMS, DRAFTS AND FAIR COPIES

David Gascoyne in the 1940s

SONNET

A SONNET FOR A.K.M.

For countless miles around us stretches air
That knows strong Southern sunshine, Northern rains,
That moves on mountains, trembles over plains
Of burning sand, yet cannot let us share
Its pulsing knowledge, cannot sudden bear
On its wings away through lovely lanes
Of ice-blue sky and swirling, pearly chains
Of cloud to that unknown, desired place, where
Midst snow, the navel of the world, the core
Of light and dark lies naked and revealed,
The secret of the kabbalistic lore,
The meaning of the cosmos, unconcealed.
There man would be consumed with piercing awe
And madly from that Truth would search for shield.

w. 1932

HINTERLAND

(1)

Damp silence and dark in the valley; above the town
brown sackcloth hillsides slope barely away
to cold peaks and snow-crags where not yet the day
has turned on its light. Cold waters flow down
from a cleft in the hills: They are quiet in the night,
moving slow through the vale past the somnolent mill
whose wheels turn no longer, whose crankshafts are still;
past the wide, empty quayside where in the halflight
a few misty figures steal secretly by;
past the darktowering powerhouse where dynamos sleep,
to the ultimate plain, where unshepherded sheep
wander grazing and bleating beneath the dim sky,
flowing out to the sea through a motionless port
whose windows are shadowy, dockyards seem dead.
Fog moves up the valley; the heights overhead

can hardly be seen; but the time is now short
till the dawn.
    All the valley is waiting.
                The sea

beats impatiently on like a preluding drum
to the dazzling symphony of light that's to come.
All the valley is waiting and longs to be free
from this stifling curtain, the prison of dark.
From her nest of wet weeds in the midst of the plain
to rise upwards singing and joyful again
to welcome the first ray of dawn waits the lark.

(2)

And now, in this listening hush before light
when the valley seems waiting, and waiting is dumb
with expectancy; in this last hour of the night
strange portents appear of renaissance to come.

From behind the dead peaks of the last mountain range
a white comet bursts from its matrix of sky
trailing glorious streamers of swift-foaming flame
and down the cold roads of the air rushes by.

From a pass in the foothills a stranger came down.
Through the valley he wanders, a messenger-ghost.
He passes through the midst of the town
to the fog-hidden plain where vague sheep wander lost.

Now piercing the veils of the fog from the sea
a stately great ship up the estuary slides.
At the sound of her engines, the song of her crew,
on all sides around her the silence divides.

In the town a clock strikes and the lights one by one
begin faintly to glimmer in windows and streets.
Like sparks among stubble they spread house to house
and slowly before them the darkness retreats.

And lo! on the mountains the snows are aflame
with a gospel of hope for this sad hinterland

The mists glow with glory, the fog sails away,
and the lark rises singing, for dawn is at hand!

w. 1932

THE VERY IMAGE

The dark sun is drowned
Floats loose as a straw
Down the torrents of light
That no man's hand can check
On any stone
In the blank space between two dawns
The dawn behind is that of too dense dark
Before it lies the dawn of too scant day.

w. 1936

ASYLUM

'Red roses, red . . .,' the impotent cripple murmurs,
'I am so tired, so tired. Give back
Our blood, our rose-red blood!' Our nerves
Are famished, too; our aching eyes
Can hardly focus [on] the street's hard brick houses
Where the newspapers are read.

The genuine anger which this crime arouses,
This dastardly attack, that treaty broken,
Does not sustain the passing on of time
From one week to the next. Next week
No doubt, a worse event will call
For further and more fervent indignation.

All the exasperation, all the shouting,
The hysteria steadily mounting day by day,
Make it more difficult to hold on, hold out
Until the swelling burst: with bursting shells,
With squadrons darkening the sky – whole towns wiped out, -
The prelude to the final overthrow.

w. 1936

THE PERPETUAL EXPLOSION

When the wall was hidden by a cloud,
we knew the treasure must be hidden on
the other side. A garden of leprosy.
The sun was made of skin.
 When we sang into the hollow sun, our
skins began to stretch. We looked like
flies. There is a wheelbarrow in Heaven.
 Rouse your stick the stones will rise,
the flowers will appear to be
sewing their nerves to the veins of the stones,
your stick will stretch to a length of
one hundred and forty-two feet, the sound
of its growing will fill the ears of the flowers,
a growth of hair will fill the mouths of calves.
 A citadel of wax destroyed by a
beam of light. Tie your tongue to your
toes. Destruction is not immanent.
 Ants' eggs eat birds, birds eat palms,
palms eat carpets, the carpets are spread
across the path of the [meandering ?] corpse
which ate the coal buried at the foot of
the cross. The cataract of brains burns out
the speed of thought which equals the speed
of trains, increased by the power
of torrential deluges of rain. Great eyes of
ruined phosphor gaze into the sound of
cities, rising from the labours of the plain,
and hollow is the midnight of the wind. The
dust of houses falling in the rain is spread
across the outstretched body of remembered torment.
 'Do not beg me to cease, my end is
my own end, I see no further than the
distance which begins to be near.'
 'I cannot bear the beating of the rain
inside your brain, nor the movements of
destruction, nor the thawing of blackness of
the Poles. I am on fire.'
 And the gradual and unbearable
[thrust ?] of the womb becomes a hideous
throbbing hidden by the sulphur throat of

the sky, in which the flight of buildings
has darkened the deepening cleft which
separates the boiling flood of thought
from the metallic wrinkles of the roaring sand.

    'Have you carved your name upon the flank
of the immense stone basilisk who guards the fiery
gates? The key which I held in my
hand was bubbling liquid dark as ink
which fell and stained the mass beneath my feet.'

    'I do not know which way the wind has
gone, and carried with it all that I forget.'

    And the home of dusk turns on to its
side in the echo of chaotic
magnetism, determined to search the
further brink of silence, when the thickness
of the bolts is as a calming hand hard
on the forehead of the red-hot metal plates.

    And the thick skins of plants preserved in
alcohol begin to breathe through their
foreshortened sex, the sound of their
putrefaction is as breaking ice, their
heads are broken and their limbs are vapour.

    At each moment the sweat of snakeskin
pours from an eyelet in the partition
of a skull, in whose bleak shadow
strikes an acid clock. Long after its
last glimmer has faded into the
lake surrounding it the fog of
numbers and conundrums continues to
bind the shrivelled gods of iodine
together in the soft ears of the shells
which are swaying slowly to and fro in
the semi-darkness of the morgue. A
rapid claw slits open the velvet
throat of a bullock's horn which is
biting like a waltzer's skate into
the frozen surface of the tropic slime.
From top to bottom falls a cyst.

    'My fingers illumine the path which
leads from emptiness to suffocation.
There is no longer any reason why
they should continue to convert rain into

the weakness which robs our sleep of
dynamite. There are no more blades
between the sheets.'
   'Paralysis has not yet invaded the
[*two illegible words*], but an
approach has already blackened the
edges of the forms which represent our
desire to poison one another as soon as day breaks.'
   But suddenly a dense falsity
envelopes the conventional replies which
give rise to so much confusion that the
heat they engender almost melts the
tenderness of children's solitude, a pulp
of snowy substance resembling oxygen
oozes out of a confession, and converts
itself into strength sufficient to deny
everything that could possibly be said
concerning the relationship between man and woman.
   If man is no less than the initial of
a vanished species, the hasty signature of a vertebrate, if man is a thistle growing out of
the concentrated essence of his own contradiction and if he stands still before the
gaping mouths of wounds caused by falling
thoughtlessly through outer space, he is to
woman what an ultra-violet ray is to an infrared ray disclosing the decimal system which
forms the main structure of red sandstone, and woman is a tigress in the
dock, defending her right to weep for
all the children she devoured before they
even issued from her body and to
lament an opportunity of making herself at least the equal of those who
gaze upon her silently as she tears their
limbs to pieces before scattering them
like melted coins across the surface of the
plain which is about to be destroyed
by an eternal earthquake.
   Man is a padded cell in which woman can
fling herself from floor to ceiling without the least
sound of her screams being heard by

the world outside. Man is the finger
of a hand extended into the night to
see whether the rain is falling. Woman,
a bright and tinkling rain like that
which falls on mountain fields and
gems the threads of gossamer stretched
crazily between the eidelweiss, man a spear
of grass forcing its way out of the crevice
of a top-most rock and silhouetted
against the blue of distant heights. The
veins are curdled by the mysterious
discussion which goes on throughout the
night, the nerves awake and sing, a dew
of honey falls. Man and woman united
by the tremulous voice which rings
across the space between two peaks, man
and woman in their unity a mountain
range, a geological system, and at the
same time a pad of wadding between
two of the hardest surfaces which
ever pressed towards one another
in an attempt to crush everything
which is most glittering and most
evasively triumphant in the world.

'Out of the rainy night, a voice, a
hand, a spear. O lightnings, sear
the wigs of all those sombre heads
which pass in a silent procession
down the gorge; strike down the
branchy pines which mar the horizon's
ghostly clarity; and charge all
the mountain streams with electric light
and let them glitter down the vale
like morning staircases.'

'Out of the Polar city, a white road
climbs up into the burning plateau; and
man and woman must traverse that road.
When we are lost we shall look
back, and everything which was only
revealed to us in a passing flash
of light will stand out clear as
boulders from the sand.'

  Lip to lip, wrenched out of
solitude by a force greater than
all their solitary resistance, forced to
see their own faces in the light
of another's mirror – the twisted
wreckage dangling, twirling lazily in
the empty space above the roofs of the enormous
city, mangled railway-lines
a conglomerate mess
of shattered metals, – (the great
destruction has already begun), –
the body of love expressed
and radiant in the gaze of eyes
enlarged to the size of inner lakes,
with a great light breaking forth in
breathless rays in all directions, the
perfume of perfect flesh smouldering
in the dilated nostrils of the assembled
tribes, - for ever.
  'Both land and sea reach up towards
the highest breaking-point of atmospheric
pressure, where a single heart, its
beating having perpetually increased in speed
and force in proportion to the
increase in height and desperation, tears
through the imagined night like a mighty
phallus, winged and glowing red as the
warning lantern of an express train,
whose thundering pistons shake the
surrounding hills. Yet the true source
of its movement remains unshaken as the gradual
and awesome flowering of some crystal, breaking with
calm and relentless intensity out of formless
clouds of matter into the eternally
predestined figuration of the star which
is at the core of all explosions. A star
with an infinite number of rays,
each of which points out towards the
unnamed location of the unification of two bodies. And the
exploding heart breaks into an infinite number of pieces each of
which [is] about to undergo a similar
process of combustion. The heart at the

heart of the heart at the heart of the heart – is
an endless series: and each part of the
series is predestined to explode.
   'Forms, barriers, torrential rain,
the bright mind breaking
the earth's crust cracking, we have lain
asleep too long, there is nothing to impede
the progress of the waking planet towards
the sun. The loaves of rain-soaked bread
shall harden in the heat; we shall put on our
many-coloured robes, the sea shall come to meet us
and the dark shall die.
   Our eyes, all eyes are
fixed upon the unfolding blossom of the
horizon, the summit too long hidden by
the intermingled bodies of the halt and
blind. The world is moss, peat,
velvet, sand, and water fired with the
reflection of its burning vapours – the world
is stigma, orange, dew-pond, metal
ragged leaf and petal's odour, – dust
and syrens, clover, sparks, tumescence
pregnancy and rock.'

w. 1936

THE HILLS AND IN THE LIGHT, DAILY

When love sequestered from the mad dream of this man
Breaks into branches that unfold
In all the bounty that the brightest sun can boast

Smooth lips declaim their names and clear eyes scan
The heroes – whose the exploits shall be told
To these to come, whom the whole earth loves most

Now in the Perfect Tense we tell what they shall do:
Who loosed the captives, burnt their prisons, who
Made what seemed false the single true.

They held the sword that cleft in twain;
They took his stolen gold and gave it back again;
They broke the torture rack and stopped the pain;

And in all places built the bright abode
Of wisdom and the wide pleasant road
Away from darkness, that ensuing races trod.

But times do not revolve so easily;
And love is still unsheltered from the dream
That comes by night to make man restless, turn
Distraught from side to side, uneasily,
Torn between quietude and the destroying scream, -
Still ignorant, unable yet to learn.

What you involve. In perfect present time,
Are sewage systems breeding plagues of crime
Sapraemic cesspools choked with stinking slime.

w. 1936

COMPLINE FOR THE OCCIDENT.

A Cantata for Choir and Solo Voice (Fragment)

First voice:
To be
Open to every influx to obey
The law that governs mercury

First voice, Recitative:
To be
The first voice, and to break
The silence, and to say:
O speak
Now, voices of the speechless, in
My voice: O let me be
More than the voice
Of a young man alone
In a suburban bedroom, writing verse,
More than the mere
Articulation of ephemeral despair:
And let my one
Be subject to your many, at the core
Of the immense confusion and distress
Which drowns us. And to cry:

Be more than my confused subjective cry,
Confused, confusing cries, let my cry be not less
Than all yours crying, let me be possessed
By your obsession, and let me confess
To a confused distress not mine alone:
To be this voice, to give voice to this cry
So that the other voices may begin,
And having spoken to give place
To each voice in its turn

Chorus of questions:
Why do we wake
Each morning into shadow and not light?
Though sunlight may still fall
Across the coverlet, we can no longer feel
A sun within us radiate response:
And where there once
Rose like a spring in us the love of life
A dry stone lies. Why does each day
To which we wake seem like a lake of ice,
Whose unsafe surface we must cross
With swift and anxious steps
To reach sleep's brief security? Bad dreams
Recur more frequently each night though no-one knows
Their real interpretation; and sometimes
They even drift across the waking mind like clouds.

w. 1937

TWO FRAGMENTS

The twilight eats the reeds
a crooked pin
breaks the water into shapes
like those of frozen shawls
with which the dawn was decked.

All in the carious mouth is ash, sand in the teeth
But were our mouths, as red as madder meant to
Kiss and communicate?

w. 1937-38

COME DUNGEON DARK (PART III: CONCLUSION)

Though now the false cheque's countersigned, the fog
Of dream's delusion lifted from the air, and split will's
Confusion, realized at last, made all too clear:

Though now the spell be broken of the drug,
The faithful dozing dog awake to find
That he's been muzzled: though each slight mistake

Be seen to form a link in a tight chain
That now binds freedom to the stake of its defeat:
Though all past struggle to defend seems in vain;

O do not think that this must mean that Man
Is fated never to transcend his servitude,
Nor that the first and last condition of his world
Made this conclusion of defeat foregone.

w. 1939

DARK'S FIDELITY

While manhood's fire still burn the blood,
And quietens with unspent desire my breath,
There come to share the shadows of my bed
Many a slim sweet girl and sleek-limbed youth,
Though never next day by my side
Remains even a wraith.

But when they come no more, I'll turn
Gratefully to the dark's great emptiness
And sink, clasped in Night's arms, more deeply than
Ever in any girl's or young man's kiss;
Nor shall I wish to rise again
From that timeless embrace.

w. 1941

EPILOGUE TO AN EPISODE

I

An adolescent brooding on a bomb
Of hatred of appearances, longing to crack
The gimcrack and exasperating crust of everyday,
Frustrated by the gunpowder's failure to explode,
I jumped on to a bus at Charing Cross
One overcast Spring dusk, clutching my latest hope
Between the covers of a just discovered book.

For the first time, on a lurching top-deck seat,
Spelling out Breton's high-flown phrases' spell
I felt the toxic thrill
Of letting-go normal surface-hold to sink, though still awake,
Into wild mental regions far beyond the pale
Of Reason and beneath the genteel veil of
Calm, commonsense and compromise. His exhortations made
South Kensington, Earl's Court and quiet Kew
Seem built above volcanoes' buried mouths,
Strained violently to bursting-point in the green sunset glow
By the tense imminence of the super-real . . .

How finely attuned the nerves were that dark Spring
To the least hint of the miraculous! The sulphur in the air,
The tinkling of faint bells beneath the skin,
Bats buried suffocating in the hair of
Aunts at tea-time! broken window-panes
Through which the sky pushed inwards with grey rain-drenched
Groping hands! Flux of provoked delusions wherein lay
This single true conviction: the sublime
Existence I aspired to was always *elsewhere*,
Unprisoned by the walls of Space and Time.

II

Behind my single-handed unripe mutiny of mind
I found the solidarity of a well-trained band
Of bandits and conspirators already sworn for years
To systematic sabotage of 'the so-called real world',
And stealthy preparation of a series of strange coups
Planned finally to culminate in the storming of the Past's

Reactionary Bastilles by massed international groups
United in their frenzy by the flag
Of Revolution, Poetry and Love.

> *L'Amour*

(In me confined still to the head) was synonym
For *Poésie*: the poetry of bed, that famous chance
Encounter there: a Man Ray dream of fair
Surrealist women, glossy, svelte and flat.

> Devotee more

Of Poetry *per se* than of its flesh, for hours each day
I'd stare at zero, trying to glimpse the 'flash
Of silver on the brain's insuperable wall'; a spark
Out of the dark of that deep crucible where 'all
Our doubts, our poor abilities, the radical idea
Of impotence, and reputation's shreds, mixed up
With other sensitive glass instruments', were to be thrown
As though into a cellar: where mysterious light
'Might one day cease to flicker . . .'

> And for hours on end

I'd listen-in to the white voice inside my skull
(Like Death each minute murmuring a name)
Announcing non-stop nonsense news: 'The Iron Starfish Kneels
Under the Thirteenth Chair . . .': make records of its drool:
Or track the automatic paper-chase through outlawed, queer
Half-baked expanses where like weeds break through
A few weak obscene puns, where verbal mist
Is rarely stabbed by any ray of daylight making plain
The lie of the obscure surrounding text.

> And often now

I was a guest at that rococo vast chateau
Which had been built up slowly, wing by wing, upon a site
Staked out in the last century by seers:
Museum, zoo or waxworks, more involved than a mad brain,
A Tower of Babel full of winding stairs,
Corridors ravelled as intestines, secret doors
And rooms more difficult to count than those of Glamis,
Each one more unexpected than the room before, like tanks
In a deep-sea aquarium, full of alarming freaks:
Anthropomorphic, ectoplasmic forms

Far too profuse and complex to rehearse:
Unwieldy objects of no earthly use
From the fleamarket of the mind, oneiric beasts
Uncatalogued by heraldry, and sculpture carved
By Sleep's instinctive and unsteady hand.
Among these shapes the visitor may stray
As through a maze and with amazement see
The drawing-room whose ceiling is a lake, the corridor
Of which the lofty windows view the mountains of the moon;
The gallery whose niche of honour shrines
The statue of Lautréamont, piano-tuned,
Perched on a pillar of quinine; the hall
Where railway-engines fight with brontosaurs;
And somewhere lost in the colossal central court,
That desecrated chapel on whose windy stone-paved floor
The Dreamer and his mistress lie star-crossed,
United at their axe as by a sword . . .

w. 1939–40

DEAD END

It has become more difficult, more
Tiresome and more painful than before
To write the poem that perverse desire
To write a poem leads to. Most
Difficult of all lines is the first;
And hard again when one has written five
Or six, to clear away the mist
And seize an image (while excitement's still
Alive) and plant it in the shallow shifting soil
Of the first stanza: like a fist,
A flag, a lantern or a door. That done,
It then should need less effort to move on:
To choose, from many possibles, the one
Route that will take me to the end
By way of the most interesting
Scenery.

　　　　　But O! what scenery can I
Now see, through all the thicknesses
Of scruple, like smoked glasses, that descend
Upon my sight as soon as I've unwound
An opening! All images reduced
To less than crumbs, soon leave no trace
Or shadow; and the inner scene I had
Hoped would appear is further than Thibet! I'm faced
With the familiar Void: a vacant space
Like the uncoloured, senseless sea or sky
That hangs under the eyelids of the dead.

w. 1939–40

A LA FENÊTRE

Immediately above my ceiling lay
The {slanting roof-slates that kept Winter's rain
　　　{sloping
From seeping down to stain the room's white walls.
And in the Summer like a lid held in
The stewing inmates' fumes; upon
The unmade bed beneath it, I
Would lie on lean days in a daze
Of weak dejection, and for hours,
On end, half-dozing, half-awake,
Would gaze across at the pale glass
Through which was in the distance to be seen
One fragmentary cornice of a corner of
Notre-Dame, ~~whose chimes~~ . . .

w. 1940–41

EPILOGUE: 1940-1941

How far that last departure out of France
Seems now; way back in a Time-Past remote as myth's
Most misty hemisphere; from memory almost
Expunged entirely by the curtain-falls of rock
That since, descending on experience, have crushed
All spirit from the substance of our hope and left it
Carrion . . .

That far-off cold night when I
Last left the capital I had so loved:
A [starry] night in early spring, after a day
Of gusty rain and chilly stillness: tears
Raw in slow streams (as I sat in the train
Watching black landscape sliding past outside
The carriage window) out of my rapt eyes.
The heart I then had in me seldom stirred
Out of the trance that held it in its thrall.

w. 1941

DEAR THOMAS ELIOT

    Dear Thomas Eliot (let's suppress
                the Stearns
    Your fame no longer needs, and make
                this rhyme):
    There is no hell-fire where a
                martyr burns.
    Stern flesh rejoices to be cleansed
               in lime.

w. 1949–50

THE PORCH BEFORE THESE POEMS IS THE ENTRANCE INTO NIGHT

The porch before these poems is the entrance into Night
Dear nameless God, must I say Thee
Though towards the suburbs the city becomes wan
To heal the sick and cast out devils, Lord
The whole world still remains
That there is justice in the world
There are no harsh laws
Really religious people are rarely looked upon as such
Our God was executed by the people's will
Listen, lover of the glistening peril
I had not dared to turn inward my gaze
I praise Thee, O God
The Son of Man is in revolt.

w. 1949–50

'THE HAND THAT IN THE DARKNESS BEFORE [COLD] DAY'

The hand that in the darkness before [cold] day
Breaks with its sad blue glimmer on the ledge
Of the wide sill, the hand that still
[with age-old tenderness]
Gentle as negligeable breath
Passes across the Christ-crossed brow
Seraphic sentence has to say
Bringing a word unspeakable of life from out of death
Dear Child, dear father, dear
      [noble warrior], O Still.

w. 1949–50

'THE SON OF MAN IS IN REVOLT'

The Son of Man is in revolt
Against the God of men
The Son of God
Has nowhere now to rest his head
But in the outcast heart in solitude:
He is shut out, forgotten and his name misused
By those who never knew Him till the sword
He came to bring had been hid deep away
(Buried Excalibur) and in its stead
A jewel-filled butcher's knife brandished aloft
To bid the comfortable come to the rich board
Where their complacency and self-deceit
Might copiously be fed.

w. 1949–50

POEM [FRAGMENT]

When I am able to think at Night,
To make use of the night-hours given to all, for rest,
For retirement apart, for meditation, not desolate solitude –
Not for feverish flight from an inner emptiness
    or guilty exile from the light, -
Then the hours of darkness bring me deep new strength,
Calm confidence with which to face the trials
    and dangers in this world
Which await every man remaining resolutely loyal
To the power of Love that he carries in him,
The hours of Night restore me to my hidden truer self.
Even here, even now, at the darkest, most desolate hour,
The Eternal is closer and simpler than breathing,
    brimming over with boundless love.

w. 1950

HAIKU

Rain globules on glass
Make sorrow recognize pain's [world's]
Tears that blur clear sight.

w. 1950

UNTITLED

And tell me, how is Christ preached now
To megalometropolitan man, and how does Christ
Strike Democrats whose victory in War
Over the forces they called Antichrist's
Might have ensured the reign of Christian peace
Over at least the nineteen-fifties, had
They all been as sincere as those who died
In battles of the early forties. These
Naked souls we see now in city streets,
What rags have to lend them, who will freeze
To spiritual death with careless grins
Unless the clad ~~can lend them garments~~
How is Christ preached to them? From vans
Through blatant tinny speakers in such tones
As a bad sergeant might use on parade
Admonishing a teen-age idiot. They have heard
That sin's wages are death, what they believe
Is that virtues make one tough and mean
That the kind heart is soft with mawkishness.

w. 1954

REMANENCES

4. A Summer Evening at Caesar's Tower

[Aix-en-Provence]

Something's burning, not
too far away. What is it?
It could be brush, but smells
of, is it resin? That would mean
pines – they're everywhere
about in Cézanne Country.
Maybe it's coming from over
Bibemus way. Crepitations,
burning branches. The Black Château
though out of sight from here
might well be the conflagration's site.
Masson's property would be threatened
too if that's the case. Let's hope there's
someone there to fight the blaze.
Each summer now these [bon]fires
break out in Bouches du Rhône.
Can you hear that distant crackling?
You can't mistake that odour, it's
almost like incense. Now smoke's rising.
Tonight the festival's bound to be crowded.
*Mozart (as usual). At least the [Virots]**
won't be frightened of fire. So cool down
the air with the Roman fountains.
Vieux Garçons will be packed as usual.
Too late to go down there now.

w. August-September 1992, and 16 October 1995

---

* This word in DG's shaky handwriting is illegible. It may be a proper name.

APPENDIX B

DRAFTS, POEMS IN FACSIMILE, TYPESCRIPTS

David Gascoyne photographed by Rollie McKenna, 1951

ELEGIAC STANZAS.

IN MEMORY OF ALBAN BERG.

David Gascoyne.

ELEGAIC STANZAS

In Memory of Alban Berg.

I.

When a rich rose falls in flakes from a thorn-spiked stem
Its petals stain the dark eroded soil;
So tears fall heavily to stain the heart's stone floor.
A grief near madness sets its sudden springs
To leap without a cause from out our sleep,
Our jarring nervous dreams,
Until we shake with sorrow that we cannot name.

The rain with turbid drops adorns the leaves
Of rose-bushes that grow among the rocks
And stifle with their scent the chilly air.
It is the hour when disembodied heads,
The faces of the lost, glide pensively
Across the misty twilight of this distant place, –
Cimmeria, the refuge of the shades.

On high
Striations of white light amaze the sky;
While round the staring lead-eyed pool below
A dull wind stirs the agony of reeds,
Concentric ripples strike the waters' rim
Like echoes of a desperate final cry;
And arrow-headed birds fly fast away.

. . . . .

EX NIHILO

[Handwritten draft:]

Ex Nihilo

~~Here am I now cast down~~
~~Beneath the eyeless glare of the dead suns~~
~~which~~
~~Beneath the black glare of this netherworld's~~
~~Dead suns~~

Here am I now cast down
Beneath the black glare of a netherwold's
Dead suns, dust in my heart; among
Dim tiers no tears refresh am cast
Down by a   hand:

Hand that I love! Lord Light,
How dark is Thy arm's will and ironlike
Thy ruler's finger that has sent me here!
Far from Thy face, I nothing understand
But kiss the hand that has consigned
to this latter world
Me ~~[illegible]~~ where I must learn
The revelation of despair and find
Among the debris of ~~(this father world)~~ all certainties
The hardest stone on which to found
Altar and shelter for Eternity.

Here am I now cast down
Among the hopeless dust of fractured
Plinths, — shrine desecrated, glory trash,
The will uncurable: am cast
Down by a violent hand:

Here am I now cast down
Among   fractured
Plinths,

Down by a ruthless hand

Here am I now cast down
Beneath the arid eyeless glare of ashen
Suns, choked with dry darkness, in the tiers

MOZART: SURSUM CORDA

Filters the sunlight from the knife-bright wind
And rarifies the rumour-laden air
The all-receptive heart in pure hands held
Towards the sostenuto of the sky.

Supernal voices, flood the ear of clay
And break through the dense skull ! reveal
The immaterial world concealed
By mortal deafness and the screen of sense.

World of transparency and utmost flight,
And world within the world : beyond our speech
To tell what equinoxes of the absolute
The spirit ranges in its long upward release.

The Plummet Heart

Down, Hart, you fell down sound-
lessly, as though through shaft of lift,
leaving the roar of world's wind-parted rift
around the topmost floor. no ground

beneath, no wreath of rock
to crown your exit from his crux;
and as you dropped through the restricted flux
of such duration as the clock

controls, on swift walls shone
in mirrors as you hurtled by
the sculpture chiselled by your heart, until
the sea received you, azure antiphon
whose octave answer is the sky
where your wrecked smile drifts still.

David Gascoyne
27·X·39

APOLOGIA

> "Poète et non honnête homme."
> <u>Pascal.</u>

(i)

It's not the Age,
Disease, or accident, but sheer
Perversity (or so one must suppose)
That makes me pace the singularly bare
Boards of this trestle-stage
Which I have mounted, and adopt the pose
Of a demented wrestler, with gorge full
Of phlegm, eyes bleared with salt, and knees
Knocking like ninepins : a most furious fool!

(ii)

Fixed by the nib
Of this inept pen to a bleak page
Before the glassy gaze of a ghost mob,
I stand to face the silent rage
Of my unseen Opponent, and begin
The same old struggle for the doubtful prize:
Each stanza is a round, and every line
A blow aimed at the too elusive chin
Of that Oblivion which cannot fail to win.

(iii)

Before I fall
Down silent finally, I want to make
One last attempt at utterance, and tell
How my absurd desire was to compose
A single poem with my mental eyes
Wide open, and without even one lapse
From that most scrupulous Truth which I pursue
When not pursuing Poetry. - Perhaps
Only the poem I could never write is <u>true</u>.

David Gascoyne.

EPILOGUE TO AN EPISODE

EPILOGUE TO AN EPISODE

(I.)

An adolescent brooding on a bomb
Of hatred of appearances, longing to crack
The gimcrack and exasperating crust of everyday,
Frustrated by the gunpowder's glum failure to explode,
I jumped on to a bus at Charing Cross
One overcast Spring dusk, clasping my latest hope
Between the covers of a just discovered book.

For the first time, on a lurching top-deck seat,
Spelling out Breton's high-flown phrases' spell
I felt the toxic thrill
Of letting-go normal surface-hold to sink, though still
                                                (awake,
Into wild mental regions far beyond the pale
Of Reason and beneath the genteel veil of
Calm, commonsense and compromise. His exhortations made
South Kensington, Earl's Court and quiet Kew
Seem built above volcanoes' buried mouths,
Strained violently to bursting-point in the green sunset glow
By the tense imminence of the super-real....

How finely attuned the nerves were that dark Spring
To the least hint of the miraculous! The sulphur in the air,
The tinkling of faint bells beneath the skin,
Bats buried suffocating in the hair of
Aunts at tea-time! broken window-panes
Through which the sky pushed inwards with grey rain-drenched
Groping hands! Flux of provoked delusions wherein lay
This single true conviction : the sublime
Existence I aspired to was always <u>elsewhere</u>,
Unprisoned by the walls of Space and Time.

(II.)

Behind my single-handed unripe mutiny of mind
I found the solidarity of a well-trained band
Of bandits and conspirators already sworn for years
To systematic sabotage of "the so-called real world",
And stealthy preparation of a series of strange coups
Planned finally to culminate in storming of the Past's
Reactionary Bastilles by massed international groups
United in their frenzy by the flag
Of Revolution, Poetry and Love.

              L'Amour
(In me confined still to the head) was synonym
For Poésie : the poetry of bed, that famous chance
Encounter there : a Man Ray dream of fair
Surrealist women, glossy, svelte and flat.

                 Devotee more
Of Poetry per se than of its flesh, for hours each day
I'd stare at zero, trying to glimpse the "flash
Of silver on the brain's insuperable wall;" a spark
Out of the dark of that deep crucible where "all
Our doubts, our poor abilities, the radical idea
Of impotence, and reputation's shreds, mixed up
With other sensitive glass instruments", were to be thrown
As though into a cellar : where mysterious light
"Might one day cease to flicker...."

               And for hours on end
I'd listen-in to the white voice inside my skull
(Like Death each minute murmuring a name)
Announcing non-stop nonsense news: "The Iron Starfish Kneels
Under the Thirteenth Chair....": make records of its drool:
Or track the automatic paper-chase through outlawed, queer
Half-baked expanses where like weeds break through
A few weak obscene puns, where verbal mist
Is rarely stabbed by any ray of daylight making plain
The lie of the obscure surrounding text.

                And often now
I was a guest at that rococo vast chateau
Which had been built up slowly, wing by wing, upon a site
Staked out in the last century by seers:
Museum, zoo or waxworks, more involved than a mad brain,

A Tower of Babel full of winding stairs,
Corridors ravelled as intestines, secret doors
And rooms more difficult to count than those of Glamis,
Each one more unexpected than the room before, like tanks
In a deep-sea aquarium, full of alarming freaks:
Anthropomorphic, ectoplasmic forms
Far too profuse and complex to rehearse:
Unwieldy objects of no earthly use
From the flea-market of the mind, chimeric beasts
Uncatalogued by heraldry, and sculpture carved
By Sleep's instinctive and unsteady hand.
Among these shapes the visitor may stray
As through a maze and with amazement see
The drawing-room whose ceiling is a lake; the corridor
Of which the lofty windows view the mountains of the moon;
The gallery whose niche of honour shrines
The statue of Lautréamont, piano-tuned,
Perched on a pillar of quinine; the hall
Where railway-engines fight with brontosoars;
And somewhere lost in the colossal central court,
That desecrated chapel on whose windy stone-paved floor
The Dreamer and his mistress lie star-crossed,
United at their axe as by a sword....

DEAD END

It has become more difficult, more
Tiresome and more painful than before
To write the poem the perverse desire
To write a poem leads to. Most
Difficult of all lines is the first;
And hard again when one has written five
Or six, to clear away the mist
And seize an image (while excitement's still
Alive) and plant it in the shallow shifting soil
Of the first stanza : like a fist,
A flag, a lantern or a door. That done,
It then should need less effort to move on:
To choose, from many possibles, the one
Route that will take one to the end
By way of the most interesting
Scenery.   But O! what scenery can I
Now see, through all the thicknesses
Of scruple, like smoked glasses, that descend
Upon my sight as soon as I've unwound
An opening! All images reduced
To less than crumbs, soon leave no trace
Or shadow; and the inner scene I had
Hoped would appear is further than Thibet! I'm faced
With the familiar Void : a vacant space
Like the uncoloured, senseless sea or sky
That hangs under the eyelids of the dead.

David Gascoyne.

AN ELEGY, last page

Elegy. 6. iv.

To end at last, in bankrupt exile, in
This sordid scene of Ulysses; and there,
While War sowed all the lands with violent
graves,
You finally succumbed to a black, wild
Incomprehensibility of fate that none could
share....

Yet even in your obscure death I see
The secret candour of that lonely child
Who, lost in the storm-shaken castle-park,
Astride his crippled mastiff's back was borne
Slowly away into the utmost dark.

June 1941.
(Revised 24. XI. 41.)

Fragment
("From A Diary")
— 2nd Draft. — { 1st draft: 27.VII.41.

- Imperfections of substance, dross of the day-by-day;
  Banality, unlove and disappointment... Grey
  Webs of attrition, and the trivial tick
- Of the nerves' run-down clock, — dank skeins of thick

  Colourless thought unravelling through the skull,
- This bitter grit of conscience, and the dull

  Pulse of internal scars... Compression: no
- Inscape or scope or space: only the flow

  Of stupor's ~~ceaseless~~ steady muffled fugue. — At night
  [While ~~unseen hours pursue their (steady flight)~~
  ~~time pursues~~ unmatched its (weightless ~~flight~~)]

- Blackness lolls on the air, as still as gas
  And denser, round each building's lonely mass

(Fragment: "From A Diary")

- Collapsing in the depths of its own dream;
  Silence suppresses every pent-up latent scream;

- And I lie like a log (as I have lain
  ~~How many~~ year-long nights?), and once again,
   mute, locked
- ~~Mute and~~ immobile, in my private room,
  ~~Afar,~~ ruminating on the ~~ ~~ doom
                                  (unwritten)

- Awaiting all men's hearts in their dumb
                                    solitude,
  Within me my heart's numb, indifferent blood.

———————

(Bridlington: 2. XII. 47.)
(20 lines)

(To replace "Variation on a Theme.")

CHAMBRE D'HÔTEL

"Chambre d'Hôtel"

While a sad Sunday's silver light
Slid through the rain of afternoon
   And slimed the town's grey stones,
We side-by-side without a word
  * Above the cobbled island quays
Round which rolled on the swollen Seine,
   Lay staring at the white
And barren ceiling : till it seemed
We'd lain forever thus entombed
   Deep in unspeaking spleen.
                          (cont.)

[Above the island's cobbled quays] ?

                                  2.

Oh, when at last I tried to take
Your hand in mine, your stranger's face
   Towards my mouth to bend,
You sprang up from the bed and went
Away, across the room, to stand
And watch through muslin'd window-glass,
   The plane-trees lean to ask
The river what you too asked then,
A riddle without answer and
   As old as earth's disgrace.
                    (July, MCMXL.)

("Reminiscences of Paris" No. 6). 1

Noctambules.

They stand in doorways; then
step out into the rain ~~word~~
~~(disappear for now)~~
..Beneath the lamplight's blue
Aurora; down the street
Towards a blood-red sign
Scrawled swiftly on the wet
Slate of the midnight sky
Then sponged away again....
Some of them stand and wait
Beside the door. I cannot ~~me~~
not see their faces; some ~~are~~
are weeping. Now I hear
The tall one say: "The band,
~~Is playing Europe I start to~~
~~The jira in this~~ recklessly
~~with~~ My dear, is playing away
Our last hours, one by one..."
And now the girl in tulle
with mauve moths ~~fluttering~~ in
Her hair, ~~crowned~~ enters the full

EPILOGUE 1940-41

"Souvenirs de Paris": (VII).

Epilogue: 1940-41.

How far that last departure out of France
Seems now; way back in a Time-Past remote as Myth;
Most misty hemisphere; from Memory almost
Expunged entirely by the curtain-falls of rock
That since, descending on experience, have crushed
All spirit from the substance of our hope and left it
Carrion...
          That far-off cold night when I
Last left the capital I had so loved:
A night in early spring, after a day
Of rain, chilly and stillness: tears
raw in slow streams as I sat in the train
Watching black landscapes sliding past outside
The carriage-window) out of my rapt eyes.
The heart I then had in me seldom stirred
it, its
Out of the France that held it

SONNET: THE BATTLE

25.III.41.

Sonnet: The Battle.

Away the horde rode, in a storm of hail
And steel-blue lightning. Hurtled by the wind
Into their eardrums, from behind the hill
Came in increasing bursts the startled sound
Of trumpets in the unseen hostile camp.
Down through a raw black hole in heaven stared
The horror-blanched moon's eye. Across the swamp
Five ravens flapped; and the storm disappeared
Soon afterwards, like them, into that pit
Of silence which lies waiting to consume
Even the braggart World itself, at last....
The candle in the hermit's cave went out
At dawn, as usual. No-one ever came
Back down the hill to say which side had lost.

AN AUTUMN PARK

AN AUTUMN PARK

The world is dark again; but such
Ubiquity of shadow is unequal. Here
At the spiked gates which crown the hill begins
A reign as of suspense within suspense:
Outside our area of sand-bagged mansions, of our tense
And inarticulate expectancy of roars,
The unhistoric park
Extends indifference through all its airs.

During the present days
None but the lonely and reflective care to walk
Through these unworldly and concealed preserves
Of vegetable integrity, where trees
Though murmurous at least are without words.
For such unsocial ones the park negates
With its consistently non-human peace
All the loud mind-polluted world outside its gates.

When sudden sunrays break the brooding haze
Which makes monotonous these grounds,
Livid the little wind-flaked lakes appear,
Vivid the fever-mottled leaves still bound
By mouldering stalks to idly-shaken boughs;
Brief light and breath intensify the scene
With glitter drifting across wet grass wastes
And odour of crushed bracken and raw sand...

These acres bordering on plains of brick
And brain and coin and newspaper and noise,
Still store for townsmen such as seek
Remembrance of the simpler earth that was
Our dwelling and contentment once, a chance
Of rebeholding that lost innocence; may show
To such as walk today there to forget, the true
And imminent glory breaking through man's circumstance.

October, 1939.

David Gascoyne.

THE GRAVEL-PIT FIELD

Notes for a poem: (1)

(~~Stones and grass~~)

~~Other~~ possible titles:
"The Wilderness" — "Terrain Vague" — "The Gravel-Pit",
"Stones and Weeds" — "Zone" — "A Barren Acre"

- demonic exhalation of sub-soil
- a Pharaoh's necklet
- dead grass white & black
- breath of world's turning

- minutiae
- birds
- grey, colour of haze
- far edge of existence, beyond names

Hole for axle at centre of wheel (Lao-Tse)

Up ~~shapeless tiers~~
shallow sloping mounds of
gradual
Up ~~double~~ shapes of clay-soil tiers

Sprawls laggard across till
they reach a ~~~~ raw ~~~~ villous rim.

~~shapeless~~
Up ~~shallow steps (tiny tiers)~~   VI. Bones of a dead dog
                                      ("une baroque")
Upwards in shallow shapeless tiers

I. Field   IV. Stones, soil
II. Pits   V. { Strength, durability, triumph
III. Weeds, grass   of the utterly impoverished & despised
                  VI. { bare; & wise — outside time,
                       like "being" at core of an
                       idols brow, ~~Buddha~~

IX

Over the scene: And in a flash
Of insight I behold the field's
Apotheosis: No-man's-land
Between this world and the beyond,
Remote from men and yet more real
Than any human dwelling-place:
A tabernacle where one stands
As though within the empty space
Round which revolves the Sage's Wheel.

17·5·41·

III

The shabby coat of coarse grass spread
Unevenly across the ruts
And humps of lumpy soil; the bits
Of stick and threads of straw; loose clumps
Of weed with withered stalks and black
Tatters of leaf and scorched pods: all
These intertwined minutiae
Of Nature's humblest life persist
In their endurance here like rock.

POEMS PUBLISHED 1941, NOTES

Poems Published, 1941.

"Farewell Chorus" — Partisan Review, Jan. '41.
"Rain and the Tyrants" — N.S. & N. — Spring '41.
"The Writer's Hand" — Penguin New Writing, 7.
"The Gravel-Pit Field" — Folios of New Writing, Autumn '41.
"Noctambules" — Daylight, No. 1. - Agonia
{ "Lines" — Poets of Tomorrow, Vol. 2. (Hogarth Press)
"A Wartime Dawn" " " " "
"Walking at Whitsun" " " "
"Chambre d'Hotel" " " "
"Jardin du Palais Royal" " " "
"The Plummet Heart" " " "
"Phantasmagoria for M.W." " " (- Agonia.
"(Farewell Chorus" " " ")

"The Open Tomb" — Modern Reading, 4.

(Notes.)

- The Cavernous Wound
- Dichotomy
- A Simple Tune
- Ode to Rimbaud
- Humilis
- An Epistle to All
- Thrice Myths: Onan, Janus, Narcissus
- Patmos
- The Fall of Kharkov.
- Poem for Ruby M.
- Dramatic Episode (protagonists, narrator, chorus)

(Poems Published 1941, continued from opposite):

"Loveland" — Agonia, Buenos Aires. September '41.
"Inferno"   "
"Epode"   "
"Sonnet" ("Morning. Full Chorus of the birds...")
"Projections of Desire"

REQUIEM

Hymn ~~Requiem~~
1.

for Frank Kainer

Voice: O Hidden Face! O Gaze fixed on us from afar,
And that we cannot see: Grant us, who wait
In the great park of tumbling monuments that is
The world, that we may meet at last those eyes,
In which the black fires burn white,
With perfect clearness, and not veiled by weary heat,
Nor in the sudden spasm of disintegrating fear
That rends the heart of hearts, and blinds
The blind and unpitying: And O instruct
Us how to ripen into Thee.

Choir: Hearts are unripe
And spirits light as straw, and in Thy light
Shall kindle as the straws and burn away
To nothing in an instant brush of smoke.

Voice: Thy light is like a darkness and thy
Joy is found in grief. And those who search
For thee shall find thee not. And hidden in thy mouth
The blinding benediction of the final phrase
Which shall not fall upon a listening ear.

Choir: For those who listen at the guarded door
Hear only their heart beating out its fault.

Voice: In the great park,
The wanderer at sundown by the weeping falls
Of bloodless spume and fine prismatic spray
Has seen across the water in the last elusive light
A figure with a bright black chalice come.

Choir: But it was not thy angel.

Voice: And another heard
A warning echo in a mountain cave,
Reverberant with distance and with an undertone of guilt

Choir: But it was not thy voice.

REQUIEM

>"Permets que nous te goûtions d'abord le
>   (jour de la mort
>Qui est un grand jour de calme d'épousés,
>Le monde heureux, les fils réconciliés."
>   Pierre Jean Jouve.

Recitative

[1] **Voice:** O hidden Face! O gaze fixed on us from afar
That we cannot meet : Grant us, who wait
In the great park of crumbling monuments that is
The World, that we may meet at last those eyes
In which black fires burn back to white,
With perfect clearness, and not blurred by fever's heat
Nor in the sudden spasm of disintegrating fear
That rends the breast of beasts and blinds
The blind and undefined : And O instruct
Us how to ripen unto Thee.

Sotto Voce

[2] **Choir:** Hearts are unripe
And spirits light as straw, that in Thy light
Shall kindle like the straw, and flare away
To nothing in an instant breath of smoke.

A Vagrant.

They're much the same in most ways, the big cities. Those that I've seen, this one is of them all easiest, the best big metropolitan area for a man to wander in when he has ceased to find shelter, relief or dream in sanatorium bed, and nothing calls to him decisively to bring an end to brain's proliferation in the void of possibility that up adolescence, even years up to the thirtieth birthday — nothing calls or seems to wait till his arrival, my arrival (I am he) that the solution now most conveniently to say has been found after spans unavoidable delay due to this state of wars that we've been having lately, — here it is,

RONDEL FOR THE FOURTH DECADE

A RONDEL FOR THE FOURTH DECADE

The mind if not the heart turns cold
Seeing the calendar's leaves flying;
Yet dare not yet cease trying
To coax the heart to accept growing old.

However often heart's fortune be told
By skeptic mind, it beats on still relying
On consanguinity for help to hold
By against age's chill and sighing.

But when the last leaves are swept flying
From our life's tree, a stone is rolled
Over the hole where as they turn to mould
The heart's remains still lie denying
That mind can know the truth of dying.

David Gascoyne

D. Gascoyne,
Hotel du Pas de Calais,
57 rue des Saints-Pères,
Paris VI.

BARCAROLLE

Three Venetian Nocturnes

1.
Barcarolle.

The day's sun-floodlit blue floats through green
Which with a flow of indigo evening into night,
stains sky, ocean and shore;
And deep in velvet folds of dark are absorbed
from the air
The orchestrated murmurs of the crowd and bursts
of bright
Abruptly ebbing brassy music bruited from the
Square.

On the lagoon drift shreds of serenade
from lanterned boats
That bob more quickly like a pulse when
from the Lido steers
Close past them the returning vaporetto; the
heart beats
More quickly for a moment, lifted on a wave
of tears
Upwelling but not breaking in the eyes of one
who floats

Reclining in a gondola alone and with
Being borne across the Bacino the tide towards where
In heaven like spilt pearls all the stars on the black
Heaving liquidly about her robe Venice wears
when as a nocturnal bride
She mourns her youthful glory long drowned
in the sea of years.

———

Three Venetian Nocturnes.
1.

Stele

The most enduring final statement
Is the Silence we don't hear.
It digests everything.

Silence that's NEVER known this side
of death.
Try for a moment to experience it
You may hear Nothing; but that's
not the Silence

For Nothing just makes its own
inquiet noise,
A sort of famished gasping in
the eardrums
An ever-ending syllable of suppressed
anguish

TERMINAL

<u>Terminal</u>.

"<u>Poetry? I too dislike it...</u>"
(M. Moore).

The most enduring massive statement
Is the silence no-one hears.
It sums up everything.

There is no silence on this side of death.
Listen to any muted moment
When all is quiet. You will not hear it.

Yet it is under all and overhead
Not less indubitable than the firmament.
It is itself the Word.

It affords vast relief
To recollect that 'tis being spoken
Making inept all tongues that would
                              compete.

ELEGIAC IMPROVISATION IN HONOUR OF PAUL ELUARD, page 1

Elegiac Improvisation.
In Honour of PAUL ELUARD

A tender mouth a sceptical shy mouth
A firm fastidious tender mouth
A Gallic mouth an assymetrical mouth

He opened his mouth he spoke without hesitation
He sat down and wrote without crossing
And as he wrote his lines
began to speak

Warmly and urgently
Gently and movingly
Simply, and convincingly
Clearly, sincerely
Bitterly, painfully
Softly, caressingly
Pensively, stumblingly
Brokenly, heartbreakingly,

ENTRANCE TO A LANE

Memento rectangled to lead the gaze
From outer levels to a log of solids,
An elsewhere that recedes from curling
leaves

Sequestered mural scene sleputed stylish,
Section's insignia reduced to stones
Of red and verdure, ceases to spray
of blotch

A static vortex in which a dim glow flows
Softly in strata licked by staseless and
Of compact shade and long stones
which light

The felt-floored lane leads to a
blank where lines
And perceptions vanish as fast as time
Into the non- beyond alerted reach

Where red is not the opposite of not
On devastation the reverse of peace
And all the things that were self cease
resume.

July 23/85
1985

APPENDIX C

NOTES TO POEMS / COLLECTIONS

David Gascoyne in a Paris bookshop, 1984

POEMS WRITTEN AT SCHOOL

Storm and **October Night**
Two of 'Four of Several Poems Written by David Gascoyne (Chorister)' written in September and published in *St. Osmund's Magazine* (December) of that year. The other poems were 'The Tear of Shame' and 'The Stork'.

ROMAN BALCONY AND OTHER POEMS (1932)

DG told Michèle Duclos: 'I was already politically aware and this expressed itself in my poetry from the outset. So the title of my first collection translates the notion of Roman decadence, the end of a civilization'. He was influenced, he said, by Walter Pater and his reading of *Marius the Epicurean*, and explained his chosen title for the collection. As far as '*Balcony*' is concerned, he thought it an unconscious reminiscence of Pater. He was to add a little to this in his introductory note to 'Mood', reprinted in Jon Stallworthy's anthology *First Lines*: 'The title reflects a concern with "the Decline of the West", a constant implicit theme in nearly all my poetry to date, the Roman Empire's decline and fall representing an immature metaphor for the continually increasing social and spiritual crisis experienced by my generation and its successors' (p. 107).

'It's obvious that at first I was under the influence of the Imagists,' DG told Michel Remy in the interview extract published in *Temenos* 7 in 1986. In a conversation with me he acknowledged, too, 'very definitely' in his first collection, the influence of T.S. Eliot's 'early Imagist poems' (he cited **Exhaustion** as an example) and *The Waste Land*, of Baudelaire in **The Bridge** and possibly that of Verlaine, 'though my discovery of Rimbaud would relegate the importance of Verlaine.'

During our conversation in 1995 DG was struck by the fact that he had chosen to use lower-case letters at the beginning of each line of verse in more than a few poems. 'I avoided it after a while,' he confided, 'because everybody else was doing it.' Significantly, however, it was his selection of form and metre in the poems which seemed to intrigue him more and more with each re-discovery. He sat across from me reading aloud and tapping out the beats in the lines on his book or the arm of his chair. 'I'm pleased to see that I used clipped lines.' Then, a few moments later, 'And I like to see the use of four syllable lines in this poem, and my experiments with different techniques.' He added with a smile, 'When I broke the rules, I always did so deliberately.'

'Transformation Scene'
Published in *Everyman*, 19 May 1932, p. 536

'The New Isaiah'
DG commented to me that he found it interesting then to realize with the benefit of hindsight that several poems had been rehearsing for and leading up to **Night Thoughts** (1956), long before its publication and first broadcast. The genesis of that 'radiophonic poem' can be found in **The New Isaiah**, and later poems listed in my note to **The Post-War Night**.

OTHER EARLY POEMS (1932–1935)

By the Sea Traditional form & Modernist form
Published in *The Quintinian*, 24, Spring of that year, on pp. 31–32.

Susan: a carving by Eric Gill
First published in *Recent Poetry 1923–1933*, edited by Alida Monro (Gerald Howe Ltd. & The Poetry Bookshop, December 1933), p. 54.

From **Ten Proses**
First published in the *New English Weekly*, 14 September under the title 'Ten Proses'. **The World of Chirico** was included by DG in his *A Short Survey of Surrealism* (1935), pp. 74–75.

From **Automatic Album Leaves**
Nine prose poems were published under the title 'Surrealist Cameos' in the *New English Weekly*, 30 November, and numbered i–ix.

Hommage à Mallarmé
First published in *The New English Weekly*, 27 July.

Oleograph
First published in *Frontier and Midland*, Vol. 14, No. 2 (January).

Night-Piece
From *The Listener*, 31 October, p. 748.

End of Peace
Published in *Tone. Modern Poetry*, No. 3, 1 March, p. 11. DG is described on the Contributors pages as follows: 'David Gascoyne,

whose home is in England, is at present working on the staff of a newspaper in Paris'. There is no evidence to support this.

They Spoke of a New City
From *The Bookman* in the March issue.

The Roots of Evil
From *The Bookman* in the August issue.

MAN'S LIFE IS THIS MEAT (1932)

A note on page 4 explains that 'With the exception of Nos.1–6, the poems in this collection are Surrealist poems.'
DG's translation of Eluard's 'Critique of Poetry' precedes the Contents page:

> Of course I hate the reign of the bourgeois
> The reign of cops and priests
> But I hate still more the man who does not hate it
> As I do
> With all his might
> I spit in the face of that despicable man
> Who does not of all my poems prefer this *Critique of Poetry*.

I asked him in 1994 about the experience of 'automatic' writing. 'In my Surrealist phase,' he said, 'I tried to make my mind a blank and wrote down whatever came into my head. It's like a session of psychoanalysis – the result will be typical of you – people have clusters of images in their minds and they come out this way – clusters of words and images and associations – what comes out is a unique combination of new words and images. Surrealist writing is the cultivation of spontaneity.' DG's 1935 review in the December issue of *New Verse* of Paul Eluard's most recent poems, *Facile* (illustrated by Man Ray), has some relevance here. 'In Eluard,' he writes (p. 19), 'there can be no question of *premeditated style* or *imagery*' (his emphases). No other living writer has achieved such perfect *spontaneity*' (my emphasis). DG also told Mel Gooding: 'I just ceased to write that sort of poem, you know, or quasi-automatic writing, without correcting what you'd written. I became more interested in creating – saying something which had form as well as content [. . .]' (MGI), p. 64.

Reintegration
First published in *The Year's Poetry*, compiled by Gerald Gould, John Lehmann, Denys Kilham Roberts, p. 138.

Charity Week, Yves Tanguy, The Rites of Hysteria, Unspoken
When I pointed out to DG the incidence of references to hysteria in these poems, he was surprised: 'I tried to write poetry that reflected the atmosphere of the times, that was typical of the febrile atmosphere of the thirties; for example, the bombardment of the workers' flats in Vienna (as in Spender's poem), the feverish, sinister atmosphere of the film *Dr. Mabuse*, smuggled out of Germany. The unpublished poem you've shown me, **Asylum**, reflects this. Another film was Pabst's of Kurt Weill's *Threepenny Opera*' (1994).
Charity Week is dedicated to Max Ernst whom DG first met in 1933. He told me that by 1934 he had seen Ernst's 'Iconographie' at the end of *Une Semaine de Bonté*. These collages constructed by the artist of Dr Charcot's hysterical women at the Salpetrière Hospital in Paris in the late nineteenth century are displayed in the last seven plates of the book and portray disjunctions of mind and body. Paul Eluard's translation into French of **Charity Week** appeared in *Cahiers d'Art*, 10 (1935).

'The Truth is Blind'
DG accepted that the title is a paradoxical expression, 'found spontaneously, which equates truth and the traditional image of Justice'. The text also expresses 'my continued preoccupation with the relationship between poetry and truth, as in Goethe's *Dichtung und Wahrheit*, Eluard's *Poésie et Vérité* or **Apologia** [1943], another of my poems. It is a collage poem where I think of myself as the inventor.' (MRUI), p. 120.

Educative Process, Antennae
'Both "Educative Process" and "Antennae" were written under the influence of Eluard's poetry' (MRUI), p. 120, and DG indicated, in particular, *L'Amour la Poésie* and *A Toute Epreuve*. Eluard was the first Surrealist he met on his initial visit to Paris in 1933.

Salvador Dalí
Originally entitled 'In Defence of Humanism' when first published in *New Republic* in October 1934. DG told me with a smile that it was an ironic title then, and that he had put himself in the poem as a David (unnamed) to Goliath who '[. . .] plunges his hand into the

poisoned well ? / And bows his head and feels my feet walk through his brain [. . .]'. 'I was also incorporating autobiographical details into the poem.'

He commented to Duclos that 'The poem on Dalí isn't a Dalian transcription [of images] but a homage' (MDC), p. 122.

'And the Seventh Dream is the Dream of Isis'
'The first authentically automatic poem that I wrote, following the orthodox Surrealist technique.' (MDC), p. 21.

See Michel Remy's brief illuminating analysis of the poem in his *On the Thirteenth Stroke of Midnight: Surrealist Poetry in Britain* (Carcanet Press, 2013), p. 8.

SURREALIST AND OTHER POEMS (1936–1938)

The Entrance to that valley stands alone
First published in a limited edition on the occasion of DG's 85th birthday on 10 October 2001. As I wrote then in a note on the text, this 'is a transitional poem on the cusp of that conscious thrust, following his growing dissatisfaction with Surrealism, to find a different kind of language. It seems to anticipate that used in the four original poems interpolated in **Hölderlin's Madness** (1938), yet in the later stanzas of this poem Surrealist imagery echoes the speaker's disjunction.' Add. 56043.

Phenomena
A prose poem 'influenced by the texts of Jennings and Charles Madge' (MRUI), p.123.

The Very Image
DG emphasized that the window is the subject which struck him most forcibly in Magritte's work (MRUI), p. 122, and explained that when, early in the 1980s, he read this poem at the Tate Gallery, he thought it would be interesting to give a title of a Magritte painting to each of the six stanzas accordingly: 1 'The Human Condition'; 2 'The Charms of a Landscape'; 3 'The Man of the Sea'; 4 'Memory of a Journey'; 5 'The Reckless Sleeper'; 6 'The Captives'. 'They are not actual Magritte paintings; I simply wanted to indicate some paintings that he would have been able to produce', (MDC), p. 22.

The Great Day
Prefaced on publication in *Janus* (January 1936) by the following, in parenthesis: '[Simulation of Paranoia: Acute Mania, Delirium of Interpretation, Delusions of Grandeur.]'. Gascoyne had purchased a copy of *L'Immaculée Conception* in Paris in December 1933 and brought it back to London with him. Before that 'momentous' first visit to the French capital, he had studied the translated texts, which made up the 'Surrealism and Madness' section of the September 1932 issue of *This Quarter*. These included André Breton's article 'The Treatment of Mental Disease and Surrealism', and passages from three of the five essays by Breton and Eluard which form the section 'The Possessions' in *The Immaculate Conception*: 'Simulation of Mental Disability Essayed'; 'Simulation of General Paralysis Essayed'; 'Simulation of the Delirium of Interpretation Essayed'. DG told Lucien Jenkins that it was 'a very brief period in my life belonging to the Surrealist Movement, writing Surrealist poetry. I disliked the label "Surrealist Poet" which was hung around my neck for years and years, long after I had stopped writing automatically.' (LJI), p. 23. Asked by Michel Remy about the importance of Surrealism, he replied: 'It's very great. Never for a moment have I regretted taking part in the movement, but I could not have remained in it for long, like many others who left it, with the exception, indeed, of [Benjamin] Péret . . .I think the spirit of Surrealism is eternal', (MRT) pp. 270–71. 'I had to begin by separating myself from Surrealism in order to develop what was in me', op. cit., p. 270.

The Symptomatic World
Five 'Fragments', first published in October 1936, pp. 113–115, were followed by two further 'fragments' that same year in the next issue of *Contemporary Poetry and Prose*, pp. 134–135. These seven sections were presented together for the first time in *Early Poems* (Greville Press, 1980) with this statement: 'This sequence originally contained XII poems, but the remaining five were never printed, and the MS is now lost.' I have seen no evidence to support the existence of the missing five. The earlier section, 'At the age of nine months I entered the world' from *Janus*, No. 1 (January 1936), became the first, when the eight appeared complete in *Collected Poems 1988*.

Eau Sifflé
DG inscribed a copy of his second book of poems 'A Georges Hugnet, grand amitié toujours, David Gascoyne, October 15th 1936.' On the rear inside blank page he handwrote the poem first

published in 1992 in *Poésie 92*, No. 41 (Paris). This copy of **Man's Life Is This Meat** is part of the Gabrielle Keiller Collection now in the Scottish National Gallery of Modern Art. Hugnet's comments in his long contribution, '1870–1936', in *Surrealism*, edited by Herbert Read (Faber & Faber, June 1936), represent a useful attempt to characterize Surrealist poetry which is 'in opposition to the usual conception of poetry'. Surrealist poetry, he suggests, can be 'roughly divided into the automatic text, the dream narrative, and the poem properly so called' (p. 214).

Goût du Jour, Cafard, Récupération
Recovered from a 1930s notebook and first published in *Poetry Review*, Vol. 86, No. 1 (Spring 1996).

Fool's Paradise
Add. 56040. First published in *Maggie O'Sullivan, David Gascoyne, Barry MacSweeney*, Etruscan Reader III (Etruscan Press, 1997).

Symptomatic World
Add. 56040. First published in Etruscan Reader III, op. cit., in 1997.

Elegiac Stanzas In Memory of Alban Berg
The first draft, Adds. 56041, 56043 is in four sections I, II, III and Elegiac Stanzas IV. The second draft in two sections is in the Berg Collection, New York Public Library. First published in *Despair Has Wings. Selected Poems of Pierre Jean Jouve*, translated by David Gascoyne, edited by Roger Scott (London: Enitharmon Press, 2007), pp. 168–174.

'Chorus' to *Procession in the Private Sector*
DG's Surrealist film scenario, 'The Wrong Procession' (1936) was first published from a notebook in the British Library by Michel Remy in *David Gascoyne, ou l'urgence de l'inexprimé* (1984). In his Author's Note, DG indicated that he 'had originally intended a Surrealist-type poem to be incorporated as a spoken commentary at a certain juncture of the film, but I do not think I was ever able to produce a poetic text suitable for this purpose.' I found the poem in 1992 out of place in the same notebook, and it was published in 1998, together with the renamed **Procession to the Private Sector**, *in Selected Prose 1934–1996*, pp. 357–72, 460–62.

The Moon Over London
From notebook 1937–8. First published in *The Independent* in 1996, and in *Nineties Poetry: Winter 1995–96* (Lansdowne Press).

An Unfinished, Post-Auden Pre-War Proem (for J[oan] S[cully]
Originally 'Proem' in a 1930s notebook and retitled by DG for publication in the *London Review of Books*, 25 January, 1996.
His 'Notes' survive: 'Proem':
This is to be a long poem, of some fifty or more six-line stanzas, on the pattern

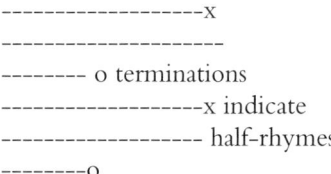

The title implies the tradition of Wordsworth's *The Prelude*. Theme of the poem is a young man addressing a young woman on the life of their times which they are to share with one another; an introduction to modern existence, sketching in the basis of an attitude, a philosophy, a morality, and taking account of all the facts, outward and inward, which are likely to mould the sensitive today. The intimate and the public world. Love and death as they appear in the light of contemporary historic upheaval.

1. Introductory
2. But think: have we filled our map?
3. This summer evening's like your country dream.
4. The City's facts
5. The Moral Journey
6.   "   "
7.   "   "
8. The Social World
9.   "   "
10.   "   "

Three Verbal Objects
Included as untitled poems in the catalogue *Surrealist Objects and Poems* for the exhibition at the London Gallery which opened in November

1937. The three prose poems were posthumously dedicated to the author of a series of 'Reports' and short texts, Humphrey Jennings, of whom Gascoyne spoke to me warmly. They first came into contact in the mid-1930s through Surrealism and Mass-Observation. 'I must have been one of the last people to see Jennings, apart from the film technicians, just before he died [in a bizarre accident when he slipped and fell on a Greek island, while filming in 1950]. "I know what I'm going to do with the rest of my life," he told me, "I'm going to paint".'

'Transparency of the vegetable world'
From a notebook dated 1937–8. First published in Etruscan Reader III, op. cit., 1997.

Phantasmagoria
In a prefatory note to a selection of his poems in *Poets of Tomorrow*, Third Selection (Hogarth Press, 1942), p. 25, DG wrote, '"Phantasmagoria" was written 'primarily as a *divertissement*, [. . .] the first Surrealist poem I have produced since I decided a few years ago, to abandon the "Surrealist" technique and general approach to poetry. It will probably be my last poem of this sort.' He added a final paragraph, dissociating himself once again at that time from Surrealism: 'I feel that poetry of the "magical" category – product of sheer imagination, unrestricted by pure design and untempered by the wisdom of disillusionment – may be more stimulating, more immediately satisfying to write; but in the long run is probably less rewarding, less consoling, than that resulting from conflict between the instinctive poetic impulse and the impersonal discipline, the unadorned sobriety of realistic "sense".'

HÖLDERLIN'S MADNESS (1938)

In 1937, DG contributed his only published short story, 'Death of an Explorer' to the anthology *Under Thirty*, edited by Michael Harrison (London: Rich & Cowan Ltd.), with an autobiographical preface of four paragraphs. In the third he wrote: 'I no longer have any desire to be connected with any particular group, ideology, or programme, but wish to be entirely free to develop my own individual preoccupations, which centre round the inner problem of modern man: the necessity for *greater consciousness of himself*: as a social being, as a psychological being and as a spiritual being – a problem too great to be perceived from a single, fixed point of view', p. 172.

His journal entry for 24.IX.37 reads: 'Until I wrote *Hölderlin's Madness* a few days ago, I had scarcely written poetry of any kind for well over a year.' He continues: 'Anything of the kind I may write from now on will be entirely different: no more themeless improvisation, no more autonomous lyricism, no more "pure" effect. I want depth, solidarity, experience. Poetry that will say something definite. Emotion, a raised voice, but clear and coherent speech' (CJS), p. 129.

On 30.V.38, DG noted that the eight months' period in Paris from August 1937 until the end of March 1938 had 'brought a definite enrichment and an *approfondissement* I did not have before, – a greater understanding of solitude, poverty and despair, and of the nature of human relationships. I wrote *Hölderlin's Madness* and "Despair Has Wings"' (CJS), p. 156.

Remy questioned DG in the *Temenos* interview: 'You say that to write creates the possibility of danger.' The reply is particularly relevant: 'Yes, that is the theme of one of Heidegger's essential commentaries on Hölderlin, who referred to writing poetry as "the most innocent of all occupations" but designated language on the other hand: "most dangerous of possessions". To create is to take risks. Hölderlin wrote that "God is near and difficult to grasp but danger strengthens the rescuing power" (opening of the poem "Patmos"), and it is true that a hard winter will produce a good harvest. That seems pitiless, Neitzschean: perhaps, but the danger lies in that as a writer one sets in motion a renewal of vision, and one can come to grief.' (MRT), p. 270.

DG had no German, and his own versions were 'made with the help of two German friends who were living in Paris at the time', as he explained in his contribution, 'A Paris, en 1937 . . .' to *L'Autre* (juin 1992), Jouve number, p. 11. In a presentation copy of *Hölderlin's Madness* from the author to John Arlott, inscribed in 1944, DG wrote: 'Entirely superceded [sic] by more recently published works, such as Michael Hamburger's and J.B. Leishmann's [sic] authoritative versions. The awful truth is, you see, that I don't really know a word of German, & all I ever understood of Hölderlin – if anything – was acquired solely through the exercise of sheer, or mere, intuition . . .'

His Introduction to *Hölderlin's Madness* (J.M. Dent & Sons Ltd., 1938), pp. 1–14, was reprinted in *Selected Prose 1934–1996*, (London: Enitharmon Press, 1998), pp. 155–162. At the end of his preface there is an important note: 'The poems which follow are not a translation of selected poems of Hölderlin, but a free adaptation, introduced and linked together by entirely original poems. The whole constitutes what may perhaps be regarded as a *persona*' (p. 162).

Orpheus in the Underworld
Gwendolyn Murphy included the poem in her anthology *The Modern Poet* (Sidgwick & Jackson, 1938) and DG told her that 'Orpheus in the Underworld' was 'from a new series of religious – or "metaphysical" – poems on the theme of Death'. This poem, he said, 'is not meant to be a transcription of the Orpheus legend but an allegory of the spiritual condition of the twentieth-century poet' [. . .] and 'refers to the poet Hölderlin exiled to the underworld of insanity.' At the same time it has the above general reference 'to the poet in the world of today' (p. 202).

POEMS 1937–42 (1943)

In his journal entry for 12 September 1939, DG had recorded his intention to write to T.S. Eliot 'to try to make him come to a final decision about the collection [of his poems] that T.S. Eliot is supposed to be considering for Fabers' (CJS), p. 272. Eliot rejected the poems. 'He said,' DG told me with a smile in 1998, 'that they "lacked sufficient objective correlativity".' Eliot also decided against publishing Kathleen Raine's first collection of poems, returning the manuscript to her. Some years later, she recalled in her autobiographical *The Land Unknown* (London: Hamish Hamilton, 1975, p. 156), Eliot admitted that he had had afterthoughts about both younger poets: '*Another* mistake I made was over David Gascoyne,' he told her.

A note by DG to the first edition (and subsequent second and third impressions, 1944 and 1948) of ***Poems 1937–42***, explains that:

'The poems in this collection were originally planned as two separate ensembles: "The Open Tomb" (1937–39) and "The Conquest of Defeat" (1939–42); but it has now seemed expedient to combine the two under the present title, and to rearrange the whole order of the poems so as to present them here in five main groups, roughly classifiable as follows: (1) Religious poems; (2) metaphysical (or "metapsychological") poems; (3) a longer poem; (4) poems on themes of a "personal" nature; (5) poems of time and place.'

Graham Sutherland's eight designs for *Poems 1937–42*
DG's illuminating description of the drawings (gouache, coloured chalks and inks) may be found in his contribution to *Tambimuttu:*

Bridge Between Two Worlds, edited by Jane Williams (London: Peter Owen, 1989), pp.113–15. Equally as interesting is Sutherland's own attempt in a handwritten letter dated Feb. 1st 1945, to reply to a correspondent's query about how the artist had set about making the drawings for DG's collection. I have retained his underlinings. 'Firstly, I don't really believe that poetry should be illustrated, unless by the poet himself, or at least by somebody who thinks very much in the same way as the poet does himself. Therefore the drawings must not actually illustrate the poems; they must merely try to give an equivalent in terms of drawing to the feeling & mood of the poems. I decided to do a full page drawing for each section:

No (**1**) Religious. This is the only drawing which has in any way an illustrative motive. The units derive from the lines 'The *Rockhewn tomb*. There is no more Regeneration in the *stricken sun*'; but it is a mood which pervades all these religious poems. In the sky a *hooded stricken* sun. The hooded sun was used in Byzantine paintings of the crucifixion to express the stricken elements of the sky. The jagged lines in the foreground – blood: a feeling of silence and emptiness.

(**2**) Metaphysical. The science which investigates the first principles of nature &. Thought. Therefore something of a primitive nature & something suggestive of thought. In my drawing a mysterious rock-like figure, half-human, shrouded: the flames emanating from the head are intended to be a symbol of thought. O This form at R.H. & repeated in the figure is an ancient symbol of the soul. Λ

(**3**) Elegiac. This should speak for itself. Song of mourning. Cromlech-like rocks: suggesting the tombstone; above: the thorns of life. Below: the reverie of the tomb.

(**4**) Personal. Perhaps the most obscure drawing. Idea: intimacy and intensity: symbol; a curved branch of thorn. The small figure on the branch perhaps has the gift in personal relationships, so enviable, of walking between thorns: i.e. the gift of nursing his friendships & avoiding the thorns of enmity.

(**5**)Time & Place. What suggests time? The sun & moon. What suggests place most fundamentally? Something immovable: stones: monoliths. What eats away place? Time. Therefore here are two monoliths: their tops eaten away symbolically by time i.e the sun & moon.

(**6**) The cover. The poet's pen, ablaze with black flame (hotter than white flame: look at the sun, close your eyes & you can see a black sun transfixes the earth (pointed mountains with long shadows).

(**7**) Back cover. The objects are moths. The circle is not an apple, but a huge sun. The idea: Tragedy (for these are in the main tragic poems) symbolized by moths attracted by the light (sun) but unable to look at it. They are covering their heads with their arms . . . they fly above a barren landscape, desert-like: (more cactus-like plant L.H.).'

I'm most grateful to Marcus Williamson for sending me a copy of this letter.

RELIGIOUS POEMS

Miserere

On Sunday 29 May 1949, DG broadcast 'A Selection from his poetry made by the author' on the BBC Third Programme. In his introduction to the 'octet of poems', *Miserere*, with which the selection began, he explained:

'The title [. . .] is intended to indicate that the poems relate to a period of spiritual death and anticipation of rebirth – of spiritual rebirth and not religious revival – and not only to such a period in the life of an individual, but to the present moment in the history of western civilization as is indicated also by the four brief lines from the French poet, Pierre Jean Jouve, chosen as an epigraph to the sequence' (which he quoted in French: *Le désespoir a des ailes / L'amour a pour aile nacre / Le désespoir / Les sociétés peuvent changer'* / 'Despair has wings / Love has mother of pearl for wings / Societies can change / Despair'). DG said that the epigraph was added *after* [my emphasis] writing the eight poems 'because of the echo they supplied' (MRUI), p. 124. Benjamin Fondane had introduced him to the work of the philosopher Chestov, who wrote: 'The abyss is our element. Flung into it [. . .] we sprout wings.' (Quoted by Brian Merrikin-Hill in *Temenos* 7, p. 273).

DG was aware that certain readers and critics have assumed that both the title and production of the poems that make up the 'dark, brooding' *Miserere* have been influenced by Georges Roualt's series of prints also known as *Miserere*. This is not so, as he explained in a talk he gave in Piccadilly at the Royal Academy of Arts in 1983, the subject of which was the importance of painting in his life and work. 'Two other painters, however, probably did condition the imagery of at least two of the eight poems: the anonymous Provençal master responsible for that superb and unique work known as the *Pietà d'Avignon*, now in the Louvre, where the poem "Pieta" is concerned; and the image of the Christ of Revolution and of Poetry that is evoked in "Ecce Homo"; the last poem in the sequence, was undoubtedly influenced by my having been presented in 1938 with a folder of black and white reproductions of the Isenheim Altarpiece of Grünewald, a work hitherto unknown to me' (pp. 2–3 of eight pages of A4 typescript). The reproductions of the triptych were given him shortly after his return from Barcelona during the Spanish Civil War in 1936 by Christian Zervos (chief editor of *Cahiers d'Art*), who had published them in his periodical. 'It is, above all, the central panel to which these texts refer [from left to right: the Incarnation of the Son of God; the Annunciation and the Resurrection, where the motif of the Open Tomb is visible; the triumph of the Ascension and of the suspension of bodily weight]', DG told Remy (MRUI), p. 124. The Altarpiece is a complex polyptych constructed on three levels: 'The Shrine', 'The Middle Position' to which DG refers, and 'The Closed Position'.

He told Remy that he had always had a liking for foreign language or Latin titles: 'Certain of these titles [in **Miserere**] refer to particular sections of the religious service, but in a very loose manner (**Kyrie, Sanctus, De Profundis**). These texts were written in the order in which they are presented, as far as I can recall.' What is particularly interesting is the following comment: 'The basic idea was to compose a sequence of *ten* texts [my emphasis].'

The completed sequence of eight was first published in *Poetry in Wartime*, edited by Tambimuttu (Faber & Faber, 1942), pp. 67–73.

Tenebrae

In *Poetry London*, Vol. 1, No. 2 (April 1939) this poem was entitled 'The Last Hour', and line 2 read: 'Has consummated the stigmata and the veil'.

See DG's 'metaphysical' journal entry for 5.III.40 (2.30 a.m.), (CJS), p. 293. On the same page he quotes from a poem by Jean Wahl: 'We are at the lowest point in the universe, unable to climb back up' (my translation).

Pieta

The poem was inspired by that visit DG made to the Louvre in 1938 and his vivid and acute response to a version of the *Pietà*, 'that amazing French primitive of the Avignon school [. . .].' See the journal entry for 31 October 1938 (CJS), p. 200. First published in *Seven*, No. 6 (August 1939), p. 21.

Ex Nihilo
DG had written in his first letter to Benjamin Fondane, 11.VII.37, about the complex relationship between despair, destruction and creativity, and addressed the notion of *creatio ex nihilo*: 'You see I, no more than you, hold that despair (or rather the negation of despair) is an end in itself. A phrase that I found in Chestov expresses my ambition "Creation *Ex Nihilo*". In the destructive element immerse said Conrad, that is what one must do before being able to create, obviously. But most people who would agree with this, do not understand how *absolute*, how extreme this really is. One can strip oneself and yet not be naked. I now hold the opinion that there is no creative work which is not, for its creator, the result of the need to find some protection against the powers of destruction, a shield against affliction. A work of art should grow like one's skin in response to the hostility of nature. To believe this is the same as believing in *the cry* which arises from us in spite of ourselves is it not?' (From 'Meetings with Benjamin Fondane', translated by Robin Waterfield, in *Selected Prose 1934–1996*, op. cit., pp. 137–138. See, too, Gascoyne's journal entry for 22.VIII.39 (CJS), p. 255.

Ecce Homo
On its first appearance, in *Poetry London*, Vol. 1, No. 3 (November 1940), and later in *Poetry in Wartime*, this poem was entitled 'Miserere', and the last three stanzas were in italics.

'Line 13, "And we must never sleep during that time", is a direct quotation from Pascal, number 553 precisely of the *Pensées*, about the Mystery of Jesus' (MRUI), p. 124.

In each of the final three stanzas DG directly addresses the 'Christ of Revolution and of Poetry', a line which has developed a particular resonance since the first publication of the poem, but which also contributed to his expulsion by Breton from the Surrealist Group after the war when he returned to Paris. DG records how, revisiting 'the Surrealist group's Montmartre meeting-place, I found myself facing a severe Breton at the head of the communal café table: "I am told that you have become not only a Communist" (meaning Stalinist rather than Trotskyite) "but a Catholic", he announced to me in his iciest manner' (CJS), p. 393. On p. 395 DG refers to 'the refusal of Breton and his followers to realize that a recognition of the all-important power of love, combining Eros and Agape, is inseparable from the discovery of the philosopher's stone, the corner-stone of a truly human society'. See Brian Keeble's insightful essay, '"Whose Is This Horrifying Face?" Reading David Gascoyne's *Miserere*', in *Temenos Academy Review* 15 (2012), pp. 153–65.

METAPHYSICAL POEMS

There are two epigraphs to the **Metaphysical Poems**, the first taken from 'The Book of the Dead', from the culture of ancient Egypt, the second from a text of Chinese wisdom, 'The Book of the Open Flower'.

Jouve's important essay, 'The Unconscious, Spirituality, Catastrophe', the preface to his collection of poems, *Sueur de Sang* (1935), was translated by DG at the end of the 1930s (published in *Poetry London*, Vol. 1, No. 4 (January-February 1941) and clearly provides his alternative heading, 'Metapsychological', for the poems collected in this section II: 'Incalculable is the extension of our sense of the tragic that is brought us by metapsychology'. I have inserted **Concert of Angels** and **Elsewhere** here where they belong. The title of the latter appears in Add. 62947 as 'Concert of Angels (Grünewald)'.

Inferno
A reproduction in colour of Graham Sutherland's powerful gouache for this poem, dated 1978, appears in *Poetry London/Apple Magazine*, Vol.1, no.1, ed. Tambimuttu (Editions Poetry London, 1979), facing p. 70. Sutherland's illustration for **Mountains** was included in *Tambimuttu. Bridge Between Two Worlds*, op. cit., between pages 76 and 77. The artist's ten images for ***Poems 1937–42*** may be found in Robert Fraser's biography, *Night Thoughts. The Surreal Life of the Poet David Gascoyne* (Oxford University Press, 2012), plate 18, between pp. 236 and 237.

Lowland
The version first published in *Delta* (April 1938), p. 18, was more than lightly modified by DG for inclusion in *Poems 1937–42*:

> Shadow was violet and brown among the rains,
> Among the rain-logged tombs. The wet fields ran
> Together in the middle of the plain; and there were heard
> Incessantly the thud of violent horses, and a cry,

More long and lamentable as the rain increased,
Which came from beyond.
O sumptuary
Appeal of our mortality out of the slow decline
Of our dark day! Among the lowlands of despair
Build us a savage and enduring monument!

Winter Garden
A direct reference to the Luxembourg Gardens in Paris. DG told Remy that the poem was written in Paris after he returned from a Montmartre nightclub to his attic flat in the rue de la Bûcherie at about 5 a.m., at the very moment when dawn was breaking and 'I was walking alongside the Luxembourg Garden which becomes this winter garden' (MRUI), p. 125.

The Fortress
'This is a text on the subject of Eros and Thanatos' (MRUI), p. 125.

I.M. Benjamin Fondane
Written in England, said DG, 'shortly before Benjamin Fondane was arrested by the Nazis and taken to Birkenau where he was gassed. It is thus, a premonitory poem because I didn't learn of Fondane's death until after the war' (MRUI), p. 125. 'Fondane was hostile to any fixed ideas; he always wanted to question everything. The state of certainty of which I speak at the end of the poem, is that of serenity, not a state of total immobility, but of accepting things as they are, of the necessity of evil if, on the other hand, there is God – "to care and not to care" Eliot would say – the idea of a paradise where everything is marvellous, is intolerable and would be a veritable source of boredom', op. cit., pp. 125–6.

Mozart: Sursum Corda
First published in *Seven*, No. 4 (Summer 1939), p. 33. It is difficult not to see here an echo of Jouve in his poem, 'Mozart' in *Les Noces* (1931). For Jouve, 'The only human parallel to this rarified emotion [the particular joy of spiritual illumination] is [...] the music of Mozart,' records Margaret Callender in her *The Poetry of Pierre Jean Jouve* (Manchester University Press, 1965), pp. 86–87. 'and he sees in its "divine gaîté" a purity that raises it on another plane from our own, [stressing] the uniqueness of the music.' An alternative version, without the dedication to Rainier, appears in a signed typescript in one of two folders in the Royal Music Academy Library (See Editor's Preface):

Filters the sunlight from the knife-bright wind
And rarifies the rumour-burdened air
The all-receptive heart in pure hands upheld
Towards the sostenuto of the sky.

Supernal voices, flood the ear of clay
And break through the dense skull: reveal
The immaterial world concealed
By mortal deafness and the screen of sense:
World of transparency and utmost flight,
And world within the world: beyond our speech
To tell what equinoxes of the absolute
The spirit ranges in its long upward release

Cavatina
In its first printing in *Delta* (April 1938), p. 8, line 3 began: 'Brutality of ecchymosis . . .'; line 16 read: 'Yet through disaster some transcendent melody'; the last line began: 'To carry starwards . . .'

Artist (later Philosophical Artisan)
'The sense of the word "artist" here,' says DG, 'is that which is used in alchemy, that is, the author of the Work. The text was written the day after these dream visions, each of which served as a basis for the successive fragments of the poem. I tried to reproduce as faithfully as possible the way the episodes unfolded and linked together' (MRUI), p. 126.

Legendary Fragment, Eve, Venus Androgyne
DG pointed out that **Legendary Fragment** is 'a mixture of the kind of mysticism and sexuality that recurs sometimes in my poetry'. Of **Eve** and **Venus Androgyne** he says: 'I think that these texts must have helped me express my nature which is deeply bi-sexual' (MRUI), p. 126. His own views on his sexuality are expressed in the *Collected Journals* in a long entry in 1938 following several sessions of psychoanalysis with Blanche Reverchon, Jouve's wife (CJS), p. 346, but he had previously attempted a case history headed 'Myself', dated 18th January 1937, that remained unpublished until my edition of *April: a Novella* [1937], (Enitharmon Press, 2000), pp. 111–112 which included this psychic profile in the Appendix.

Venus Androgyne
First published in *Delta* (1938), p. 14, where lines 3–4 read: 'The breast is female and the fist is male / The red-eyed sphinx . . .'. In the second stanza, lines 10–15 read:

> The gentle athlete flank,
> That sacrificial blood may flow,
> Atone
> The secret heresy of human seed:
> The twin spasmodic tides of our desire
> Incarnate in this third apostasy.

DG told Remy that the myth of Androgyne is 'one of the poles of Surrealism' (MRUI), p. 126.

Amor Fati
'The expression must have come from my reading of Fondane then probably of Chestov. It relates to "the need to submit oneself to destiny, to one's own destiny, the idea that each of us must accept his own sexuality". I admit that this doesn't represent a very optimistic view of sexuality' (MRUI), pp. 126–7.

Post-Mortem
Add. 56045. First published in *Despair Has Wings*, op. cit., p. 182. The poem was 'written under the influence of Jouve', and planned as part of a sequence, 'Cortège and Hymn of Death', which has not survived. DG grimaced in what seemed almost like distaste when I showed him it.

The Fault
Also published in *Delta* (1938) where lines 5–7 read as follows:
> An hour in the condition of our blood
> And not known how a sacred wound and black
> And ever more irreparable.

DG's comments to Arta Lucescu-Boutcher are enlightening: 'The theme of the Garden of Eden and the Fall of Man, the nostalgia of the origins, is the fundamental theme of European literature [. . .]. The Garden of Eden is just a symbol for the pure state': 'Interview with David Gascoyne on Benjamin Fondane' (typescript dated February 1992), p. 8. Earlier in that interview, he had remarked:

'To me, man and God are one; man and God were one; the source of being. And religion is turning back to this source. After the disaster which man called "la chute" – the Fall, this pure being (that is, man and God together) no longer existed. Religion is thus binding back to the pure being' (p. 3). He explained that 'When we refer to Original Sin we are referring to the idea of breaking away from the source of being. The word "sin" means "separation" – which is the result of breaking away,' op. cit.

The Descent and The Open Tomb

DG remarked to Remy that he'd never met anyone who properly understands the sense of these two poems. 'They refer to the Prophecy of the Great Pyramid in which I've never wholly believed, but it is something that you could call a vision of the artist, an aesthetic symbol, which was very popular at the beginning of this century.'

'According to this myth,' says DG, 'the Great Pyramid contains a passage, a double corridor ["shaft" in the poem]: one section descends and the other rises towards the surface. The descent is measured from the entrance in "pyramid inches" (slightly different from the British inch), each of which corresponds to a year; the length of this descent thus corresponds to the time which separates the moment when the pyramid was built and the moment of reincarnation, of the death and Resurrection of Christ. If we calculate it, we are at this moment in the ascending section. It should be made clear, too, that the pyramid was not designed to be the tomb of a pharaoh but to be a temple of initiation' (MRUI), p. 127. The initiate 'must climb the stairs and lie down in the tomb which wasn't looked upon as a sarcophagus but as a bed; he was, perhaps, rendered unconscious by a drug' (MDC), p. 36, then 'plunged into a state of suspended animation, hypnotized, if you like. After having spent three days and three nights in the Great Pyramid, the initiate left the illuminated open tomb. Reading behind all that, mankind descends towards sleep and death and what follows in the progressive illumination of the soul' (MRUI), p. 127. The poem, **The Descent**, 'is a kind of fusion of Egyptian and Christian mythologies: as far as I know, the Egyptians didn't have angels in their religion . . .' op. cit. 'In Egyptian mythology, as in the fundamentally Christian concept, it's a question of death and resurrection. I'm trying to show that we pass through what Carlyle calls Palingenesis' (MDC), p. 36.

DG explained that **The Open Tomb** isn't ambiguous but has a double meaning, as is frequent in English poetry, and he references Empson's *Seven Types of Ambiguity* (MDC), p. 36. He commented that Piranesi's imagery continues to fascinate him, how the painter's *Prisons* 'represents the unconscious, the open tomb', op. cit., p. 39.

Duclos commented: 'Your Christ seems to me sometimes a bit

pagan, and appears to be identified with the sun.' DG replied: 'Yes, I attach great importance to Anaktaton, the heretical pharaoh who instituted the religion of the sun which, on his death, was suppressed' op. cit., p. 38. His uncollected poem **Oleograph**, from 1934, confirms the accuracy of this, with the emphasis on the sun and its association with ancient Egypt.

The Plummet Heart

Norman Cameron, poet and translator, and DG's close friend whom he saw almost every weekend for a period during the 1930s, introduced him to the poetry of John Crowe Ransom and Allen Tate, and to that of Hart Crane. In 1938 DG bought the first English edition of *The Collected Poems of Hart Crane*, edited by Waldo Frank (London: Boriswood, November 1938), which had just been published. 'Before long I knew most of the poems by heart' ('Anniversary Epistle to Allen [Ginsberg]', published in *Kanrecki: A Tribute to Allen Ginsberg*, Part 2, edited by Bill Morgan (New York: Lospecchio Press, 1986). While in Paris that year he commented in his journal: 'Have been reading rather a lot recently: among other things the horrifying life of Hart Crane' (CJS), 31.XI.38, p. 234. He handwrote his own poem with its punning title 'The Plummet Heart (for Hart Crane)'[1] on the front free endpaper of his copy, signing and dating it 'David Gascoyne 27.V.39' [See **APPENDIX B**]. He used the first words of the fourth line in the fifth quatrain of Crane's 'Recitative'. There are minor variations in the printed version in the punctuation of lines 4 and 11. In his copy of Crane's *Collected Poems*, 'Cape Hatteras', Part IV of *The Bridge* (pp. 51–56) is annotated in pencil by DG, with directions for reading the poem aloud. The date is significant because 'The Plummet Heart', unaccountably, was not included in *Poems 1937–42* (1943), though it had appeared in print for the first time in 1942 in *Poets of Tomorrow* 2 (London: The Hogarth Press), then not until twenty-three years later in *Collected Poems* (Oxford University Press, 1965). I am grateful to the late Peter Jolliffe of Ulysses Bookshop in Bloomsbury for showing me this copy and for providing photocopies of the pages mentioned.

The Three Stars, A Prophecy, Epode (initially 'The Prophetic Mouth')

Termed 'crisis poems' by DG, and written like **Artist** on II.IX.39. According to the poet **The Three Stars** 'refers to the Three Wise Men, but more than anything, it represents the very simple application of dialectic in a spiritual sense' (MRUI), p. 128.

Epode
DG did not recall precisely what 'gave birth to this image, but the main theme is certainly that of the oracle which etymologically comes from the mouth. But I also had in mind the enormous statue of Pharoah or a photograph of Memnon, or even the immense statue commissioned by Rameses II in Shelley's poem "Ozymandias"' (MRUI), p. 128.

PERSONAL POEMS

The epigraph to the **Personal Poems** comprises two quotations from Marcel Jouhandeau whose work had interested DG very much before the two writers met. 'He has written some beautiful texts, like *Jeunesse sous l'Occupation*, or *Monsieur Godeau Intime* which I associated then with the problem of the condition of the artist,' he told Remy (MRUI), p. 128.

'The poems of this last section reflect civilian experience of the early years of the war', he said. He found an affinity in Sutherland's last drawing with some of Paul Nash's wartime paintings: 'the chalky quality of a dead moon, the desolation of Nash's dead sea of crashed planes,' op. cit., pp. 114–5.

Sonnet: From Morn to Mourning
Published as 'A Sonnet – Morning' in *New Road* (1943).

The Fabulous Glass
With regard to the lines, 'A Peacock, which lit up the glass / By opening his Fan of Eyes', DG acknowledged that the peacock comes from alchemy: 'I'm convinced that alchemical symbols are produced in the collective unconscious' (MRUI), p. 128.

Camera Obscura
First published as 'The Projections of Desire' in the polyglot bi-monthly *Agonía*, Revista literaria, No. 8, Julio – Septiembre (Buenos Aires, 1941), pp. 82–83. This title was included in the planned collection *The Conquest of Defeat: Poems 1939–40*, in the second section, 'Personal and Confessional Poems', of three sequences. The poem would seem to belong to a group alongside **Legendary Fragment**, **Eve**, **Venus Androgyne** and **Amor Fati**, and confronts sexual ambivalence.

Another poem with the title 'Camera Obscura' exists in draft form in Add. 56045 (1940–44): 'Documentary Poem (Experimental Text), Plan of contents: Documentary poem / Phenomena / The Lion's Mane / Extension of Reality' / Mirror – Fugue / Enigmatic Communication / Soma / The Great Day.' The first section begins: 'Reverie made up of a sequence of unco-ordinated bestial and archaic elements. Emerges gradually from a tight mucous-coloured "atmospheric" sheath situated somewhere at the centre of the partially-concealed zone of Secondary Consciousness (Accompanied during later stages of development by occasional sub-luminous vibrations and a certain amount of intermittent auditory disturbance in the higher registers).'

The Sacred Hearth
Dedicated to George Barker, one of DG's closest friends in the 1930s and 1940s, and after. For a full treatment of their friendship, see *The Fire of Vision: George Barker and David Gascoyne*, edited and introduced by Roger Scott (Tragara Press for Enitharmon, 1996). Gascoyne told the publisher and bookseller Alan Clodd that he couldn't understand why this visionary poem was not included in *Poems 1937–42*. The basis of the poem is DG's experience 'one night when I had just left George Barker's house for only a few moments' (MRUI), p. 133.

An Elegy. Roger Roughton (1916–1941)
First published as 'In Memoriam' in *Today's New Poets* Resurgam Books, n.d., 1941?), then as 'Elegy' in *Poems of This War by Younger Poets* (Cambridge University Press, 1942), pp. 37–38.

Roger Roughton, DG's senior by one month, gassed himself in his birthplace, 70 Wellington Road, in 'that sordid city', Dublin. See my article with DG, 'Roughton, Roger Edmund Heude', for the new *Oxford Dictionary of National Biography* (2004). They first met during the winter of 1933–4 in the famous left-wing Parton Street Bookshop in Holborn, London, where they were introduced by the proprietor David Archer. Shortly afterwards, DG visited Roughton in Hampstead where he was living with his half-sister and his mother, with whom relations were strained. Eventually Roughton moved to share DG's small flat in Southwark for a short period (CJS), pp. 345–48. The latter stressed his friend's utter despair; he told me that for Roughton the last straw was the betrayal of Czechoslovakia by Chamberlain's policy of appeasement: 'Seeing the world's damnation week by week / Grow more and more inevitable'. The closing lines of the sixth and last stanza refer to a Surrealist prose poem, 'The Journey', published by Roughton in his review *Contemporary Poetry and Prose* No. 8 (December 1936), pp. 152–54, in which a child journeys through a large park on the back of a huge Saint Bernard whose legs have been broken: 'that lonely child [. . .] was borne / Slowly away into the utmost dark'. Several of DG's poems and translations were published in Roughton's review.

Fête
'This is the direct transcription of an experience following a long walk along the canal Saint-Martin [. . .] in the spring of 1938 a short time after I had moved to the rue de la Bûcherie' (MRUI), p. 130.

Chambre d'Hôtel
'It's the direct transcription of a personal experience with Bent von Müllen, a young Dane whom I knew then. It happened in the hotel in which I was living in the rue de la Bûcherie in Paris after August 1937. I have dated this experience as July 27 1938 in my *Journal 1937–1939*' (MRUI), p. 130. See (CJS), pp. 165–66. Earlier, on II.V.38, DG had written in French of his love affair (CJS), pp. 153–155. He was to learn of von Müllen's death after the war, but his account (CJS, p. 397) differs from that of his biographer, Robert Fraser, who managed to discover the precise circumstances of von Müllen's murder in Denmark under Nazi occupation: *Night Thoughts*, op. cit., pp. 210–211.

Jardin du Palais Royal
Dedicated to von Müllen, 'my friendship with whom was closer to my ideal than that with anyone else I ever met' (CJS), p. 370.

Noctambules
First published in *Daylight – European Arts and Letters*, Vol. 1 (January 1941).

On 18 September 1938, DG sat for 'R.' for a couple of portrait-sketches, the second of which, 'bolder and more harsh in style, made me look like a Parisian *noctambule*', haunter of cafés, slightly '"diabolic"', probably drugged: a vicious, androgynous face with enormous eyes and a sensual mouth' (CJS), p. 181.

The poem is dedicated to the American author of *Nightwood*, Djuna Barnes, whom DG knew through Antonia White and Peggy Guggenheim. 'The reference at the end to the "snarling lions" which are in the Place Saint-Sulpice in Paris suggests the Freudian notion of the angry father because the son arrives home so late. I think it was 5 a.m.,' he told Remy (MRUI), pp. 130–1.

The Anchorite
Add. 56046. Written Spring-Summer of that year, and planned in five sections, only two of which were begun. First published, together with the later incomplete **The Bomb-Site Anchorite**, in *Encounter With Silence: Poems 1950*, with an introduction by Roger Scott (London: Enitharmon Press, 1998), pp. 26–28, 29.

TIME AND PLACE

Snow in Europe
First published in *New Writing* n.s. II (1939), p. 175.

The epigraph for the first poem in the final section, **Time and Place**, is taken from Jouve: 'Au temps où la douceur / Est cruelle et le désespoir est brillant' ('At a time when sweetness / is cruel and hope is shining'). The time in question for Gascoyne was Christmas 1938. He and Denham Fouts, to whom he dedicated **To a Contemporary**, were living in the rue de Bac in Mégève 'during the winter that followed Munich; we realized that war was inevitable' (MRUI), p. 131. They had met for the first time at the lecture given at the Sorbonne by W.H. Auden. DG wrote in his journal: 31.X11.38 'There has been a lot of snow, but now it has all melted away. Have written a new poem [. . .]' (CJS), p. 234.

The last three lines invoke James Joyce's description of the altered Irish landscape in the final paragraph of his story *The Dead*. In this visionary sequence, Gabriel's mind is on the brink of sleep, and the snow falls 'faintly through the universe [. . .] upon all the living and the dead' covering all things with a neutral whiteness. As in DG's poem, it erases all differentiating details, effaces frontiers with indifference. But if, in *The Dead*, the snow symbolises the egotistical protagonist's accommodation with the world, in a sense of total unity, 'Snow in Europe' has no such optimistic ending.

Zero (formerly **Zero: September 1939**)
The poem can be read with the journal entry for 1.IX.39: 'When reality is as painful as it is at this hour, how can the disillusioned few who are capable of seeing it hope to be able to make other men open their eyes to what they see. Is the "ordinary man" even capable of a moral suffering great enough to force itself inescapably upon his consciousness and to make him admit its existence openly?' (CJS), p. 260. Two pages later DG refers to the 'stunning blow struck by the horror of actuality.' Following Jouve, he employs the Spanish *'nada'*

(the 'nothing' of the Spanish mystics, like St John of the Cross) in the second stanza, linking the words 'zero', 'the Void' and 'Negation'. Two days later, he wrote: '*Zero is over.* [. . .] I feel today that midnight has struck and [. . .] the worst of the night is still to come [. . .]', p. 262.

An Autumn Park
Written a month later, this is, in effect, Richmond Park which DG often crossed on his way back to Twickenham, not far from a house for disabled ex-servicemen from the First World War, where they made paper flowers (MRUI), p. 131.

The Conspirators
DG told Lucien Jenkins that 'My poem [. . .] is not exactly Audenesque but it is an attempt to write a narrative poem which was not out of key with the kind of poetry Auden was writing' (LJI), p. 24.

Farewell Chorus
First published in *Partisan Review*, Vol. VIII, No. 1 (January-February 1941), pp. 20–23.
'The basic metaphor is that of the departing trains full of servicemen, but essentially it is, of course, a goodbye to the 1930s' (MRUI), p. 131. 'And that poem of mine "Farewell Chorus". It's Thirties political poetry by someone who has read and loved Guillaume Apollinaire' (LJI), p. 24.

A Wartime Dawn
The setting is his parents' house in Teddington. ' [. . .] "A Wartime Dawn" would probably never have been written had I not by then already become an inveterate benzedrine user' (CJS), p. 384. He told Remy: 'In the garden there was a mulberry bush and beyond the garden extended a housing estate for the Shell Mex employees with houses completely white and lawns in front with a thick chain like a fence. Our house was very large because it was situated on a corner' (MRUI), p. 131.

The Gravel-Pit Field
The terrain described in this poem is in the suburbs of Teddington, and mentioned in a journal entry four years earlier: '26.IV.37: We all went down to the weir the other night and sat on the island till two in the morning, talking and watching the moon scatter its light

across the water – then withdraw behind a film of cloud. There was a mysterious fire blazing in the middle of the Ham gravel-pit fields on the other side of the river' (CJS), p. 100. Of all the drafts for published and unpublished poems (and translations) that I have examined in the notebooks in the British Library and elswhere, this (Add. 56045) is the most assiduously worked over. See **APPENDIX B**. The final scene seems to chime with Yves Bonnefoy's notion of the *arrière-pays*.

Strophes Elégiaques à la mémoire d'Alban Berg
Originally written in English in the summer of 1936, not long after Berg's death, in two versions, **Elegiac Stanzas I.M. Alban Berg** which DG found 'unsatisfactory'. The earlier attempt is in a notebook in the British Library and the second in the Berg Collection in New York Public Library (See **APPENDIX A**). He began a translation into French just before the outbreak of the war (the MS is dated 'Eté 1939'), following his return from Paris in March to his parents' home, and it was published the following year in *Cahiers du Sud* (Marseilles) No. 220 (janvier 1940), pp. 49–52.

Three of the subtitles for the five sections are, DG explains in his essay on Sutherland's illustrations, 'borrowed from movements of the composer's *Lyric Suite* for String Quartet (p. 114). These are "Andante Amoroso" (first section), "Tenebroso" (the second), and "Misterioso" (the fourth); the third and fifth are entitled "Intermezzo" and "Epilogue". Berg's six movements are: "Allegretto giovale", "Andante amoroso", subtitled "trio estatico", "Allegro misterioso" (subtitled "trio estatico"), "Adagio appassionato", "Presto delirando" (subtitled "Tenebroso"), and "Largo desolato", which denote successive psychological states.'

A VAGRANT AND OTHER POEMS

A Vagrant
Composed in a Paris hotel room. DG characterizes the poem as 'a distinctly "anti-bourgeois" poem, whose approach is comparable to the freer and more declamatory poetic style of [Allen] Ginsberg and his American companions': 'Le surréalisme et la jeune poésie anglaise: souvenir de l'avant-guerre' by David Gascoyne in *Encrages* No. 6 (Eté 1981), Departement d'Etudes des Pays Anglophones, Université de Paris VIII Vincennes, p. 23. DG met the Beat poets in the 1950s, and again in San Francisco many years later, after his marriage.

Innocence and Experience
The setting here is the private mansion of Madame Edwards, in the Faubourg Saint-Germain district in which she had lived for many years, including the period of Occupation. She was South American by birth, and wife of the owner-director of one of the famous Paris department stores, 'Les Magasins du Louvre'. Before the war, Madame Edwards was persuaded to give the poet a small monthly allowance, and she became 'a sort of patron' (MRUI), p. 133. This long poem (sixty-three lines) commemorates the second visit made there by DG, this time in 1947 after a gap of ten years, accompanied by Jenny de Margerie, and is 'almost a transcription' of the visit, written immediately afterwards, as he told Duclos (MDC), p. 31. He invented the notion that Madame Edwards was the daughter of a South American dictator (MRUI), p. 133.

The line, 'To play the cello to a foreign bard's guitar', 'was suggested by the famous portrait by Augustus John of Suggia, the celebrated Spanish violincellist of the 1920s, a very beautiful woman', op. cit., p. 133. The 'sad lady' is Mme de Margerie as Mme Edwards smoked her cheroots.

The speaker tries to see behind the masks. See **Saturnalia** below.

DG critiques the world of private art collectors who own paintings which no one sees: they are 'wasted, these valuable paintings which ought to be available for everyone to look at because too often reproductions lie'. He is also criticising bourgeois society, and told Duclos that he was lower-middle-class by birth and upbringing, but considered himself to be classless; however, he admitted to having a conscience about it, because he had read Marx and Engels, op. cit., pp. 31–32.

Photograph
DG said that the inspiration for the poem came from the portrait of Soupault taken by the famous American photographer, Bérénice Abbott, which appears in *Philippe Soupault*, no. 58 in the 'Poètes d'Aujourd'hui' series, selected by Henri-Jacques Dupuy, between pp. 128 and 129. 'This text isn't specifically about Philippe Soupault; it is concerned above all,' said DG, 'with an ideal modern face. It begins with a concrete image of a photograph and doesn't include any metaphor or image; you could say that it's an "ethical poem"' (MRUI), p. 133.

This poem was first dedicated to Soupault in **Collected Poems 1988**, after DG had written asking his permission. Like René Crevel, Soupault was one of the Surrealist group in Paris whom he was unable to meet in the 1930s. Soupault had gradually severed contact with the Surrealists, concentrating on poetry as well as novel writing and travel journalism, which were unacceptable to Breton as he considered they must be intended for commercial gain. DG and Soupault met eventually when the French poet was in his mid-80s (c.1982), not long before DG completed his remarkable translation of *Les Champs Magnétiques* by Breton and Soupault, published in 1985 (Atlas Books) as *The Magnetic Fields*. DG translated several poems by Soupault, including his 'Ode à Londres bombardée'.

Eros Absconditus
DG told me that this poem (two stanzas of nine and six lines) was written in memory of Bent Von Müllen, to whom he dedicated **Jardin du Palais Royal**. The later poem takes a line from Hölderlin for its epigraph: 'Wo aber sind die Freunde? Bellarmin / Mit dem Gefahrten . . .' ('But where are the Friends? Where Bellarmine / And his companion'). The translation from the poem 'Remembrance' is Michael Hamburger's, from his *Friedrich Hölderlin: Selected Poems and Fragments* (Penguin Books, 1998), p. 253. David Constantine suggests that Hölderlin 'may have had his own friend Sinclair in mind' in Friedrich Hölderlin: *Selected Poems*, translated by Constantine (Bloodaxe Books, 1990), p. 78. Hölderlin had first met Isaak von Sinclair in 1793; after they met again in 1800, 'Sinclair was to prove a most loyal and helpful friend to Hölderlin in the next few years' (Hamburger, 'Introduction', op. cit., p. xxv.

   DG indicated that 'the central idea is that of male friendship', clarified in the final lines of the poem: '[. . .] The squalid inhibitions of those only half alive. / In blind content they breed who never loved a friend'. He insisted to Remy that 'it is not a "gay" poem' as the kind of love he describes 'exists over and above homosexuality' (MRUI), p. 134.

The Goose Girl
Previously 'No End in Sight' in *Botteghe Oscure*, No. IV (1949). The title comes from a fairy story DG read when he was a child, and 'is probably a reflection on desire or on the chances I had of getting married' (MRUI), p. 134.

Beware Beelzebub
This sonnet 'is an ironic poem, satirical if you like, against British puritanical hypocrisy' (MRUI), p. 134.

Rondel for the Fourth Decade

Here DG uses two four- and one five-line stanzas, thirteen lines, like Charles d'Orléans's development of the form, but instead of his Rondel rhyming abba, abba, abbaa, DG's version follows abba, abab, baabb. The poem was published in *12th Street: Poetry Issue 1* (USA, 1949), together with **Absconded Eros** and **Rex Mundi** (pp. 17–19). DG made substantial modifications to the first before it appeared the following year in *A Vagrant and other poems*:

> The mind if not the heart turns cold
> Seeing the calendar's leaves flying;
> Still dare not cease trying
> To make the heart resigned to growing old.

> However often heart's fortune be told
> By sceptic mind, it beats on still relying
> On consanguinity for help to hold
> By against age's chill and sighing.

> But when the last leaves are swept flying
> From our life's tree, a stone is rolled
> Over the hole where as they turn to mould
> The heart's remains still lie denying
> That mind can know the truth of dying.

In the typescript (see **APPENDIX B**), line four reads: 'To coax the heart to accept growing old'.

September Sun

At the time he wrote it DG was living in Paris in the Hôtel du Pas-de-Calais, and 'it was a magnificent day during an Indian Summer. I went for a walk in the gardens at Versailles' (MRUI), p. 134. He added that he had always loved public gardens and parks. DG told Mel Gooding that before taking the train from Montparnasse he had bought 'a little selected poems by O.V. de L. Milosz' from 'a little bookshop which was also a publisher, André Silvare [. . .]' and 'during all of this wonderful afternoon I read Milosz for the first time, and it was very exciting to me. And that resulted in a poem called "September Sun"' (MGI), p. 87. An additional verse (written in 1981) was first published in 1983 in Michael Horovitz's *New Departures*, Third International Poetry Olympics, Number 15. The contribution, including the original poem, was headed 'An Old Poem Updated', p. 58, as it was in *Lo Spezio Humano*, No. 6 (gennaio-marzo 1983).

The Post-War Night
One of those poems which DG recognized with hindsight in conversation with me in 1995, were 'rehearsing for, leading up to *Night Thoughts*' throughout the 1930s, 1940s and early 1950s, effectively a long gestation period. The other poems are: **They Spoke of a New City**; **Noctambules**; **The Moon Over London**; **Phantasmagoria**; **The Anchorite** (incomplete); **The Conspirators** (incomplete); **A Vagrant**; **Fragment of an Unfinished / Unpublished Poem**; **Metropolis By Night**, **Nightwatchers' Ruminations**; **Night Thoughts** (an earlier version).

Demos in Oxford Street
This poem 'was actually originally intended to be called . . . to be about the Edgware Road, because I was living at that time with Robin Waterfield in Paddington. And I felt that the Edgware Road was one of the most dreary streets in London or any modern capital [. . .] and I changed to "Oxford Street". Somebody once asked me, "What were those demos in Oxford Street about?"' (MGI), p. 88.

DG said that 'There is in this text a kind of deception and disillusionment' (MRUI), p. 134, his own disillusionment stemming not from Socialism itself, but from dissatisfaction with 'the Socialists in power after the Second World War' (MDC), p. 33. He added in that same conversation with Duclos: 'this is an ironic and satirical poem.' The statement is clarified in the final lines where 'those who say at the end of the text "We're not the Working Class" are actually the workers who've become "petit bourgeois" and consider themselves superior now' (MRUI), p. 134.

Evening Again
The original title was 'The Unfulfilled' in *Botteghe Oscure*, No. IV (1949). The poem recalls a journey DG made with his friend, Jenny de Margerie, mother of the French Ambassador to England, to visit her cousin, Jean Rostand, near Saint-Germain-en-Laye. On their return they crossed the Seine on a level with the Ile de la Cité. He found the buildings he could see on the other side of the river very impressive (MRUI), pp. 134–5.

Three Venetian Nocturnes
'I knew that Princess Marguerite Catani, editor of the review *Botteghe Oscure*, paid well for material written for her, and I wrote them in one week and sent them to her' (MRUI), p. 135.

On the Grand Canal: There were 39 lines in the version printed in *Points*, No. 8 (Paris, Dec.1950-Jan.1951), pp. 43–4. The poem as published in *A Vagrant*, shows a large number of alterations.

The lines 'a young girl's head / In a near window, her sweet fresh-coloured face / Vividly lit with eagerness, whose aspect made / Me wonder what it was she held before her,' replaced the following in *Points*: '[. . .] and I observed / Was imaginatively moved by, a girl's head / Fresh and vivid with an earnest eagerness / That made her face seem rescued out of time / As by some novelist's or painter's genius'.

Fragments Towards a Religio Poetae

The epigraph is taken from Meister Eckhart whom DG had read before and during the war. He also had a copy of Jacob Boehme's *Aurore* which he read from time to time (MRUI), p. 135. He added, 'There are perhaps too many upper-case letters.' See my note to the unpublished '*The Porch before these poems is the entrance into night*' and '*The Son of Man is in Revolt*'.

When **The Bomb-Site Anchorite** was published for the first time in *An Enitharmon Anthology for Alan Clodd*, edited by Stephen Stuart-Smith (Enitharmon Press, 1990), p. 23, there was a note by DG about this uncompleted poem on the facing page which is particularly relevant to *A Vagrant and other Poems*, and to matters such as tone and DG's state of mind:

'[. . .] My reluctance to give any definite expression of my persistent residue of faith resulted in the fragmentary nature of the **Religio Poetae** section of *A Vagrant and Other Poems*, and prevented me from elaborating the kind of discourse it would have been appropriate for my anchorite to deliver to the impartial narrator of my poem. Awareness of the pitfalls besetting specifically philosophical poetry inhibited me from risking the completion of this particular poem altogether,' op. cit.

MAKE-WEIGHT VERSE

A second section in *A Vagrant* styled, self-deprecatingly, 'Make-Weight Verse', not included in the **Collected Poems** (1965), but restored to the **Collected Poems 1988**, and to **Selected Poems** (1994) under the heading 'Light Verse', comprises seven light pieces, three of which: **An Unsagacious Animal or The Triumph of Art Over Nature**, **The Decay of Decency** and **With a Cornet of Winkles**, are fully developed. DG very much enjoyed reciting the first at poetry readings. The **Three Cabaret Songs** include one (unidentified) which is all that remains of DG's satirical one-act play, *The Hole in the Fourth Wall*, produced in 1950. He does not name the song, but it seems likely that he is referring to the second, **What a Way to Walk into my Parlour, Little Man!** since a draft of the poem with a different heading, 'Cabaret Song: De Haut en Bas' appears on two pages in Notebook IV.

With a Cornet of Winkles
First published that year in *Botteghe Oscure*, V, pp. 304–306.

DG's apparently effortless homage in the form of a parody to Wallace Stevens whom he had long greatly admired. The mimicry is self-conscious and playful. At the same time there is an element of pastiche to highlight Stevens's 'gaudy' language, eccentric word-play and humour, with a seductive collation of examples of the more extreme aspects of the American poet's diction. DG recreates the rhythms and sounds created by players of the lute, mandolin and clavier.

ENCOUNTER WITH SILENCE. POEMS 1950

A limited edition, published in 1998, edited and introduced by Roger Scott (Enitharmon Press), comprising a selection drawn from an orange manuscript Notebook, *Poems, 1950*, which has been for some years in the Berg Collection at the New York Public Library. The catalogue description reads: '31 holograph poems, unsigned, 66 pp. (Bd. 25cms.). Contains translations and some prose passages'. It seemed before my visit to America in 1997 that these must represent no more than the draft pages of *A Vagrant and other poems*, rather than any new or forgotten work. However, my assumption was proved wrong.

The relationship of these *Poems, 1950* to the collection brought out by John Lehmann in that same year is both interesting and problematic. DG himself had no recollection of the notebook which contains drafts of two of the poems in the Lehmann publication, **A Tough Generation**, and **Three Venetian Nocturnes**, together with **Sentimental Colloquy** (first published in the *Times Literary Supplement*, 2 April 1954, p. 215) and 'Elegiac Improvisation. In honour of Paul Eluard' (sic), (published that same year in *Botteghe Oscure*, XIII, pp. 118–21 as **Elegiac Improvisation on the Death of Paul Eluard**). The poem 'Recitative from an Oratorio in Commemoration of the Dead' appeared in 1959 as **Remembering the Dead** in *X*, Vol. 1, No. 1. In addition to several unpublished poems and translations, and light verse (in the vein of the 'Make-Weight Verse' in *A Vagrant*), there are fragments, and half-completed, never developed plans.

The chosen selection echoes in miniature the format of *A Vagrant* in that original poems are followed by translations and light verse. However, another section is added after the translations, offering two versions of a poem neither of which was completed, begun at different times during the 1940s: DG's original plan for and first draft of **The Anchorite**, dating from Spring-Summer 1941, and the later fragment, **The Bomb-Site Anchorite**, written then abandoned c.1948/9 according to the poet.

The title, **Encounter With Silence**, is mine, appropriated from that of Section 3 of *Night Thoughts*, as silence is a recurring theme, addressed much earlier in two unpublished poems from the 1930s: **Compline for the Occident, a cantata for choir and solo voice**, the long 'automatic' Surrealist poem *The Perpetual Explosion*, and **The Entrance to that valley stands alone**.

Silence is explored in several poems, some complete, others unfinished, in the Berg notebook (DG also chose to translate Char's 'Affres, Detonation, Silence'). Apart from **Give Up Dead Words**, **Stele** and **Terminal** there are fragments which also engage with the state of being silent or unable to speak, as in 'Silence in Heaven' which begins, 'To be as nothing, being unable to speak', and the incomplete draft, 'Silence on Earth': [. . .] Cramped in a rambling house / With blinded windows / Assailed by constant sounds / On the edge of an abyss / How can one speak / Or know what to say?'

Concerned to address the nature of language and to ask whether it still has validity or whether silence must be the choice of the writer, DG quoted both Hölderlin and Heidegger on the significance of language in *Encrages*, op. cit., p. 24.

In one of his orange notebooks from c. 1950, I found two separate and somewhat enigmatic jottings relating to silence: 1. 'Silence. Shutupness. The daemonic testimony withheld / Refusal of acknowledgement. Tacit negativity. Unspoken falsehood. / Silence, confidence, acceptance of transcendence, realization of temporal and approximate, limited and partly confusing nature of all verbal communication. Faith in reciprocity. Deliberate repose. Fulfilment.' 2. 'Equivocal evasion of theological conclusions in Platonic idealist approach to "problem of Being", beyond a certain point. Silence eventually equivalent to dissimulation. / Notion of silence in H[eidegger]. Two experiences of silence. Anguish – plenitude. Wrath or bliss pre or post articulate silence' (no pag.).

Give Up Dead Words
George Steiner, often quoted by DG, points to the situation of a writer who may feel that 'the condition of language is in question, that the word may be losing something of its humane genius'. One of the choices he faces is 'the suicidal rhetoric of silence', in 'Silence and the Poet', *Language and Silence: Essays 1958–66* (Faber & Faber, 1967), p. 69. The title, 'Give Up Dead Words', appears to address these issues.

Stele and **Terminal**
These are interdependent texts which appear on facing pages in the Berg notebook, compelling in their concision and steely rejection of any false consolation. DG is writing two versions of the same kind of poem: an epigraph or inscription. His choice of 'Stele' refers to an upright stone slab or tablet decorated with inscriptions or figures. It also references Victor Ségalen's *Stèles*, 'undoubtedly a neglected book [. . .]. To me, I must say, it is worth all the poetry Claudel ever wrote (with the exception of "Cinq Grands Odes" perhaps)'. In one of the orange 1950 notebooks Gascoyne goes on to emphasize 'the virtues of compression and reticence displayed' in *Stèles* [1912] some of which 'I feel I can identify myself with in every word' (no pag.).

Fragment of an Unfinished, Unpublished Poem
Another attempt by the poet to examine his vision of the modern metropolis, – '(here all wear masks)' – and predates **Night Thoughts** by six years.

Saturnalia
DG acknowledged the Modernist fondness for masks and for creating personae. Here, the constant blare and din of everyday living, the anxiety and alienation in contemporary urban society, require the necessary adoption of masks to hide our vulnerability.

  The incomplete poem is an early version of the passage in 'Megalometropolitan Carnival' in **Night Thoughts**, which begins: 'Smoothburnt by artificial sunrays, cold with sweat . . .'. Another draft (undated) of the opening 13–14 lines is in the McFarlin Library at the University of Tulsa.

  In an unpublished fragment in the Berg notebook, 'The Rahjah's [sic] Rite', the wearing of masks is again an accepted requirement for living: '[. . .] And all we, merchant, clerk, comedian, / Housewife and handy-man, shopkeeper and whore, / Teacher and business-woman, soldier sailor, all / Must wear the same mask of disguise: a smile / To reassure the inquisition that we are employable, / A cloak of small-talk, and a shield of brass / To hide too shifty eyes / To draw across the eyes, when it's / expedient, and gloves / Of skintight antiseptic scepticism, lest / Our getting too involved leaves the palms stained . . .'

The Bomb-site Anchorite
The character was invented by DG 'in order to give utterance through him to my own meditations on the question as to whether it is possible any longer to envisage the divine in the second half of the 20th century', *An Enitharmon Anthology*, op. cit..

MAKE-WEIGHT VERSE

A Post-Card from Venice to T.S.E.
My transcription of the draft in *Poems, 1950*.

However, the version below is the poem that was written on the postcard actually sent by Gascoyne to Eliot from Venice in 1950. It was sold at Bonhams from Roy Davids' catalogue in April 2013, described as follows: 'Item 169, GASCOYNE, DAVID (1916–2001) [. . .] AUTOGRAPH IMPROMPTU VERSE ON A POSTCARD TO T.S. ELIOT, 6 lines, beginning 'Though some pigeons and tourists seem to fraternize, the birds / Got too absorbed in grain to pay attention to their class . . .', with two lines on the picture side showing the Lion of St Marco in Venice, *2 pages, small octavo*, Venice, June 1950 almost certainly unpublished [. . .].'

> Though some pigeons and tourists seem to fraternize, the birds
> Get too absorbed in grain to pay attention to their class.
> I pose among them Baedeker in hand, with a cigar,
> Wishing a Princess predatory as Volupine would pass.
> P.S.
> Lucky for B. it was not on the bell-tower
> He was together with her in that fell hour.

I am most grateful to James Fergusson who drew my attention to this sale and transcribed for me some words on the card.

OTHER POEMS 1950–56

Qu'est-ce que la decadence?
Published in *84*, Numéro 13 (Paris, Mars, 1950), p. 28. This issue also included DG's translations of three poems by Kathleen Raine.

Yes, You! and **'Yes, thank you. Now I can start the day'**
Add. 56057. At the end of the 1940s, DG was still trying to come to terms with the virtual disappearance of the verbal facility he had enjoyed throughout the 1930s and the early years of the war. He was, too, beginning to recognize painful signs of the silence that can be enforced by 'writer's block', and there was for him the unavoidable question, that faced by Samuel Beckett, too, in the post-war condition: is the living truth no longer sayable, capable of utterance? In addition he had to contend with his post-war disillusionment, neurasthenia, and the unrelieved nagging of accusatory inner voices which had to be silenced. **Yes, You!**, the poignant poem addressed these voices in a notebook dated c. 1950. DG explained in his contribution to *Encrages* that he didn't find it strange that he 'could always distinguish the words "the gods, the gods",' because of what he knew of Hölderlin's experience, op. cit., p. 23 (my translation). In 'Guilt by Association', her review of *Painted Shadow: A Life of Vivienne Eliot* by Carole Seymour-Jones, Hermione Lee observes that T.S. Eliot 'wrote a prayer for himself which ran, in part, "Protect him from the Voices / Protect him from the Visions / Protect him from the tumult / Protect him in the silence".' *Times Literary Supplement* (30 November 2001), p. 3.

In another notebook from 1950, the heading 'Bile and spleen, nausea, self-reproach' precedes a further attempt to produce another poem in which he confronts the intolerable, tormenting voices. At least there is a recognizable rhythm and a regular rhyme scheme, but some passages are disturbing to read, revealing a tenuous hold on reality; it is as if the need to write and the practice of jotting (in a large, wandering and spidery hand) are barely enough to stave off mental collapse. The fragment of a projected poem, 'Silence in Heaven', in the notebook in the Berg Collection in New York Public Library indicates DG's continued mental instability, abandoned with the words 'Poem sabotaged by demonic raving and impatience, 29.XII.52'. Another, longer fragment of what was intended to be a companion piece, 'Silence on Earth', begins: 'Always the voices [. . .].'

Remembering the Dead
From *Poems, 1950*, where the draft was entitled 'Recitative from an Oratorio in Commemoration of the Dead'. Unpublished until 1959 in *X*, Vol. I, No. 1 (November), p. 77.

Haiku: Urban Autumn After the War
From an orange notebook. First published in Etruscan Reader III, op. cit., Limited Edition 1996.

Haiku: 'My own sophistry'
Untitled in the orange notebook. First published in Etruscan Reader III, op. cit.

Cartesian Haiku
Entitled 'Sum' in the same orange notebook. First published in the *Haiku Quarterly*, No. 16, edited by Kevin Bailey, 1995.

Amiguous Haiku
From the orange notebook. First published with title in the *Haiku Quarterly*, op. cit.

Metropolis by Night, Night-Watchers' Ruminations, Night Thoughts
Early versions of the 'radiophonic poem'. The first two poems appeared in *Points*, No. 19, Paris (Spring), the third in *Botteghe Oscure* XVII (Spring).

Elegiac Improvisation on the Death of Paul Eluard
For an earlier version deemed 'unsatisfactory' by DG, entitled ***Elegiac Improvisation in Honour of Paul Eluard***, see **APPENDIX B**.

At some point, DG drafted a preface that was never published to his new poem:

'Introductory Notes to *ELEGIAC IMPROVISATION ON THE DEATH OF PAUL ELUARD*'

He cancelled the first three paragraphs that follow:

[The French poet Paul Eluard died suddenly towards the end of last year (1954), to be mourned by countless numbers of his fellow countrymen and by lovers of France and of poetry all over the world, as one of the best loved among the famous modern men of letters.

Paul Eluard was a poet whose life and writings expressed all the love, warmth and tenderness so conspicuously lacking in most of the French literature of his time. His emotions were pure. His heart was true, it was just, as it refused nothing. He therefore inspired love in far more readers than modern poets are able as a rule to reach.

I would call this poet above all an *imagier français*.]

Paul Eluard had served as a very young man as a soldier in World War One, and his very earliest poems were written out of his experience, and then as the expression of joy at the Armistice: the joy of finding that the simple everyday happiness of ordinary things, flowers and objects, could be returned to once again by men who had discovered during the War that they had brothers. He wrote then, already, from the first one might say, not for himself merely but for all men, or for a perhaps ideal common man, and that was the reason for his effort then and later to use a simple language, a language of clear, colloquial expressions, candid and purified by ardent appreciation of the pristine originality of the utterance that is unhesitatingly spontaneous.

I first met Eluard in 1935. I had by that time already made a few translations from his poetry and, having written to him asking his permission and advice, had received letters from him having a mysterious magical virtue (as it then seemed to me and indeed does still), in the beauty of the almost anonymous yet unique personal clarity and simplicity of the author's handwriting and the unforgettable signature in which the Christian and the surname were as though married by a large superalgebraic 'X' formed by a line continuing the 'l' of Paul and the beginning of the letter 'E' of Eluard. The address at the head of these letters was in the rue Legendre, and it was at his apartment in that street that I saw him for the first time. It is a not at all remarkable street, situated somewhere off the railway cutting by the rue de Rome running north from St Lazare, but at that time the word 'Légendre' was for me not a proper name that could be taken to mean and was in fact the name of the son-in-law, but the French for 'Legendary' (this would of course have been 'Légendaire', but I never stopped to think of that, as it seemed so entirely appropriate that the poet should have his elected domicile in Legendary Street.)

Albert Schweitzer says somewhere in one of his writings on Bach: 'Painting is suffused with poetry and poetry with painting. The quality of either of the arts at a given moment depends on the strength or the weakness of this intercolouration. As regards their means of expression each of them passes into the other by imperceptible gradations.' These observations are particularly *à propos* in relation to any consideration of the poetry of Eluard. No poet living in Paris in the 20th Century can have had a more intimate relationship with all that was most alive in modern painting than Eluard. Many of his books are devoted to painting and painters, above all to Picasso – *mon grand ami, mon bon ami, Picasso, mon vieux ami*. A great many of the limited editions of his poems were accompanied by drawings, lithographs, engravings, photos, collages by a large and varied number of contemporary artists; a very large number of his poems scattered throughout his whole output were about or inspired by painters who were his friends.

And this was in spite of the fact that like Picasso, he had been a member of the Communist Party and for some time before his death a devoted humble follower of the 'party line'. He even wrote a routine poem, I say 'routine', for it is really not a distinguished piece of writing in any way, for Stalin's ?60th birthday, which was printed in a book of similar offerings about the size of a telephone directory. It simply is not possible to suppose that the late Russian 'Father of his country', leafing through this volume, suddenly exclaimed 'Oh, there's a poem by the great French poet Paul Eluard, who used to be a Surrealist, and how very gratifying!' [*Draft ends here*] David Emery Gascoyne Special Collection, McFarlin Library, University of Tulsa.

See DG's comments on Eluard in his 'Introductory Notes' to *Collected Poems 1988*, his review of Eluard's *La Rose Publique* in *Selected Prose 1934–1996*, and references in the *Collected Journals 1936–1942*.

NIGHT THOUGHTS

This '*A Radiophonic Poem*' in verse and prose was commissioned in 1953 with the working title of 'Night and the Watchman' by Douglas Cleverdon for the BBC Third Programme. The work, for voices and orchestra, in three parts or movements, was 'written in a relatively short space of time' in 1954 although DG was struggling with writer's block, and first broadcast on 7 December of the following year with music specially composed and conducted by Humphrey Searle. DG said that he used the title because Edward Young's poem 'Night Thoughts' had been illustrated by William Blake and the phrase fitted what he wanted to say (MDC), p. 51.

In his memoir *Quadrille with a Raven*, Humphrey Searle writes: '*Night Thoughts* was probably one of the first BBC productions to use musique concrète. There was no BBC electronic workshop in 1955 and only discs, not tape, were available. To accompany the long dream sequence in the centre of the feature, we asked the famous percussionist James Blades to record all possible kinds of percussion sounds. We then played them backwards at various speeds; we could only make the speed either twice or four times as fast or slow; the

BBC had no variable speed control in those days. In spite of these technical handicaps we produced some very interesting sounds and were later congratulated by a French composer of electronic music on what we had been able to achieve with such meagre resources' (online at http://www.musicweb-international.com/searle).

'**Night Thoughts**,' DG told Remy, 'is the struggle of the individual to reach his true self, in order to distance himself from the man in the street and from the world of statistics. The city, it's the creation of Cain, he is the first creator of the city; so that is linked in part to the notion of transgression in Christian mythology, whereas for the Greeks, it is linked to the idea of reconciliation, with the figure of Athene, protector of cities, a parthenogenetic figure, you know: so not tainted by Original Sin. I have always been interested in the Oedipus cycle, this trilogy which explains the birth of urban civilization, of what we call civilization, and which is developed in a crime scene. This has been well realized by the French filmmaker, Jean Luc Godard in *Deux ou trois choses que je sais d'elle*, particularly in the famous scene where two characters are talking while a pneumatic drill is operating beside them. In **Night Thoughts**, London isn't the sin, but a multiplicity which is a breaking of the spirit and a place of temptation . . . The section of dreams isn't London any more, but an oneiric city that a Londoner would be capable of seeing in a dream. I refer also to the Garden of Eden, to the primordial forest . . . The word "omphalos" is an interesting word, at once a boss (in Greek) and a hollow. "Boss" is ambiguous and could signify a chief, and the chief of Hell, that's Pluto, whom I introduce later. The character who makes a speech, it's the devil with his tail. The whole metropolis is a labyrinth where the individual's personality and the possibility of becoming a person are dissolved, in the sense employed by Keats and Kierkegaard . . .The third part of **Night Thoughts**, it's the third part of a dialectical movement, it's a resolution' (MRUI), pp. 134–35.

See the following: DG's essay, 'The Poet and the City' in *Selected Prose 1934–1996*, op. cit., pp. 126–132; Roger Scott, 'David Gascoyne's *Night Thoughts*: "The Infernal Megalometropolis"' in *Temenos Academy Review*, 4 (Spring 2001), pp. 107–22; Alan Munton, 'Night Thoughts: David Gascoyne's Excess', in *Cambridge Quarterly*, 31, 1 (March 2002), pp. 33–55.

LATER POEMS 1956–1995

Half-an-Hour
First published in *Isle of Wight Poets*, 1.

On Rereading Jacob Boehme's 'Aurora'
A modified, retitled poem first written in 1953 as *Lines After Reading 'The Aurora'*
It was read by Dennis McCarthy on BBC Radio in *New Soundings* No. 12, edited and introduced by John Lehmann, broadcast on 11 March 1953. DG re-titled the poem when it was first published in 1975, and the date of composition was given misleadingly as 1969. There are small differences in what is, in effect, a later version of the earlier composition.

> None are can now deny
> All that the blessed shoemaker foretold
> Is come about indeed. Babel is builded high
> About us. Nothing avails to save
> The old world like a brand from burning. We must die
> Before our eyes can see. The dead must live
> Before the sound or mourning cease to be.
> All that is is heard to rise from earth's vast grave.
>
> Of chaos. Out of the triple void
> Of no religion, no communion, no hope, Boehme
> Foresaw the sun at midnight would be seen
> To rise with rays like healing wings and shine
> On all the world men's fears had else destroyed.

Three Verbal Sonatinas
First published in *Adam International Review*, Vol. XXV, 337–339 (1970).
  DG said of the third poem: 'The last one [. . .] really reverts to a kind of surrealism [. . .] and at the same time it also refers to my interest in music [. . .] finally I think I have understood modern music.' The poem is intended to be amusing. Based on the atonal music of Schonberg (*David Gascoyne and Anne Ridler Read and Discuss Selections of Their Poems*, Critics Forum Series, cassette tape, Norwich, 1983).

Speechlessness
In a rare occasional poem, DG would confront the choice as a writer to be silent, the route taken by his early hero Arthur Rimbaud who

renounced poetry, or the very condition forced upon Hölderlin: **Speechlessness** was written August-September 1979, after the murder of Lord Mountbatten by the IRA on 27 August, then published in *The Listener* (4 October) that year.

Whales and Dolphins: a Poem for the Greenpeace Foundation
First published in *A Garland of Poems for Leonard Clark* (Enitharmon Press & Lomond Press, 1980). Again, with typical honesty and forthrightness, DG engages with the question of language.

His prose piece, 'Departures', offered in 1983 what is effectively a mission statement: 'If I choose to think of our time in terms of a metaphor such as The World's Midnight, and thus risk seeming to be inclined to the speciously dramatic, that is my own affair. I would only submit that it has become increasingly difficult to ignore the blatant contemporary reality of violence, aggressive hostility, terror, dehumanisation, polarisation, explosive disruption and all the other all too familiar phenomena presented to us daily as evidence of what such words must inadequately be used to express. How can any of us ever suppress some longing to depart from such an overtly catastrophic ambience and from the nihilistic hegemonies of power, self-interest and autonomously proliferating technology – or avoid expressing, however indirectly, some symptom of this longing in the poems we manage to produce?' First published in *New Departures*, 15 (1983), edited by Michael Horovitz, and reprinted in *Selected Prose 1934–1996*, pp. 45–46.

Prelude to a New Fin-de-Siècle
First published in Italy in *Nuova Rivista Europea*, No. 19–20 (October-December 1980) in English and in Italian. I'm grateful to James Fergusson who sent me copies of this first publication of the poem with DG's corrections to the text, incorporated in the final version published in *Collected Poems 1988*: in the third stanza the Italian printing read: '[. . .] Chile, Cambodia, Iran, Afghanistan, / Belfast's Bogside, Derry and Crossmaglen / Up in Strathclyde or down on Porton Down, / On Three Mile Island or in Northern Italy [. . .]'. The poem then appeared in Summer 1981 in *Poetry in the Town*, Third European Festival of Poetry, Cahier no. 30 (Leuvense, Scheijversaktie).

Variations on a Phrase
First published in *Poetry Review*, Vol. 72, No. 3 (September 1982), and in *La Nuova Rivista Europea*, No. 29/30 (giugno-agosto 1982).

Charles Seluzicki issued a broadside in 1984 with a magnificent lithograph, *Figure Caught in a Net*, by Stanley William Hayter. See DG's obituary for his long-time friend in *Selected Prose 1934–1996*, op. cit., pp. 250–51. I am indebted to Charles Seluzicki who sent me copies of letters to him by DG and Hayter regarding the project, together with a master copy of the engraver's original design. Seluzicki recalled that DG 'felt it was his most successful poem in a long time' (email dated 25/6/2002), and it would be difficult to disagree. DG's 'passionate interest' in Rimbaud in the 1930s developed into a less intense but lifelong admiration and fascination for both man and poet. It seems reasonable to assume that **Variations on a Phrase** represents in effect DG's late *hommage* to the writer. The first two lines of DG's poem are a translation of the slightly modified epigraph, whereas Rimbaud's opening line in 'Après le Déluge' from *Illuminations* is as follows: *Aussitôt que l'idée du Déluge se fut rassise*' ['As soon as the idea of the Flood had subsided']. In a letter to Seluzicki dated 12 October 1983 DG wrote: '[. . .] the rainbow [. . .] is central I suppose to the poem as a symbol of hope (with regard to which the poem is open-ended) [. . .]. To me, the key word (or image) of the poem is connected with the syllable *fil*, from the Latin *filum*, a thread, and the idea of the substantial world as woven, [. . .].' DG chose an interesting form: rhymed couplets with a blank line in-between.

Rare Occasional Poem
At the end of his response of 'inordinate length' to *Authors Take Sides on the Falklands* (London: Cecil Woolf Publishers, 1982), DG addressed the editors Cecil Woolf and Jean Moorcroft Wilson as follows: '[. . .] I must quench my explanatory verbal flow. Just in case you should find, understandably enough, that this contribution to your dossier is too long to print as it stands, I now append a short poem which you might care to use in place of the preceding pages [in the event, both prose piece and poem were published]. It was hastily written on the day mentioned in the title and revised the day after. The rather feeble intended pun contained in the title refers to the quite insignificant fact that I have seldom written what are generally known as "occasional poems". It is clearly a non- or apolitical poem, and is distanced from the burning Falklands issue by the use of a deliberate form, which is that of a verbal square made up of 144 syllabic units as follows [. . .]', pp. 43–44.

Arbres, Bêtes, Courants d'Eau: Improvisation (for Salah Stétié)
DG met Stétié through the Jouves. Poet, essayist, art critic and diplomat, Stétié was born in Beirut in 1929. This poem was published in *Poésie 92. La Poésie entre les langues*, No. 41 (février 1992), pp. 61–63. DG read it at the Institut Français in London in 1996 when he was presented with the prestigious award of Chevalier dans l'Ordre des Arts et des Lettres. He translated Stétié's essay, 'On Novalis and the Night' for publication in *Temenos* 9 (1988), pp. 115–16.

Hague Haiku
Originally 'Hai-Ku for Stétié'. Written at Wassenaar, The Hague, 5 September 1984 when the Gascoynes were staying with Stétié who was then the Lebanese ambassador to the Netherlands.

Entrance to a Lane
Written 22–23 July 1985, this was DG's contribution to the Tate Gallery Anthology *With a Poet's Eye*, edited by Pat Adams (The Tate Gallery, 1986). He was offered three choices: Constable's *Salisbury Cathedral from the Meadows*; Dubuffet's *The Busy Life*; Sutherland's painting, which had convinced DG in 1942 that he should suggest to Tambimuttu that the artist might undertake to illustrate **Poems 1937–42**, just accepted for publication by Poetry London Editions.

Ivy
First published in *The Independent* on DG's birthday, 10 October.

UNPUBLISHED POEMS

'Sonnet to Alida Monro' and 'Hinterland'
Two poems sent to Alida Monro in 1932 were accompanied by a letter, now in the British Library Manuscript Department:

402 Richmond Rd.
East Twickenham
M'sex

Dear Mrs. Monro.

I want to thank you again (the first time was before I had read it) for your kind letter. I have always wanted someone to read my work whose opinion I can revere and respect. But I am sorry that you should think that I neglect technique. It has always been my goal, my ideal. Just recently I have been devoting my entire attention to it, you will be glad to hear. I am sending you a new poem, which I think is, technically, the best thing I have done so far, and would be very glad to know what you think of it. I shall probably never write another poem in free verse, except by way of recreation. It is my belief as a poet that every poem, or rather poetic *germ*, or idea, gives birth spontaneously in the poet's mind to its own, individual form and cadence, suitable only to that idea, being its only possible expression. So I do not *yet* regret all the poems in my book. But of that I should like to talk with you at length. I have asked Miss Wright and we should both love to come to supper with you one night. Technique is really a thing that calls for length, discussion and cannot be treated with justice in letters.

Yours very gratefully,
David Gascoyne

The Very Image
Add. 56042.

Asylum
Add. 56043.

The Perpetual Explosion
Add. 56043. DG told me he had no recollection of this. He wrote in his journal on 1.X.36: '[. . .] "Something great and obscure is striving to express itself through me." One day, perhaps, I shall genuinely explode. A perpetual explosion would be my ideal mode of life. I must be very repressed after all' (CJS), p. 20. In that year DG planned a collection of surrealist poems, *The Winged Victory*, in three sections:

I 'The Symptomatic World – 30 poems' (sic). Published as a sequence of 8 poems only. A single poem, ***Symptomatic World*** exists in draft form. See **APPENDIX A**.

II 'Reflected Violence', published as **Reflected Vehemence**; 'Invitations to the Voyage', unpublished; **The Great Day**, published; **The Light of the Lion's Mane**, published; '"I" is another', unwritten (refers to Rimbaud's 'Je est un autre'); **Phenomena**, published; 'Sleep & Riches: Crime & Sleep', unwritten; **The Perpetual Explosion**,

here published for the first time; 'Inverted Coma' (sic), written; 'The Winged Victory' became the third of **Three Verbal Objects**.
III The Lycanthrope – a poem. Unwritten.

The Hills, and in the light, daily
Add. 56042.

Compline for the Occident: a cantata for choir and solo voice
Add. 56044.

Two Untitled Fragments
Add. 73537.

Come Dungeon Dark
The poem to which DG refers twice in his journal: '1939. April to the end of June: [. . .] First part of "Come Dungeon Dark"' (CJS), p. 248; in one of the entries for 12.XI.39 he writes: '*New Writing*'s next issue is still supposed to be coming out this Winter, and if it does, it will contain part of "Come Dungeon Dark"', p. 272. He is referring to part I, **The Conspirators**. The incomplete section first published here is, in effect, Part III.

The Dark's Fidelity
Add. 56046. Like **Post-Mortem**, the poem was 'written under the influence of Jouve,' as DG told me.

Epilogue to an Episode **and** *Dead End*
Previously known to me only as titles of projected or completed poems in a notebook entry headed *The Conquest of Defeat – Poems 1939–40*. Add. 62947:

I DEDICATORY AND COMMEMORATIVE POEMS (15)

Lives of the Poets	To George Barker	To the Young Poets of America
	(September 1st)	Letter to Jean le Louët
The Plummet	Poetry's Evidence	Lines for Stephen Spender
Heart (Hart Crane)	(to Paul Eluard)	
The Urn (P.J. Jouve)	To Antonia White	

Ode to Rimbaud	Elegy for Léon Chestov	
		An Epistle to All

II PERSONAL AND CONFESSIONAL POEMS (20)

Paris Remembered (inc.)		
In 1937	Apologia	The Projections of Desire
A November Night	**Dead End**	The Fabulous Glass
Chambre d'Hôtel	The Writer's Hand	Sotto Voce
Fête in February	To a Contemporary	My Road is Flight!
Jardin du Palais Royal	Odeur de Pensée	Destination
Les Noctambules	Dichotomy	**Epilogue to an Episode**
Epilogue 1940	Inside the Whale	
	Three Poems of Childhood	

III POEMS ON CONTEMPORARY AND GENERAL THEMES (15)

Snow in Europe	Farewell Chorus	Zero
An Autumn Park	A Wartime Dawn	'Wozzeck' Act III, Scenes 4–5
Spring MCMXL	Walking at Whitsun	Tobias
Apocalyptic Ode	Barcelona 1936–39	The Conquest of Defeat

Epilogue 1940–41 and ***A la Fenêtre***

In notebook 56045 Gascoyne planned a sequence of poems, 'Paris Remembered' or 'Reminiscences of Paris', on a page headed *Miscellaneous Notes / 1940*: 1. In 1937; 2. A November Night; 3. Chambre d'Hôtel; 4. Fête in February; 5. Au Jardin du Palais Royal; 6. Noctambules; 7. Epilogue (June 1940).

'**Fête**, **Chambre d'Hôtel**, **Jardin du Palais Royal** and **Noctambules** are in the section 'Personal Poems' in *Poems 1937–43*. The draft of ***Epilogue: 1940–1***, was recovered from a different notebook, and the incomplete draft of another poem in the series has come to light:

A La Fenêtre may possibly be 'In 1937' retitled.

Dear Thomas Eliot
My transcription from a draft in the Berg notebook, *Poems 1950.*

The Porch before these Poems is the Entrance into Night

The unpublished poem of eleven lines was added to the script during rehearsal for the BBC programme, 'David Gascoyne: A Selection from his poetry made by the author', broadcast on 29 May 1949 and produced by Frank Hauser. The script was written and read by DG with Cathleen Nesbitt. [Poems included 'Miserere', 'Zero (September) 1939', 'The Post War Night', 'Rex Mundi', 'Birth of a Prince'.] This is the only extant version of the poem, with a slightly different first line, handwritten in Add. 71704, and in thirteen rather than eleven lines. A rehearsing of ideas and themes for *Night Thoughts.*

The Hand that in the darkness

Add. 71704. Given that DG also composed a French version of the poem, it is possible that he wrote it under the inescapable influence of Pierre Jean Jouve whose verse he had continued to translate since the end of the 1930s. I'm not suggesting, however, that this is a work of conscious imitation.

The Son of Man is in Revolt

Also handwritten in the same notebook.
It seems that in these two poems Gascoyne rehearsed some of the ideas that he wished to develop in what became **Fragments Towards a Religio Poetae**. It is clear that he incorporated several lines or parts of lines in different sections of that poem. He took seven lines from 'The Porch . . .' and inserted them in each of the sections 2, 3, 5, 6, 7, 9, 10. Five lines from 'The Son of Man . . .' are employed with modifications in sections 1, 2, 3, 4, 5.

When I am able to think at night

Written in a notebook c. 1950, like the two preceding poems.

Haiku: Rain globules on glass

From an orange notebook, c. 1950.

And tell me, how is Christ preached now?

Unpublished draft from 'ledger-sized manuscript notebook' held in the McFarlin Library, University of Tulsa. Undated, but probably c. 1954, and a rehearsing of themes and ideas for **Night Thoughts** because of the jottings that follow on a separate page:
'Megalometropolis / City: Troy: Rome: Labyrinth, arena, / Circus, games, dances, gates of entrance to the / Underworld, the earthly city, Vanity / Fair, Babel-civilization under / the rule of Pluto. Carnival by Night: / Sleep: dreams / Descent into Cavern, cave / Night as Womb, or Cave / of Initiation Mystery through experience / of vision'.

A Summer Evening at Caesar's Tower

This is a composite of three drafts in Gascoyne's final notebook '1988–1996', the first dated 'August-September, 1992', and two later incomplete, one of which is dated '16.X.95 – 4 p.m.' A series originally planned as *Fading Snapshots*, then became 'Prose Poems' to be entitled *Snapshot Album* (November 11th '95.). This may well be the very last poem he planned and began to compose. *Remanences*, comprising three poems, was published by Enitharmon in 1996.

David Gascoyne in the late 1990s